American Silver

1655-1825

in the Museum of Fine Arts

Boston

Portrait of Paul Revere
by JOHN SINGLETON COPLEY, painted c. 1768-1770.
MUSEUM OF FINE ARTS, BOSTON.
Gift of Joseph W., William B., and Edward H. R. Revere. 30.781

American Silver
1655-1825
in the Museum of Fine Arts
Boston

by Kathryn C. Buhler

Museum of Fine Arts, Boston
Volume I

Distributed by New York Graphic Society
Greenwich, Connecticut

Standard Book Number: 0-87846-064-0
Library of Congress Catalogue Card Number: 75-190547
Copyright © 1972 by Museum of Fine Arts, Boston. All rights reserved.
Designed by Carl F. Zahn and Barbara Hawley
Typeset by Craftsman Type Inc. in Jan Tschichold's Sabon.
Printed in the United States of America by The Meriden Gravure Company,
Meriden, Connecticut on Mohawk Superfine.

CONTENTS *Volume I*

PREFACE

THE AUTHOR'S INTEREST in silver was first aroused in the late twenties by answering the questions of Miss C. Louise Avery for her volume *Early American Silver,* which rightfully has since been reprinted. Mrs. Thayer's, Mr. Spalding's, Mr. Pickman's and Mr. Holmes's possessions are included therein as well as a generous number of pieces that the museum owned at that time. One sees in the list of photographs supplied by the Museum of Fine Arts, those pieces then on loan that were subsequently and regrettably diverted to other collections, largely through Francis Hill Bigelow who had transferred his interests to the Mabel Brady Garvan Collection at Yale.

In 1938 the museum permitted me to edit the book of silversmiths' marks begun by the late Ernest M. Currier, *Marks of Early American Silversmiths;* interleaved copies of this were kept abreast of regional studies of silversmiths and made the careful comments herein on makers' marks possible at the suggestion of Miss Patricia Alward for whose editorial patience in this production I express my gratitude. (The quantity of documented marks by Samuel Edwards has been a surprise!) The late John M. Phillips, of Yale University Art Gallery, who brought his classes in American Art to Boston when Yale had football and hockey games here, assisted in the Currier work and was a friend and correspondent for two decades. His service in England in World War II did not dim his interest in Massachusetts silversmiths and the notes thereon, begun by F. H. Bigelow, as his letters to my late husband and me attest. His colleague to whom he introduced us, Josephine Setze, has been a friend of long standing and was of great assistance in the 1956 exhibition. Church pieces therein that had escaped the eagle eye of E. Alfred Jones were included and in part illustrated to give the "book-sized catalogue," which was Perry T. Rathbone's requirement for the fiftieth anniversary exhibition, lasting usefulness. For that catalogue, as for others, I have wished for greater information on certain pieces than has been published.

Therefore detailed in the extreme, the notebooks whence came these entries were filled in my year before retirement with the hope of being useful to the Department of Decorative Arts and Sculpture and were not planned for publication. Approached for their opinion of the notes' possible interest, Messrs. Firestone and Parson generously responded and sought other contributions from friends and firms for a publishing plan about which I then learned. A grant from the Ford Foundation removed the necessity for further personal solicitation and was most gratefully received. Publication has kept me in touch with the museum collection far longer than I had anticipated.

The first editing left owners' names of comparable or related pieces intact, and these are available for the department. The requests of some owners not to be identified seemed prudent, and a second editing after a considerable lapse of time has eliminated all such names, but allowed to be included such diversions as Rev. William Bentley's comments on the goldsmith John Andrew. There is, if correctly remembered, a quantity of overlooked minutiae in those notebooks including statements of condition that have seemed unnecessary here; illustrations sometimes show the dents not mentioned.

Space has necessitated limiting the catalogue to men working in the seventeenth and eighteenth centuries, the exception being the few pieces of church silver from the nineteenth, for their wider interest to descendants of a congregation. Repetitive spoons took to an appendix. English pieces, although brought when new to this country and probably models for our local goldsmiths, are occasionally mentioned in the text but could not be catalogued. It seemed wise to leave September 1966 as a cut-off date, and references to books and exhibitions since then are not included. However, gifts and a bequest in the last five years have been of such importance that an addenda includes them even as page proof is being read.

Frequently visible, owners' initials unless otherwise mentioned are in the familiar and usual block lettering, with a device sometimes centered between the initials. The catalogue is arranged first regionally and then chronologically by makers' birth dates, with each man's wares, judged by style and sometimes engraving, also chronological.

Brookline, Massachusetts KATHYRN C. BUHLER
August 1971

INTRODUCTION

THE COLLECTION of American silver in the Museum of Fine Arts in
Boston is unmatched for its wealth of documented New England plate.
Its importance is amply evidenced in these volumes, which also include
the few pieces from New York and a family's holdings from eighteenth-
century Philadelphia. To those generations who preserved their silver
intact but for a sometimes inevitable dent or handle out of line, we must
be as grateful as to their descendants who in the museum's first century
so generously parted with their treasures.

Oddly, the first piece of American silver to be given to the museum, in
1877, was not early but a Tiffany piece from the Philadelphia Centennial
Exhibition, and the range of decorative arts' exhibitions has rarely allowed it to be shown. In 1888, however, Mrs. M. A. Elton bequeathed
her ancestral silver: a London made coffee urn and teapot on stand of
the 1780s, London salts with their American made spoons (Cat. no. 481),
and a small gold button then unrecognized as the work of Samuel Casey
(Cat. no. 490).

In 1892, at the conversion of the variously termed Lynde Street, West, or
West Boston Church into a branch of the Boston Public Library, the
West Boston Society presented its locally made baptismal bowl and com-
munion plate—the earliest piece thereof dating from the church's found-
ing in 1737. In 1895 and 1896, Dr. Buckminster Brown and James
Longley made the first gifts to the museum of silver by the patriot Paul
Revere II. A two-volume biography entitled *The Life of Colonel Paul
Revere* had been published in Boston in 1891. It was dedicated to the
"People of Boston, in whose service he spent his life; whose rights he al-
ways championed; and whose liberties he aided so nobly in preserving."
The author, Elbridge H. Goss, capsuled Revere's activities as a gold-
smith in the contents of the first chapter: "Learns his Father's Trade—
Makes and Embellishes Silverware" and illustrated in line drawing a
few pieces that the goldsmith would find difficult to recognize.

In 1906 the first museum-held exhibition of American silver was un-
dertaken by the Museum of Fine Arts at the suggestion of Francis Hill
Bigelow of Cambridge. It was perforce largely a loan exhibition, but
peculiarly the only lenders named in the catalogue were Harvard Uni-
versity and churches. The catalogue's introduction was by R. T. Haines
Halsey, the notable New York collector; its technical description by
John H. Buck, Curator of Metalwork at The Metropolitan Museum of
Art. Two "anonymous friends" contributed to the cost of publication.
One wonders if they ever knew how eagerly the book was sought when
it was no longer available at the museum. An anniversary exhibition,
Colonial Silversmiths: Masters and Apprentices, was held in 1956 and
it was a pleasure to be then able to fête Mrs. Henri Leon Berger, who, as
Florence V. Paull, had been the behind-the-scenes worker on the 1906
exhibition and on one held in 1911.

Under the rather misleading title *American Church Silver,* the 1911 catalogue included the Revere pieces from Dr. Brown and James Longley; the
domestic plate bequeathed by Mr. and Mrs. George W. Hammond in
1908, which included the only New York piece (Cat. no. 497) owned until
Mr. Tyler's bequest in 1932; and spoons by Ezekiel Burr given in 1910.
A goodly portion of the pieces were lent by private owners, among them
Arthur W. Wellington whose name had unaccountably been omitted
from the same loans in 1906 (now through the generosity of his widow,
catalogue numbers 102 and 304).

In 1911 and ensuing years gifts of church plate were made; individual
pieces from a number of churches and two groups of considerable importance: the New South Church group in 1912 and the silver of the
Brattle Street Church in 1913. This latter great gift, by a benevolent fraternity that still carries on its good work, included the four fine early
flagons—the possible source of which is here explored for the first time
(*see* Cat. no. 71, Notes). Presumably at that time was begun the custom
of a church lending its silver for exhibition and safekeeping yet to be
available on request for special church services. (The author remembers
preparations for Easter week when it was her pleasure to select and record close to two hundred home-going pieces.)

Private gifts of great renown came in 1913: "Grandmother Norton's"
sugar box (Cat. no. 33); the rare forks by John Noyes (Cat. no. 92); and
the punch bowl presented to Captain Thomas Dawes by his regiment
(Cat. no. 231), a possible model for the patriot Revere's famed Sons of
Liberty Bowl fashioned five years later. Also, the first of the Storer family pieces catalogued in 1911 as lent by Miss Georgianna G. Eaton were
now given in her name. Dr. Samuel Abbott Green's bequest in 1919 included his share from these Storer ancestors. Storer family plate was
added by William Storer Eaton in 1937, the estates of the Misses Cruft
in 1942, by Miss Mary O. Bowditch in 1947, Miss Gertrude Townsend
at various times, and in 1956—to be gratefully included as gifts in the
catalogue of that year's exhibition—from the Misses Rose and Elizabeth
Townsend pieces on loan since the 1911 exhibition. Much of the Storer
family plate was made by members of the related Edwards family.

Many other important gifts will be found to have been given before, in
1920, its semicentennial year, the museum made its first purchase of
American silver. Of the more than six hundred pieces recorded in this
catalogue, fewer than thirty (counting sets and pairs as one) are purchases. The first investment was the fluted ladle by Paul Revere subsequently found to have been made for Burrell Carnes in 1793 (Cat. no.
395) and, by sheer coincidence, now associated with the first gift made
by a collector rather than an inheritor. Henry Davis Sleeper had been a
rival of Revere's great-granddaughter, and others, in amassing the silver
of the patriot. In 1925 he gave his collection to the museum in memory
of his mother with the proviso that it be returned to him for study of its
origins. After his untimely death his notes were not found, and his silver
was published with rather unlikely ownerships for most of the pieces.
The estate of Mrs. W. B. Rogers had lent the fluted ladle as well as the
unique fluted coffee urn, teapot and stand, and sugar bowl to the 1911

exhibition. When the hollowware was to be sold by her heirs and the museum had no money for it, certain pieces from the Sleeper Collection that had been superceded in importance by family gifts were sold to enable the Sleeper name to be on pieces virtually assured of permanent exhibition.

In 1931, Mr. and Mrs. Dudley Leavitt Pickman gave family plate representing three generations of purchasers, the newest acquisitions in the generation of Mr. Pickman's great-grandparents. This silver is still shown as a unit and is testimony to the taste and generosity of the family. John Coney served one generation as John Coburn equipped another; Timothy Dwight and Henry Hurst, excellent craftsmen both, have each been known by only two pieces; the Pickmans' gift included their salver (Cat. no. 26) and tankard (Cat. no. 64) respectively. Mr. Pickman had been elected a trustee of the museum in 1918 and was also a donor in fields other than silver; one of his gifts was the handsomely wallpapered room from Bath, Maine, and its furnishings. He was a member of the Department of Decorative Arts' Visiting Committee and the author of charming books on ceramics. He was a frequent as well as official visitor to the department until his death in 1938. To celebrate both the Pickman gift and what was Hermann F. Clarke's first monograph, on John Coney, a summer exhibition was held in 1932 of 106 items by that master goldsmith. The catalogue for the exhibition, a small printed pamphlet, grouped the objects by maker's marks and noted contemporary engraving, original owner when known, and one dimension. It was valuable chiefly in that it included the silver owned by Philip Leffingwell Spalding, none of which had been in Mr. Clarke's book.

Other pieces of Pickman plate came with the M. and M. Karolik Collection of Eighteenth-Century American Arts. As Mrs. Karolik was a generation younger than Mr. Pickman, her inheritances from Derby and Codman families were enhanced by the gifts of more descendants in these lines. Also in 1931 was received the family plate of Mr. and Mrs. Henry W. Cunningham. His bequest ties in with family pieces from other sources and even Mr. Sleeper's gifts.

In 1932 Charles Hitchcock Tyler, one of the pioneer collectors of American arts and artifacts, bequeathed his collections to the museum to be kept at its discretion. Richard H. Randall in *American Furniture in the Museum of Fine Arts, Boston* (1965) wrote that his furniture was the "virtual keystone of the Museum's holdings." His silver includes such outstanding pieces as one of the three known standing salts of American make (Cat. no. 20), by Jeremiah Dummer; a Coney sugar box (Cat. no. 48); and the second New York piece to enter the museum's collection, a porringer by Elias Pelletreau (Cat. no. 508). His name also is found on purchase funds and on pieces acquired "by exchange."

It was the author's privilege to know and study with two early collectors and benefactors: Mrs. Nathaniel Thayer (née Pauline Revere) and Philip Leffingwell Spalding. Mrs. Thayer, whose interest was in her ancestors' skill, shared her photostatic copies of the patriot's daybooks with the department, which led to definite dating of a number of her own and other pieces. Her bequest in 1935 included a few notable fakes that she had recognized and bought to protect the good name of her craftsman-ancestor Paul Revere II. The pieces are useful for study purposes, but how futile her effort has proved to be in the light of subsequent faking.

Philip Leffingwell Spalding, whose own discriminating collecting is now represented in the museum through the generosity of his family, had made a few gifts in the early 1930s. He also found among his friends several donors for special pieces of silver as they came on the market, at the time when much Boston-owned silver was being diverted to Francis P. Garvan in New York and to Henry F. du Pont in Delaware. In 1938 he celebrated his appointment as Honorary Curator of Early American Silver by making the then anonymous gift of his standing salt by Edward Winslow (Cat. no. 67). (It has pleased me to find since the identity of the crest thereon and the fitting names for its initials.) His honorary post was brief for he died in December of that year; his family's gift of his silver was made in 1942. Two of his pieces have been found to bear an English maker's mark, although they lack hallmarks.

In 1935 Mr. Edward Jackson Holmes, who served both as director and president of the museum, had inherited from his uncle, Oliver Wendell Holmes, treasured silver that he promptly lent to the museum. Nine years earlier he had purchased and given the unique Coney chocolate pot (Cat. no. 50) when the depression had forced it on the market — though at a far from depressed price for those days. After his death in 1950 his widow began giving the pieces that all knew were destined for eventual museum ownership. Jackson possessions also reached the museum through Patrick Tracy Jackson and the widow of the museum architect, Guy Lowell.

Grace Williamson Edes Stedman in 1936 bequeathed her first husband's possessions as gifts of Mr. and Mrs. Henry Herbert Edes; a second deed of gift was from Mr. and Mrs. Ellery Stedman. The Edeses' family silver from their Wood ancestors has been augmented by gifts from Miss Penelope Barker Noyes.

In 1938 Dr. George Clymer inherited from maiden aunts a range of Philadelphia silver from the earliest makers to representatives of its best-known family of goldsmiths. The silver, which for Philadelphia smiths is comparable to the Pickman collection for Boston ones, was immediately lent anonymously. It remained on loan for almost twenty years by which time Dr. Clymer had died. When the museum asked Mrs. Clymer's permission to illustrate certain pieces in the catalogue for the 1956 exhibition, she gave in that year and the next the entire collection. A purchase in 1959 of the Simmons urn and the gift of the important Christian Wiltberger tea service in 1961 further enriched the museum's Philadelphia holdings. The service was first shown publicly in Chicago in 1949 and had been lent to the museum by Mr. and Mrs. Farovid when they moved to Boston in 1958.

In 1939 Arthur D. Foss, the Boston jeweler, gave pieces he had collected, which gave the museum then "new" marks for John Burt and his son Samuel.

In 1949 when the curator and department visitors despaired of acquir-

ing the Sons of Liberty Bowl by Paul Revere, the collector Mark Bortman
secured an option on it and rallied to the cause. As a child he had contributed to the restoration of the frigate *Constitution,* and he had repro-
ductions of the bowl passed around in Greater Boston public schools
for the pennies children might care to give. Thus donations actually
ranged from a penny to one of several thousand dollars, and the museum
assumed the balance.

In 1951, the silver of the First Unitarian Society of Revere was given with
the proviso that the museum also treasure the church's manuscript records. A perusal of the records disclosed no reference to their plate but
did prove, in the minister's handwriting, that the *Dictionary of American Biography* errs in the birth date of his son, Horatio Alger.

Purchases in the decade of the 1950s, which included the Soumain and
Fueter pieces from New York, were, comparatively speaking, lavish.
Many gifts coinciding with the 1956 exhibition have already been noted;
a later outcome of the exhibition was the presentation to the museum
in 1964 of the unique New York kettle that had been lent for the occa-
sion. In 1958, Miss Marion E. Davis bequeathed the first fund for the
purchase of American silver. The initial purchase in her name, in 1963,
was the very important caster by John Coney (Cat. no. 62) that had
long been on loan and seemed a fitting tribute to a generous donor, who,
strangely, had never made herself or her intentions known to the
department.

Important pieces, mostly long known, have been given in the closing
years of the 1960s and are included in an addenda to this catalogue.
A happy surprise, the Charles L. Boehme tea set, extends the collection
geographically to Maryland and one hopes will encourage further
expansion of the collection.

SHORT TITLE INDEX

BOOKS AND PERIODICALS

Avery 1920 Avery, C. Louise. *American Silver of the Seventeenth and Eighteenth Centuries: A Study Based on the Clearwater Collection.* New York: The Metropolitan Museum of Art, 1920.

Avery 1930 Avery, C. Louise. *Early American Silver.* New York and London: Century Co., 1930.

Bell 1930 Bell, N. S., comp. *Pathways of the Puritans.* Framingham, Mass.: published by Old America Company for the Massachusetts Bay Colony Tercentenary Commission, Boston, 1930.

Bigelow 1917 Bigelow, Francis Hill. *Historic Silver of the Colonies and Its Makers.* New York: Macmillan Co., 1917.

Buck 1903 Buck, John H. *Old Plate: Its Makers and Marks,* new and enl. ed. New York: published by The Cheltenham Press for The Gorham Manufacturing Company, 1903.

Buhler 1932 Buhler, Kathryn C. "Some Silver by John Coney." *Bulletin Museum of Fine Arts, Boston* XXX, no. 179 (June 1932), pp. 45-48.

Buhler 1934 Buhler, Kathryn C. "Silver Bequeathed by Charles Hitchcock Tyler." *Bulletin Museum of Fine Arts, Boston* XXXII, no. 191 (June 1934), pp. 46-50.

Buhler 1936 Buhler, Kathryn C. "The Ledgers of Paul Revere." *Bulletin Museum of Fine Arts, Boston* XXXIV, no. 203 (June 1936) pp. 38-45.

Buhler 1939 Buhler, Kathryn C. "Gift of American Silver." *Bulletin Museum of Fine Arts, Boston* XXXVII, no. 224 (December 1939), pp. 114-115.

Buhler, Antiques, no. 5 (1945) Buhler, Kathryn C. "Some Engraved American Silver: Part I, Prior to about 1740." *Antiques* XLVIII, no. 5 (November 1945), pp. 268-271.

Buhler, Antiques, no. 6 (1945) Buhler, Kathryn C. "Some Engraved American Silver: Part II, From about 1740 to about 1810." *Antiques* XLVIII, no. 6 (December 1945), pp. 348-352.

Buhler 1947 Buhler, Kathryn C. "Colonial Furniture and Silver: A Study of Parallels and Divergences." *Antiques* LI, no. 1 (January 1947), pp. 36-39.

Buhler 1950 Buhler, Kathryn C. *American Silver.* Cleveland and New York: World Publishing Co., 1950.

Buhler 1951 Buhler, Kathryn C. "John Edwards, Goldsmith, and His Progeny." *Antiques* LIX, no. 4 (April 1951) pp. 288-292.

Buhler 1955 Buhler, Kathryn C. "Masters and Apprentices: Some Relationships in New England Silversmithing." *Antiques* LXVIII, no. 5 (November 1955), pp. 456-460.

Buhler 1956	Buhler, Kathryn C. *Paul Revere, Goldsmith, 1735-1818*. Boston: Museum of Fine Arts, Boston, 1956.
Buhler 1957	Buhler, Kathryn C. "The Philip Leffingwell Spalding Collection of Early American Silver." *The Walpole Society Notebook*, pp. 37-52. Portland, Maine: printed by The Anthoensen Press for the Walpole Society, 1957.
Buhler 1959	Buhler, Kathryn C. "Philadelphia Silver Given in Memory of Dr. George Clymer." *Bulletin Museum of Fine Arts, Boston* LVII, no. 307 (1959), pp. 21-32.
Buhler 1963	Buhler, Kathryn C. "Three Teapots with Some Accessories." *Bulletin Museum of Fine Arts, Boston* LXI, no. 324 (1963), pp. 52-63.
Clark [Buhler] 1931	Clark [Buhler], Kathryn. "Pickman Family Silver." *Bulletin Museum of Fine Arts, Boston* XXIX, no. 173 (June 1931), pp. 43-50.
Clarke-Coney 1932	Clarke, Hermann Frederick. *John Coney, Silversmith, 1655-1722*. Boston: Houghton Mifflin Co., 1932.
Clarke-Dummer 1935	Clarke, Hermann Frederick, and Foote, Henry Wilder. *Jeremiah Dummer, Colonial Craftsman and Merchant, 1645-1718*. Boston: Houghton Mifflin Co., 1935.
Clarke-Hull 1940	Clarke, Hermann Frederick. *John Hull, A Builder of the Bay Colony*. Portland, Maine: Southworth-Anthoensen Press, 1940.
Comstock 1958	Comstock, Helen, ed. *The Concise Encyclopedia of American Antiques*. "Silver 1640-1820" by Kathryn C. Buhler, pp. 79-93. New York: Hawthorn Books, 1958.
Currier 1938	Currier, Ernest M. *Marks of Early American Silversmiths*. Portland, Maine: Southworth-Anthoensen Press, 1938.
Curtis 1913	Curtis, George Munson. *Early Silver of Connecticut and Its Makers*. Meriden, Conn.: International Silver Co., 1913.
Eberlein and McClure 1927	Eberlein, Harold Donaldson, and McClure, Abbot. *The Practical Book of American Antiques*. Philadelphia: J. B. Lippincott Co., 1927.
Ellis 1961	*The Ellis Memorial Antiques Show*. "The Pickman Silver" by Kathryn C. Buhler, pp. 19-29. Boston, 1961.
Ensko 1948	Ensko, Stephen G. C. *American Silversmiths and Their Marks, III*. New York: Robert Ensko, Inc., 1948.
Forbes 1942	Forbes, Esther. *Paul Revere and the World He Lived In*. Boston: Houghton Mifflin Co., 1942.
French 1939	French, Hollis. *Jacob Hurd and His Sons, Nathaniel and Benjamin, Silversmiths, 1702-1781*. Cambridge, Mass.: published by the Riverside Press for the Walpole Society, 1939.

Goss 1891	Goss, Elbridge Henry. *The Life of Colonel Paul Revere,* 2 vols. Boston: Cupples Bookseller, 1891.
Halsey 1925	Halsey, R. T. H., and Tower, Elizabeth. *The Homes of Our Ancestors.* Garden City, New York: published by Doubleday, Page and Co. for The Metropolitan Museum of Art, 1925.
Hipkiss 1931	Hipkiss, Edwin J. "The Paul Revere Room." *Bulletin Museum of Fine Arts, Boston* XXIX, no. 175 (October 1931), pp. 84-88.
Hipkiss 1941	Hipkiss, Edwin J. *Eighteenth-Century American Arts: The M. and M. Karolik Collection . . . .* Cambridge, Mass.: published by Harvard University Press for the Museum of Fine Arts, Boston, 1941.
Hipkiss, MFA Bulletin, no. 234 (1941)	Hipkiss, Edwin J. "Recent Gifts of Silver." *Bulletin Museum of Fine Arts, Boston* XXXIX, no. 234 (August 1941), pp. 58-61.
Hipkiss, MFA Bulletin, no. 236 (1941)	Hipkiss, Edwin J. "American Arts of the Eighteenth Century." *Bulletin Museum of Fine Arts, Boston* XXXIX, no. 236 (December 1941), pp. 79-87.
Hipkiss 1942	Hipkiss, Edwin J. "Boston's Earliest Silversmiths: The Philip Leffingwell Spalding Collection." *Bulletin Museum of Fine Arts, Boston* XL, no. 241 (October 1942), pp. 81-86.
Hipkiss 1943	Hipkiss, Edwin J. *The Philip Leffingwell Spalding Collection of Early American Silver.* Cambridge, Mass.: published by Harvard University Press for the Museum of Fine Arts, Boston, 1943.
Jones 1913	Jones, E. Alfred. *The Old Silver of American Churches.* Letchworth, Eng.: published by the Arden Press for the National Society of Colonial Dames of America, 1913.
Jones 1928	Jones, E. Alfred. *Old Silver of Europe and America from Early Times to the Nineteenth Century.* Philadelphia: J. B. Lippincott Co., 1928.
McLanathan 1956	McLanathan, Richard B. K. "American Silver: A Fiftieth Anniversary." *Bulletin Museum of Fine Arts, Boston* LIV, no. 297 (Autumn 1956), pp. 49-66.
Morison 1930	Morison, Samuel Eliot. *Builders of the Bay Colony.* Boston: Houghton Mifflin Co., 1930.
Norman-Wilcox, Antiques, Part I (1944)	Norman-Wilcox, Gregor. "American Silver Spice Dredgers: Part I." *Antiques* XLV, no. 1 (January 1944), pp. 20-22.
Norman-Wilcox, Antiques, Part II (1944)	Norman-Wilcox, Gregor. "American Silver Spice Dredgers: Part II." *Antiques* XLV, no. 2 (February 1944), pp. 80-84.
Paull 1913	P[aull], F[lorence]V. "Gifts of American Silver." *Bulletin Museum of Fine Arts, Boston* XI, no. 62 (April 1913), pp. 22-25.
Phillips 1949	Phillips, John Marshall. *American Silver.* New York: Chanticleer Press, 1949.

Phillips, Antiques, *no. 6 (1948)*	Phillips, John Marshall. "Masterpieces in American Silver in Public Collections: Part I, Seventeenth-Century Traditions." *Antiques* LIV, no. 6 (December 1948), pp. 412-416.
Phillips, Antiques, *no. 2 (1949)*	Phillips, John Marshall. "Masterpieces in American Silver in Public Collections: Part II, 1700-1750." *Antiques* LV, no. 2 (February 1949), pp. 116-120.
Phillips, Antiques, *no. 4 (1949)*	Phillips, John Marshall. "Masterpieces in American Silver in Public Collections: Part III, Ecclesiastical Silver." *Antique*s LV, no. 4 (April 1949), pp. 281-285.
Phillips, Antiques, *no. 1 (1949)*	Phillips, John Marshall. "Masterpieces in American Silver in Public Collections: Part IV, Rococo and Federal Periods." *Antiques* LVI, no. 1 (July 1949), pp. 41-45.
Wenham 1949	Wenham, Edward. *The Practical Book of American Silver*. Philadelphia and New York: J. B. Lippincott Co., 1949.
Winchester 1956	Winchester, Alice. "Colonial Silversmiths—Masters and Apprentices." *Antiques* LXX, no. 6 (December 1956), pp. 552-555.

EXHIBITIONS

Art Treasures 1955	Cancer Crusade. Parke-Bernet, New York, 1955 (no catalogue).
Baltimore 1959	The Age of Elegance: Rococo and Its Effect. Baltimore Museum of Art, 1959.
Buffalo 1965	Religious Art. Albright-Knox Art Gallery, Buffalo, 1965.
Chicago 1949	From Colony to Nation. The Art Institute of Chicago, 1949. "American Silverware of the Seventeenth and Eighteenth Centuries" by Meyric R. Rogers.
Columbus 1947	Exhibition of Colonial Arts. Columbus Gallery of Fine Arts, Columbus, Ohio, 1947 (no catalogue).
Concord 1950	One Hundred Seventy-fifth Anniversary of Concord. Concord Antiquarian Society, Concord, Massachusetts, 1950 (no catalogue).
Cranbrook 1952	American Church Silver. Museum of Cranbrook Academy of Art, Bloomfield Hills, Michigan, 1952.
Dallas 1958	Religious Art in the Western World. Dallas Museum of Fine Arts, 1958.
Detroit 1951	The French in America, 1520-1880. The Detroit Institute of Arts, 1951.
ESU 1960	American Silver and Art Treasures. The English Speaking Union, London, 1960.
First National Bank *1934*	Loan Exhibition. First National Bank, Boston, 1934.
Hartford 1946	Wadsworth Atheneum, Hartford, 1946 (no catalogue).
Hartford 1947	Exhibition of Silver of Colonial Connecticut. Wadsworth Atheneum, Hartford, 1947.

Harvard 1936	Decorative Arts of the Period 1636-1836. Harvard University Tercentenary Exhibition, 1936.
Jamestown 1907	Massachusetts Colonial Loan Exhibit at the Jamestown Ter-Centennial Exposition, 1607-1907. Hampton Roads, Virginia, 1907.
Johns Hopkins 1940	Exhibition of History in Gold and Silver. The Johns Hopkins University, Baltimore, 1940. George N. Batz.
Kansas 1950	William Rockhill Nelson Gallery, Kansas City, Kansas, 1950 (no catalogue).
London 1954	Exhibition Honoring the Ancient and Honorable Artillery Company. Victoria and Albert Museum, London, 1954; The Manchester Gallery, 1954-55 (no catalogue).
MFA 1906	American Silver: The Work of Seventeenth and Eighteenth Century Silversmiths. Museum of Fine Arts, Boston, 1906. Introduction by R. T. Haines Halsey. Technical description of objects by J. H. Buck.
MFA 1911	American Church Silver of the Seventeenth and Eighteenth Centuries with a Few Pieces of Domestic Plate. Museum of Fine Arts, Boston, 1911. Introduction by George M. Curtis.
MFA 1932	Exhibition of Silversmithing by John Coney, 1655-1732. Museum of Fine Arts, Boston, 1932.
MFA 1956	Colonial Silversmiths: Masters and Apprentices. Museum of Fine Arts, Boston, 1956. Kathryn C. Buhler.
Minneapolis 1956	French, English and American Silver: A Loan Exhibition in Honor of Russell A. Plimpton. Minneapolis Institute of Arts, 1956.
MMA 1909	The Hudson-Fulton Celebration. The Metropolitan Museum of Art, New York, 1909. "American Silver" by Florence N. Levy.
MMA 1941	Exhibition of American Arts. The Metropolitan Museum of Art, New York 1941 (no catalogue).
N.Y. 1946	American Presentation Silver. New York Historical Society, 1946-47. H. Maxson Halloway.
Park Square 1925	Loan Exhibition of Early American Furniture and Decorative Arts. Park Square Building, Boston, 1925.
Pocumtuck 1950	Colonial Silver. The Pocumtuck Valley Memorial Association, Deerfield, Massachusetts, 1950 (no catalogue).
Presentation Silver 1955	Upon This Occasion. The Towle Silver Company, Newburyport, Massachusetts, 1955.
R.I. 1965	The New England Silversmith: An Exhibition of New England Silver from the Mid-Seventeenth Century to the Present, Selected from New England Collections. Museum of Art, Rhode Island School of Design, Providence, 1965. Hugh J. Gourley III.

Richmond 1960	Masterpieces of American Silver. The Virginia Museum of Fine Arts, Richmond, 1960. Kathryn C. Buhler.
Towle 1953	Early Silver Owned in Essex County. The Towle Silver Company, Newburyport, Massachusetts, 1953 (no catalogue).
Towle 1954	Exhibition of Church Silver. The Towle Silver Company, Newburyport, Massachusetts, 1954 (no catalogue).
Towle 1956	The Odd and the Elegant. The Towle Silver Company, Newburyport, Massachusetts, 1956.
Towle Revere 1955	An Exhibition of Paul Revere Silver. The Towle Silver Company, Newburyport, Massachusetts, 1955-56 (no catalogue).
Washington 1925	Exhibition of Early American Paintings, Miniatures and Silver. National Gallery of Art, Washington, D.C., 1925-26. Section on silver by Elizabeth B. Benton.
Worcester 1916	Colonial Furniture, Silver, Miniatures . . . . Worcester Art Museum, 1916 (no catalogue).
Yale 1939	Masterpieces of New England Silver, 1650-1800. Gallery of Fine Arts, Yale University, 1939. John Marshall Phillips.
Yale 1963	American Gold, 1700-1860. Yale University Art Gallery, 1963. Peter J. Bohan.

Massachusetts

ROBERT SANDERSON
1609–1693

ROBERT SANDERSON was born in England, served his apprenticeship to William Rawlins of London, and emigrated to Hampton, now New Hampshire, in 1638. Here his first wife died, and he soon moved to Watertown, Massachusetts, where his nephew William was living and where he married Mary, widow of John Cross. Two sons were born in Watertown, Joseph in 1642 and Benjamin in 1649; two other children were baptized there, Sarah in 1651 and Robert in 1652. In 1654 Sanderson was "of Boston" when his daughter Lydia was married.

In 1652 John Hull, on being appointed mintmaster, recorded, "I chose my friend, Robert Sanderson, to be my partner, to which the court consented." Sanderson was a member of the First Church in Boston, which now owns seven pieces of silver by the partners and the only piece known bearing only Hull's mark. Through receiving the silver of Boston's Hollis Street Church, the First also owns one of the four pieces known to bear Sanderson's mark alone; three of these pieces surely were made within the period of the partnership. The fourth, dated 1685, was probably not new when presented to the First Church in Quincy. Of his three silversmithing sons, only Robert survived his father, and only Benjamin's work is known today. Sanderson married a third time; his will in 1693 mentions his widow Elizabeth; son Robert Sanderson, goldsmith; daughter Anna West; grandchildren, and a great-grandchild. He appointed "loving friends," including Jeremiah Dummer, to be "overseers" and left 115 oz. of plate, £20 in New England money, and £9-14 in English money.

Sanderson is known to have used two marks in this country: his initials in shaped punches (a) with a rayed circle above, and (b) with a sun above (courtesy of Old South Church, Boston).

a   b

1

1 Tankard, 1670–1680

H. 8³⁄₁₆ in. (inc. thumbpiece); D. of base 6⅝ in.; D. of lip 5½-5¹¹⁄₁₆ in. (uneven); Wt. 41 oz., 11½ dwt.

MARKS: *a* above and below center point on base.

Straight tapering sides, incised lines at lip, and narrow applied molded base-band with unusual punched design on lower edge. Flat cover with wide low step from flange with paired incised lines near edge slightly scalloped at front and back (cracked). Cast double spiral thumbpiece with shaped and decorated support, its modeling suggestive of the head of a bird or dolphin; meander wire in plates for five-part hinge. Outer plate has V-shaped drop from the tip of which three incised lines converge to a point over curve of scroll handle; rattail drop on body from upper joining. The broad end of the flat handle surface is scalloped and extends over an engraved shield-shaped plaque covering the rounded tip. A small vent hole is in a slit beneath.

Pricked with decorated medallions enclosing *V* on the hinge plate; *I* and *M* flanking the chased lines below, which are worn by the thumbpiece. The cover is engraved with a whorl of four flowers, their leafy stems curving from a central asymmetrical rosette; one is recognizably a tulip, one perhaps a carnation. Scratched weights on bottom, very indistinct: oz/42-0 oz dwt/41-15.

HISTORY: Isaac (1637-1710) and Mary (Balston) Vergoose (1648-1690), Boston, m. about 1668 (see *MFA Bulletin* reference below); their daughter Anna (d. 1774); her nephew William Fleet (d. 1784); his sister-in-law (d. 1827); owned in 1911 by Mrs. Alexander Fairfield Wadsworth, Boston, from whom it was bought.

NOTES: Aside from a tankard with the marks of Sanderson and Hull but with considerable alterations, this is the only one known today by this first generation of American goldsmiths.

REFERENCES: *Jones 1913,* p. xli; *Jones 1928,* p. 15, pl. II, no. 2; *Avery 1930,* p. 298; K. C. Buhler, "The Robert Sanderson Tankard," *MFA Bulletin,* XXXV, no. 209 (1937), pp. 33-35, illus.; Mrs. Russel Hastings, "Verifying a Hull & Sanderson Porringer," *Antiques,* XXXII, no. 3 (1937), pp. 116-118; *Clarke-Hull* 1940, pp. 128, 216, no. 30, illus. frontispiece, mark in error; *Buhler, Antiques,* no. 5 (1945), p. 268, fig. 4; *Ensko 1948,* p. 21; *Phillips 1949,* p. 30, pl. 3b; *Phillips, Antiques,* no. 6 (1948), p. 413; *Buhler 1950,* p. 20, illus. frontispiece; *Buhler 1955,* illus. p. 457.

EXHIBITIONS: *MFA 1911,* no. 934, pl. 22; *Yale 1939,* no. 182, fig. 5; *Minneapolis 1956,* no. 279, fig. 35; *MFA 1956,* no. 129, fig. 5; *Richmond 1960,* no. 129.

GIFT OF JOHN S. AMES AND MARY AMES FROTHINGHAM 37.263

I

JOHN HULL
1624–1683

JOHN HULL was characterized by Samuel Eliot Morison as one of the
"Builders of the Bay Colony," a phrase adopted by Hermann F. Clarke
as a subtitle for his monograph on Hull. Born in England, Hull was
brought to Boston in 1635 with a half-brother who had served five
years' apprenticeship under a London goldsmith, James Fearne. In his
diary, Hull recorded: "I fell to learning (by the help of my brother)
and to practising the trade of a goldsmith, and through God's help
obtained that ability in it as I was able to get my living by it."
Shipping interests and his appointment as mintmaster added to his
living, as is attested by the diaries he kept. In 1647 he married Judith
Quincy; of their five children, their births and deaths duly noted in the
diary, only Hannah lived to maturity. Hannah married another diarist,
Judge Samuel Sewall, who wrote of "Robert Sanderson and all that
wrought in the shop under him," suggesting Hull's lesser activity while
he so diligently served his country in important public offices including that of mintmaster.

In 1658 Hull was chosen by the Selectmen, of whom he was one, "to
receive, keep, and dispose of the town's stock or treasure." He was a
member of the First Church, Boston, until the establishment of the
Third, now Old South, Church in 1669. He died intestate in 1683 and
was eulogized in pulpit and print.

Hull used his initials (a) with a rayed circle similar to his partner's
mark; (b) over a device (a cinquefoil or star?) in a heart; and (c) with
four pellets in a square above in a conforming punch, the lower
edges squared.

a   b   c

2

2 Porringer, c. 1655

H. 1⁹⁄₁₆ in.; D. of lip 4¾ in.; L. of handle 2 in.; Wt. 6 oz., 15½ dwt.

MARKS: Sanderson *a,* Hull *b* at left of handle.

Thick straight sides curve to almost flat bottom. Center point in bowl. Cast trefoil handle has four simple piercings to form center shield, knob on tip, and thickened bar at joining three-sixteenths of an inch below rim.

Engraved AMI at rim, not quite centered opposite handle. Modern lettering on bottom: *M.B.LeM.* above very slight dome, *M.LeM.W./1917,* below. Other modern engraving was stoned from handle by the eminent Boston craftsman, George C. Gebelein, before the porringer came to the museum.

HISTORY: Arthur (d. 1707/8) and Johannah (Parker) Mason (d. 1704/5), m. May 5, 1655; their daughter Mary, m. Rev. John Norton; their grand-daughter Elizabeth Quincy, m. Rev. William Smith; descended to Mrs. Strafford (Margaret LeMoine) Wentworth, from whom the piece was bought.

NOTES: Neither F. H. Bigelow (writing in 1917) nor E. Alfred Jones (in 1928) knew of the existence of the piece, and both claimed that no porringer by these earliest silversmiths was known. Another porringer with similar bowl by the partners but with an ornate cast handle came on the market in the mid-thirties and is now in the Henry Francis du Pont Winterthur Museum, Delaware.

REFERENCES: Philip L. Spalding, "A Porringer by Hull & Sanderson," *Walpole Society Notebook,* 1937, pp. 59-63, illus. opp. p. 60; *Clarke-Hull,* pp. 126, 213, no. 23, pl. XI; *Hipkiss 1943,* pp. 13-14; *Phillips 1949,* p. 28, line drawing of handle p. 9; *Phillips, Antiques,* no. 6 (1948), p. 413; *Buhler 1950,* p. 14, fig. 2; *McLanathan 1956,* p. 64, fig. 25a; *Buhler 1957,* pp. 38-39.

EXHIBITIONS: *Yale 1939,* no. 117, fig. 1; *Chicago 1949,* no. 176, illus. p. 108; *Richmond 1960,* no. 71.

THE PHILIP LEFFINGWELL SPALDING COLLECTION. GIVEN IN HIS MEMORY BY KATHERINE AMES SPALDING AND PHILIP SPALDING, OAKES AMES SPALDING, HOBART AMES SPALDING 42.252

3

3 Dram Cup, 1652–1680

H. 1⅜ in. (inc. handle); D of base 1⁹⁄₁₆ in.; D. of lip 3⅛ in. (uneven);
Wt. 1 oz., 10½ dwt.

MARKS: Sanderson *a*, the *R* almost obliterated, at right of one handle; Hull *b*, very worn, at left of same handle.

Thick sides curve to slightly domed bottom, center point beneath. Rope-twisted wire handles probably bent from their original form. Mended at handle, broken at side opposite marks.

Crudely chased lines form ICE on bottom. Heavily chased and engraved IHM on side. Scratched on bottom, *Hall*, twice in script, *1790* three times.

HISTORY: Early history unknown; owned by Jacob and Mary Hall, m. Medford, Massachusetts in *1772*, great-grandparents of the donor; descended to their daughters, Mary and Elizabeth Hall; thence to their great-niece, Mary Elizabeth Hall, mother of the donor.

NOTES: Other examples: Yale University Art Gallery, Garvan Collection; Private collection; see also Cat. no. 6.

REFERENCES: *Bell 1930*, pl. II; *Clarke-Hull 1940*, p. 210, no. 12.

GIFT OF MISS MARY ELIZABETH LOMBARD IN MEMORY OF MARY ELIZABETH HALL *13.561*

4

4 Caudle Cup, 1660–1670

H. of body 3¾₆ in. (uneven); D. of base 2⅝ in.; D. of lip 3⅞ in. (uneven); Wt. 5 oz., 10½ dwt.

MARKS: Sanderson *a,* Hull *b* on bottom.

Bulbous body with flaring lip and convex sides ornamented with panels of flat chasing between three clustered rows of punches above and a row of spaced dots below, which is repeated above stepped flat base, which has been repaired. Center point on bottom. The panels, three to a side, are formed of narrow vertical banners; each contains a wide stylized tulip on a matted or pounced ground, two leaf forms flanking each tenuous stem. In two panels, on the *BB* side (see *Notes*), the stem has additional curls at the base of the flower, and in one of these the tulip has corresponding curls. On the other side, only one stem has curls. The cast scroll handles have freestanding scroll tips, a decorative device along the shoulder to a small inner scroll, below which are lines of graduated beading on each side. Handle joinings resoldered.

Pricked designs centered on the slightly concave rim are horizontal with tangent circles enclosing respectively, *BB* and *ED* on opposite sides. In modern engraving, near the handle of the *ED* side over the curled stem, is *M.LeM.W.* (see Cat. no. 2). *ED* remains unidentified.

HISTORY: Beriah Bright (b. 1649), m. Isaac Fowle; their grandson Rev. William Smith, m. Elizabeth Quincy, granddaughter of Rev. John and Mary Norton; their daughter Abigail, m. John Adams; descended to Mrs. Strafford (Margaret LeMoine) Wentworth, from whom the piece was bought.

NOTES: This is the only known use by the partners of this cast handle, but it is found on cups made by their apprentice, Jeremiah Dummer (see Cat. no. 11). Another style of cast handle, apparently now unique, is on the partners' caudle cup which descended in the Mascarene family.

REFERENCES: E. J. Hipkiss, "Minor Arts in New England," *MFA Bulletin,* XVIII, no. 109 (1920), p. 47; *Avery 1920,* pp. cxvi, cxviii, fig. 35; *Halsey 1925,* pp. 47, 57, fig. 16; *Avery 1930,* pp. 40, 245, 291, pl. IV; *Bell 1930,* pl. II; *Clarke-Hull 1940,* p. 208, no. 9; *Hipkiss 1942,* p. 84; "The Almanac," *Antiques,* XLII, no. 5 (1942), p. 264, illus; *Hipkiss 1943,* pp. 11-12; *Buhler 1947,* pp. 36-37, fig. 4; *Phillips, Antiques,* no. 6 (1948), p. 414; *Buhler 1950,* p. 19 and fig. 3; *Buhler 1955,* p. 456, fig. 1; *McLanathan 1956,* p. 64, fig. 25b; *Buhler 1957,* p. 41, fig. 3.

EXHIBITIONS: *Chicago 1949,* no. 174, illus. p. 109; *Richmond 1960,* no. 72; *R.I. 1956,* no. 99, fig. 1.

THE PHILIP LEFFINGWELL SPALDING COLLECTION. GIVEN IN HIS MEMORY BY KATHERINE AMES SPALDING AND PHILIP SPALDING, OAKES AMES SPALDING, HOBART AMES SPALDING 42.226

5

5 Miniature Caudle Cup, 1660–1670

H. 2³⁄₃₂ in. (inc. handles); D. of base 1¾ in.; D. of lip 2⅜ in.; Wt. 2 oz., 2 dwt.

MARKS: Sanderson *a*, Hull *b* near handle on neck.

Bulbous body with very slightly flaring rim, curved sides ornamented with four panels of flat chasing between a row of widely spaced dots above and more tightly spaced ones below. A third line of dots above the slightly stepped base is somewhat obliterated by repairs but can be seen distinctly from inside. Center point on bottom. Pairs of chased lines beneath the handles, centered front and back, divide the sides into panels for very broad tulip forms with leaves spreading from the base of the stem, against a pebbled background. The handles, their surfaces curved and insides flat, are in scroll form with freestanding tips. Their joinings have been repaired and are thickly resoldered, but X-ray spectrographs show them to be contemporary with the body. Flower stems and base repaired.

Engraved on bottom WTD around center point. Added on neck, the Wentworth arms and *1891* over *Dorothea.*

HISTORY: Early history unknown; purchased by William H. Wentworth and engraved for his daughter, the donor.

NOTES: A very similar English piece with London date letter of 1619 was shown in Christie's *Catalogue of Highly Important Old English Silver and Rare Early Spoons,* March 28, 1962, no. 122, pl. XI.

REFERENCES: *Avery 1930,* p. 291; *Clarke-Hull 1940,* p. 209, no. 10, illus. pl. VI (when the authenticity of the handles was queried).

EXHIBITIONS: *MMA 1909,* no. 369, illus.; *R.I. 1965,* no. 100.

GIFT OF MRS. JAMES STUART SMITH IN MEMORY OF WILLIAM H. WENTWORTH *58.1360*

6

6 Dram Cup, c. 1670

H. 1⁷⁄₁₆-1⁹⁄₁₆ in. (inc. handles); D. of base 1¾ in.; D. of lip 2⅝ in.; Wt. 1 oz., 4½ dwt.

MARKS: Sanderson *a,* punch worn, Hull *b;* both at rim.

Shallow bowl, sides curve to stepped flat base. Center point in bowl. High scroll handles, wrought and chased in spirals and three upright lines, give the effect of twisted wire. Mended at each handle and twice on rim.

Engraved IGA on bottom.

HISTORY: Rev. Joseph (Harvard 1669) and Ann (Waldron) Gerrish, m. before 1673; their daughter Elizabeth (1673-1747), m. Rev. Joseph Green (Harvard 1695); their son Joseph, Jr. (1703-1765), m. Anna Pierce (1702-1770) of Portsmouth, N.H., 1727; their great-great-grandson was the donor.

NOTES: Other versions: Yale University Art Gallery, Garvan Collection (chased and engraved for Ruth Brewster); private collection, a very shallow one; see also Cat. no. 3.

REFERENCES: *Bigelow 1917,* pp. 249-50, fig. 153; *Bell 1930,* pl. II; *Currier 1938,* in "From the Author's 'Note Book' "; *Clarke-Hull 1940,* p. 210, no. 13, pl. XV.

EXHIBITIONS: *MFA 1911,* no. 587, pl. 19; *Richmond 1960,* no. 74; *ESU 1960,* no. 2, pl. 1.

BEQUEST OF SAMUEL ABBOTT GREEN *19.1386*

JEREMIAH DUMMER
1645–1718

JEREMIAH DUMMER is the first native goldsmith whose work is known to us. He was born to the emigrant Richard Dummer of Newbury, Massachusetts and his second wife, Frances, widow of Rev. Jonathan Burr, on September 14, 1645. In 1659 John Hull recorded, "I received into my house Jeremie Dummer and Samuel Paddy to serve me as apprentices eight years. The Lord make me faithful in discharge of this new trust committed to me, and let his blessing be to me and them." Dummer continued to work in Boston, and among his outstanding pieces are the columnar candlesticks and Portuguese-type bowl at the Yale University Art Gallery and the "great basin" presented by his pupils to William Brattle in 1693, who bequeathed it to the First Church in Cambridge. He seems to have made a greater variety of porringer handles than any other American goldsmith. In 1672 Dummer married Anna, daughter of Joshua and Mary (Blakeman) Atwater. Their fourth child (of nine) was Lieutenant Governor William Dummer, who bequeathed the family farm in Newbury to be the boys' school which bears his name. Jeremiah Dummer held a number of town offices and served as Justice of the Peace. There is, however, no contemporary evidence to support the contention that he executed a group of portraits to which his name was added (described by Henry Wilder Foote in Clarke's monograph). He survived his wife and all but four of his children and died in 1718, "after a long retirement under great infirmities of Age and Sickness."

Dummer used two marks; the most frequently met one (and that on the MFA pieces) shows his initials, a pellet between and broken line across, over a fleur-de-lis, all in a heart-shaped punch *(a)*. His second and very small mark is of his initials in a rectangle.

a

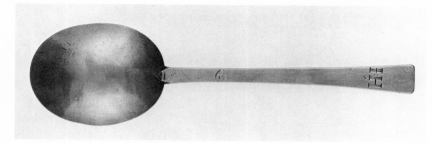

7

7 Puritan Spoon, c. 1670

L. 5³⁄₁₆ in.; Wt. 12¼ dwt.

MARKS: *a* in bowl and on back of stem.

Porringer size. Flat handle, rectangular in section with broad straight tip, tapers to V-shaped drop on back of elliptical bowl.

Engraved *IH* on back of handle.

HISTORY: Purchased from Mrs. Ann R. Woodall, whose father had found the spoon in the foundations of a building when and where the Salem Post Office was built in the late nineteenth century.

NOTES: Similar versions in large size by Hull and Sanderson and by John Coney (Yale University Art Gallery, Garvan Collection).

REFERENCES: *Phillips 1949,* p. 28; *Buhler 1950,* p. 13, fig. 1.

EXHIBITION: *Richmond 1960,* no. 41.

SETH K. SWEETSER FUND 39.553

8

8 Porringer, 1670–1680

H. 1¼ in.; D. of lip 4⅝ in.; L. of handle 2 in.; Wt. 4 oz., 13 dwt.

MARK: *a* overstamped at right of handle on body.

Slightly everted narrow rim, curving sides, trace of a step, domed bottom. Center point in bowl. Trefoil handle affixed with bar, incised lines accentuate scrolls of heart tip and rounded sides. Small triangular cuttings above plate with initials.

Engraved *NG* on top of handle away from bowl (Nabby, a common contraction of Abigail, Gardner); EBM beneath handle.

HISTORY: Probably Abigail Gardner, spinster; her sister's son Ebenezer Bowditch (1702/3–1768), m. Mary Turner (1706–1785) in 1728; descended in family to Mrs. Henry Ingersoll Bowditch, from whom it was bought.

NOTES: This is, insofar as we know, a unique handle cutting.

REFERENCES: *Winchester 1956,* illus. p. 554.

EXHIBITION: *MFA 1956,* no. 51, fig. 15.

DECORATIVE ARTS SPECIAL FUND *55.194*

9

9 Dram Cup, 1670–1690

H. of body 1⁵⁄₁₆ in.; D. of base 1¾ in. (uneven in height and diameter); D. of lip 2½ in.; Wt. 1 oz., 18½ dwt.

MARK: *a* on side.

Slightly tapering sides curve sharply to stepped flat base. Center point on bottom. Ropelike handles in scroll form, circular in section, have freestanding tips, lower tips flattened. Battered and one handle bent.

Engraved *IL* on bottom above center point.

HISTORY: Early history unknown; owned by the donor by 1917.

NOTES: Dram cups published in *Clarke-Dummer 1935* included the Cheever one in the Harrington Collection, Dartmouth College; a very shallow one (privately owned); and one recorded as a caudle cup, deeper than this one and with plain handles (Yale University Art Gallery, Garvan Collection); each with a stepped base. Clarke did not record the Dummer silver owned by Philip Leffingwell Spalding. A similar dram cup with plain handles was made by William Cowell (Edward E. Minor, "Notes on Early American Silver," *Antiques,* XLIX, no. 4, [1946], p. 239, fig. 6). Another, but shallow, one was made by Edward Winslow (*MFA 1911*, illus. fig. 36).

REFERENCES: *Halsey 1925*, pl. 16; *Clarke-Dummer 1935*, no. 37; *Hipkiss 1943*, p. 20; *Buhler 1957*, p. 42.

THE PHILIP LEFFINGWELL SPALDING COLLECTION. GIVEN IN HIS MEMORY BY KATHERINE AMES SPALDING AND PHILIP SPALDING, OAKES AMES SPALDING, HOBART AMES SPALDING 42.228

10

10 Caudle Cup, c. 1680

H. 3⅛ in. (inc. handles, uneven); D. of base 2⁹⁄₁₆ in.; D. of lip 3³⁄₁₆ in.; Wt. 4 oz., 15½ dwt.

MARKS: *a* on neck and twice on bottom.

Bulbous body, slightly flaring rim, stepped flat base, no center point. Lower body embossed with running design of flowers and foliage; pounced scrolls in open areas and short lines of graduated punches form upper edge. The concave neck is less planished than Dummer's plain caudle cups in the MFA. Cast handles, the upper halves tightly scrolled at the joining, have bird's-head shoulders swallowing lower sections, with midway scroll and upturned birds' heads on lower tips (both bird necks looking more scaled than feathered). One handle almost broken from neck.

Engraved RHM in early block lettering on bottom; faint trace that different initials may be beneath.

HISTORY: Unknown.

NOTES: The Old Colony Historical Society, Taunton, Massachusetts, has a plain caudle cup with the same handles. The MFA cup is the only floral-embossed caudle cup by Dummer which has been published.

REFERENCES: *Halsey 1925*, fig. 16; *Avery 1930*, pp. 40, 293, illus. pl. IV; *Hipkiss 1942*, p. 84, illus.; *Hipkiss 1943*, p. 18; *McLanathan 1956*, p. 65 and fig. 26b; *Buhler 1957*, fig. 4.

THE PHILIP LEFFINGWELL SPALDING COLLECTION. GIVEN IN HIS MEMORY BY KATHERINE AMES SPALDING AND PHILIP SPALDING, OAKES AMES SPALDING, HOBART AMES SPALDING 42.229

11

12

11 Caudle Cup, c. 1680

H. of body 3³⁄₁₆ in.; D. of base 3⁵⁄₁₆ in.; D. of lip 3⅞ in.; Wt. 8 oz., 5½ dwt.

MARKS: *a* on bottom and side.

Bulbous body with flaring lip and characteristic stepped flat base reinforced later with narrow applied molded baseband (slight repairs inside). Cast scroll-ornamented handles appear to be from the mold of the caudle cup by Hull and Sanderson but are slightly shorter (see Cat. no. 4).

Engraved BGS on bottom just above center point.

HISTORY: Early history unknown; owned by the donor by 1917.

NOTES: Other uses of this handle: gadroon-based cups, First Parish Congregational (Unitarian), Chelmsford, Massachusetts; The Henry Francis du Pont Winterthur Museum, Delaware; and Deerfield, Massachusetts; plain cup (one handle a replacement), private collection; with heads on the handles, First Church of Christ, New Haven, Connecticut.

REFERENCES: *Halsey 1925*, fig. 16; *Hipkiss 1942*, p. 84; *Hipkiss 1943*, p. 19; *Buhler 1955*, p. 456, fig. 2; *McLanathan 1956*, p. 65, fig. 26a; *Buhler 1957*, p. 42.

THE PHILIP LEFFINGWELL SPALDING COLLECTION. GIVEN IN HIS MEMORY BY KATHERINE AMES SPALDING AND PHILIP SPALDING, OAKES AMES SPALDING, HOBART AMES SPALDING 42.227

12 Spout Cup, c. 1680

H. 4⅞ in. (inc. finial); D. of base 2⁵⁄₁₆ in.; D. of lip 3¹⁄₁₆ in.; Wt. 8 oz., 5 dwt.

MARKS: *a* on neck and cover.

Globular body on small molded foot rim, cylindrical neck with incised lines top and bottom. Molded strap handle with rounded and everted tips not quite at right angles to the spout, which is broad at the base over a small tear-drop hole and with curved tubular tip. Flat stepped and molded cover; incised lines on wide flange; narrow bezel; turned finial, broad at base, on slight dome in center (center point inside). Trace of ring on step of cover.

Engraved SCE around center point on bottom. *1680* added on side, below maker's mark, opposite handle.

HISTORY: Stephen Codman, m. Elizabeth Randall, 1674; their son John (1696-1755), m. Parnell Foster; their son John (d. 1792), m. Abigail Asbury; their son John (d. 1803); his son John (d. 1847); his son John (d. 1900); his daughter Mary, m. Francis V. Parker; their daughter Gertrude, m. Sir Gilbert Carter; gift to her cousin Stephen Hurd Russell Codman, m. Mary J. Sullivan, 1905; their daughter was the donor.

NOTES: This and Cat. no. 16 are the only known spout cups by Dummer.

REFERENCE: V. Isabelle Miller, "American Silver Spout Cups," *Antiques*, XLIV, no. 2 (1943), p. 74, fig. 3.

EXHIBITIONS: *Yale 1939*, no. 73; *R.I. 1965*, no. 64, fig. 6.

GIFT OF MRS. EUGENE C. EPPINGER IN MEMORY OF STEPHEN H. R. AND MARY J. CODMAN 63.273

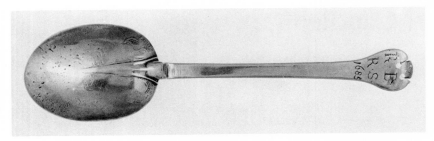

13

13 Spoon, 1685

L. 7³⁄₁₆ in.; Wt. 1 oz., 7 dwt.

MARK: *a* in bowl only, heart pointing to handle.
Stem rectangular in section, thinner at rather sharply curved short trifid
tip (point at one side broken, the center bent forward). Very worn elliptical
bowl stamped with rounded drop in grooved rattail, scroll and foliate design
shown in other examples to taper at tip, each scroll lined with a row of dots.
Engraved on back, *RB* over *RS* over *1685;* added on front in script, *L.R.P.*

HISTORY: Unknown.

NOTES: The original engraved initials, divided back and front, are on Hull
and Sanderson's death's-head spoon, dated 1661 or 1667, Hollis French
Collection, Cleveland Museum of Art. Same initials and date on Dummer's
rather similar trifid spoon with another bowl stamp (illus. Edward E.
Minor, "Notes on Early American Silver," *Antiques,* XLIX, no. 4 [1946],
p. 238). Same bowl stamps used for trifid spoons by Dummer in two private
collections; and for a wavy end spoon in The Henry Francis du Pont
Winterthur Museum, Delaware.

REFERENCES: *Hipkiss 1943,* p. 23, photographed with Edwards spoon, the
back illustrated p. 39; *Buhler 1957,* p. 44.

THE PHILIP LEFFINGWELL SPALDING COLLECTION. GIVEN IN HIS MEMORY BY
KATHERINE AMES SPALDING AND PHILIP SPALDING, OAKES AMES SPALDING,
HOBART AMES SPALDING 42.254

14 Tankard, c. 1685

H. 7⅛ in. (inc. thumbpiece); D. of base 5½ in.; D. of lip 4¾ in.;
Wt. 31 oz., 4 dwt.

MARKS: *a* on cover and at left of handle.
Straight tapering sides, sharply everted rim with incised line below, applied
molded baseband. No center point on body; one on cover. Flat stepped
cover, plain flange serrated at front and sides flanking hinge plate, under
which flange curves (bezel seamed at front). Three-part hinge with rectangular
plaques outlined in row of punched circles; double spiral thumbpiece with
modeled support, its base tangent to step of lid; scroll handle with a
relatively short heavy V-drop on body. Wide flat handle surface overhangs
very slightly the hexagonal applied tip (vent slot). Slight wear of thumbpiece
on upper handle but no sign of initials. Lower joining and hinge plate
resoldered. Inexplicable surface texture.

HISTORY: Early history unknown; owned by donor by 1928.

REFERENCES: *Hipkiss 1943,* p. 17; *Buhler 1957,* pp. 43-44.

14

15

15 Caudle Cup, 1680–1700

H. 3¹³⁄₁₆-4 in. (inc. handles, uneven); D. of base 3½ in.; D. of lip 4⁵⁄₃₂ in.;
Wt. 9 oz., 9 dwt.

MARKS: *a* on body and on bottom.

Bulbous body, slightly flaring rim, three-eighths-inch step to flat base. Two
cast scroll handles, upper surface ridged, forked at lower joining with
scroll tips, slight grip on shoulder, and freestanding rounded upper tips,
one broken.

Engraved TOD on bottom near center point.

HISTORY: Early history unknown; owned by the donor's wife by 1907.

NOTES: All other published Dummer cups with these handles have
scroll tip at upper joining also.

REFERENCES: *Morison 1930*, opp. p. 164; *Clarke-Dummer 1935*, no. 30;
Wenham 1949, pp. 22, 190, fig. 28.

EXHIBITIONS: *Jamestown 1907*, no. 89; *MFA 1911*, no. 366; *American Furniture and Decorative Arts*, Milwaukee Art Institute, June 30-July 31, 1960.

GIFT OF HERBERT F. WILLIAMS-LYOUNS IN MEMORY OF HIS
WIFE, HELEN WILLIAMS 21.286

16 Spout Cup, 1680–1700

H. 5¼ in. (inc. finial); D. of base 2⁵⁄₁₆ in.; D. of lip 3³⁄₁₆ in.; Wt. 8 oz., 13 dwt.

MARKS: *a* twice on neck and once on cover.

Globular body on finely reeded ring baseband; cylindrical neck with incised
lines below rim; mid-group of four lines. Two molded strap handles affixed
between lines on neck with pointed tip and upcurved rounded lower tip
at midbody. Spout, not quite evenly between handles, over tiny heart-shaped
hole, is broad at base, tubular and curved at tip. Flat, stepped, and molded
cover has incised lines on flange and ring for missing chain, applied
bezel, turned finial molded at base is soldered through cover (once badly
bent, and probably originally domed as is Cat. no. 12). Center point on
bottom of body.

Engraved DHE on body at left of spout (area shows evidence of earlier
initials in the same place).

HISTORY: Early history unknown; Daniel and Elizabeth (Gerrish) Henchman,
m. 1713; their daughter Lydia (1714-1777), m. 1730 Thomas Hancock (d.
1764); his nephew John Hancock; bought by Benjamin Waldo Lamb at
the sale of John Hancock's possessions; his daughter Rosanna, m. Joseph
Warren Revere; her cousin, Horatio Appleton Lamb.

NOTES: Mrs. Thomas (Lydia Henchman) Hancock in her will left ". . . a
Silver Bowl [Cat. no. 179], a Silver Spout Cup [this piece], and a large
Two-Handled Silver Cup which I give to my Nephew, John Hancock, Esq.
. . . " The two-handled silver cup was made by George Wickes, London
and is also owned by the MFA. This is the only two-handled spout cup known.
It was once badly dented and was straightened by George C. Gebelein.

REFERENCES: *Clarke-Dummer 1935*, no. 76, pl. XII; Edwin J. Hipkiss,
"Recent Gifts of Silver," *MFA Bulletin*, no. 234 (1941), pp. 58-60; V. Isabelle
Miller, "American Silver Spout Cups," *Antiques*, XLIV, no. 2 (1943), p. 74,
fig. 4; *Ensko 1948*, p. 41; *Phillips 1949*, p. 52; *Wenham 1949*, pp. 27, 192,
fig. 35; *McLanathan 1956*, p. 63, fig. 23.

16

EXHIBITIONS: *MFA 1911*, no. 345, pl. 10; *London 1954; Minneapolis 1956* (not in catalogue).

GIFT OF MRS. HORATIO A. LAMB *41.221*

17

17 Porringer, 1680–1700

H. 1¾ in.; D. of lip 4⅞–4¹³⁄₁₆ in. (uneven); L. of handle 2⅛ in.;
Wt. 5 oz., 11½ dwt.

MARK: *a* at right of handle on body.

Everted rim, curved sides, stepped and domed bottom. Center point in
bowl. Handle pierced in simple design with heart near tip, open circles at
sides, double-arched opening flanked by circles at bowl.

Engraved *AP* high on handle toward bowl; other initials erased.

HISTORY: Unknown.

NOTES: Other examples: one owned by Yale University Art Gallery,
Garvan Collection; one with a variation in the form flanking the heart,
Phillips Academy, Addison Gallery of American Art, Andover, Massachusetts;
same handle with an extra tip, Heritage Foundation, Deerfield, Massachusetts.

GIFT OF MISS ESTHER JACKSON AND MRS. PERCY O. DALEY *59.1000*

18

18 Porringer, 1680–1710

H. 1¹⁵⁄₁₆ in.; D. of lip 5³⁄₁₆ in. (uneven); L. of handle 2⅝ in.; Wt. 8 oz., 5 dwt.

MARKS: *a* on back of handle and (rare) on step of bowl.

Narrow slightly everted rim, curved sides, slight step slants to domed base. Center point in bowl. Geometric handle pierced in quatrefoils, circles, and shaped holes (resoldered at broken rim); three circles punched in tip at front and back. Edge of domed base broken opposite handle.

Engraved ESP on handle away from bowl.

HISTORY: Perhaps Erasmus Stevens, m. Persis Bridge, September 1707; subsequent history unknown.

REFERENCE: *Hipkiss 1943*, p. 21.

THE PHILIP LEFFINGWELL SPALDING COLLECTION. GIVEN IN HIS MEMORY BY KATHERINE AMES SPALDING AND PHILIP SPALDING, OAKES AMES SPALDING, HOBART AMES SPALDING 42.255

19

19 Plate, 1690–1700

D. 5⅜ in.; Wt. 4 oz., 10½ dwt.

MARK: *a* on rim.

Of heavy stock, circular with molded or scribed edge, almost horizontal flat rim, stepped center with center point on top.

Engraved in center of back ICS.

HISTORY: Probably John and Sarah (Shrimpton) Clarke, m. April 30, 1691; subsequent history unknown.

NOTES: The engraving is the same as that on a mug by Dummer (private collection) which bears the Clarke crest as on the Dummer candlesticks.

REFERENCES: *Halsey 1925*, pl. 16; *Hipkiss 1943*, p. 22, illus.; *Buhler 1957*, p. 43.

20 Standing Salt, 1690–1700

H. 5½ in. (inc. scrolls); W. of base 4¹¹⁄₁₆ in.; Wt. 10 oz., 12 dwt., 6 gr.

MARKS: *a* in bowl and on side of lower spool.

Spool-shaped circular body, both sections raised and joined by molded midband; molded octagonal top and base separated from spool by bands of reeding. Shallow circular flat-bottomed receptacle for salt in top has torus rim within slight step of octagonal hollow moldings. Faint center point in bowl. Four cast scrolled and paneled projections, their tapering stems octagonal, affixed at alternate points of inner octagon. Reeding of lower half in one with stem, molded octagonal step has added strengthening band beneath forming tiny flange; upper reeding probably in one with spool also.

Engraved lightly *Rebe* at right of most dented support; *RR-* slightly left on stem below *ufsell* (Russell), perhaps added (centered neither on point or panel of octagon below); scratched on side above, *RR 10 oz. 15 dwt.*

HISTORY: Unknown (see *Notes*).

NOTES: Possible ownership conjectured from a tankard in the Harrington Collection, Dartmouth College would be: Rebecca Russell, m. Enoch Greenleaf, 1715. Another Rebecca Russell is recorded in Suffolk Probate Court in 1690 in the will of Eleazer Russell: "I Eleazer Russell of Boston

20

goldsmith . . . to my loveing kinswoman Rebecca Russell daughter of my brother Jonathan of Bastable . . ." One of the witnesses to this will was Jeremiah Dummer. Two other salts of American workmanship are known: one by Edward Winslow (Cat. no. 67); one by Edwards and Allen made for Solomon Stoddard (Harvard 1662), see *Harvard 1936*, no. 115, pl. 21.

REFERENCES: *Avery 1930*, pp. 39, 342; *Buhler 1934*, pp. 46-47, illus.; *Clarke-Dummer 1935*, no. 77 and p. 130, pl. XV; H. F. Clarke, "Jeremiah Dummer, Silversmith (1643-1718)," *Antiques*, XXVIII, no. 4 (1935), pp. 142-145, fig. 4; "The Almanac," *Antiques*, XXXIV, no. 5 (1938), pp. 262, illus.; *Currier 1938*, line drawing, p. 4 of "From the Author's 'Note Book' "; "The Almanac," *Antiques*, XXXV, no. 6 (1939), pp. 302-303; *Ensko 1948*, p. 112, illus.; *Phillips 1949*, p. 51, pl. 10a; *Phillips, Antiques*, no. 2 (1949), p. 116; *McLanathan 1956*, p. 60, fig. 17; *Comstock 1958*, p. 90, fig. 19.

EXHIBITIONS: *Yale 1939*, no. 77; *Chicago 1949*, no. 163, illus. p. 109; The Currier Gallery of Art, Manchester, N.H., February 20-April 14, 1956; *ESU 1960*, no. 3, pl. 1.

BEQUEST OF CHARLES HITCHCOCK TYLER 32.371

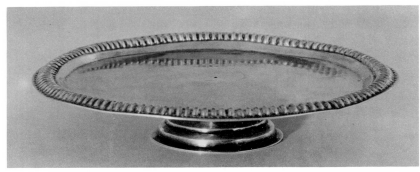

21

21 Salver, 1695–1700

H. 1¼ in. (uneven); D. of base 2½ in.; D. of dish 6¹³⁄₁₆ in.; Wt. 4 oz., 10 dwt.

MARK: *a* near rim of dish.

Circular dish angled just below raised edge of embossed convex reeding with punched dots and half circles on narrow outer flange. The low trumpet foot has tiny flange for fastening and is molded at convex curve to narrow flange. The dish is battered and broken across the rim, slightly left above mark. The center point is now a hole.

Engraved WᴮM on back of dish. Added at varying (recent) times: *William Bowditch/born at Salem/Sept./1663* [sic] *d./May 28, 1728;* and in ray formation underneath: *Joseph Bowditch/b. August 21, 1700, d. October 6, 1780./Elizabeth* [*Bowditch*] *Jeffry./b. Feb. 8th 1735, d. October 1797./ Elizabeth* [*Jeffry*] *Read./b. Feb. 10, 1772, d. March 21, 1855./Jonathan Ingersoll Bowditch./b. October 15, 1806, d. Feb. 19, 1889./Alfred Bowditch/ b. September 6, 1855, d. Feb. 22, 1918./William Ernestus Bowditch./b. April 10, 1850, d. May 22, 1918./William Ingersoll Bowditch 2ᴅ./b. Dec. 8, 1893. d.*

HISTORY: William (c. 1665-1728) and Mary (Gardner) Bowditch; descended in the Bowditch family.

NOTES: Captain William Bowditch, born at Lyme Regis, Dorset County, England, c. 1665, came with his mother to Salem about 1679. He married in Salem, August 30, 1688, Mary, daughter of Lieutenant Thomas and Mary

(Porter) Gardner. She was born February 14, 1669/70 and died in May, 1724. He died May 28, 1728.

A salver was defined in Blount's *Glossographia* (1661) as "... a new fashioned peece of wrought plate, broad and flat, with a foot underneath, and is used in giving Beer, or other liquid thing, to save the Carpit and Cloathes from drops."

REFERENCES: *Avery 1930*, p. 70; *Clarke-Dummer 1935*, no. 63 and pl. XI; K. C. Buhler, "Three Early American Salvers," *MFA Bulletin*, XXXIII, no. 198 (1935), pp. 52-54, illus.

H. E. BOLLES FUND 35.636

22

22 Tankard, 1695–1705

H. 6¹⁄₁₆ in. (inc. thumbpiece); D. of base 4¾ in.; D. of lip 4³⁄₁₆ in.; Wt. 22 oz., 17 dwt.

MARKS: *a* on cover and at left of handle.

Slightly tapering straight sides, incised lines below everted lip, applied molded baseband, domed bottom. Center points on bottom and in lid. Flat stepped cover, triple incised lines on flange serrated at front and at sides of hinge plate. Chased cusped thumbpiece, its support modeled above tapering base and tangent to step of lid; meander wire in molded hinge plates; loose pin in five-part hinge. Slight shaping on flat shoulder of scroll handle with seamed ring soldered below curve and shaped shield tip over (splitting) end with slot vent hole. Upper joining broad with curved rattail below, bisected by a slight horizontal channel. Cut-card decoration on lid, its forked tip over step; same size and pattern at lower handle joining. Large spout has been removed which probably cut into flange of cover (repairs visible).

Cracks at handle joining.

ENGRAVED: ICR on handle.

HISTORY: Early history unknown; William F. Wharton by 1916; the donor by 1928.

NOTES: Other Dummer tankards with cut-card decoration at handle and lid are owned by The Metropolitan Museum of Art, New York; Phillips Academy, Addison Gallery of American Art, Andover, Massachusetts; The South Parish, Portsmouth, New Hampshire; private collection; The Henry Francis du Pont Winterthur Museum, Delaware (cut-card only on cover).

REFERENCES: *Halsey 1925*, pl. 16; *Jones 1928*, p. 16; *Bell 1930*, pl. III; *Avery 1930*, pp. 44, 52, 244, 300-302, pl. VII; *Hipkiss 1942*, p. 85 illus.; *Hipkiss 1943*, pp. 15-16, illus.; *Buhler 1957*.

EXHIBITION: *Exhibition of Old Silver Owned in Worcester County*, Worcester Art Museum, June 15-September 15, 1913, no. 33.

THE PHILIP LEFFINGWELL SPALDING COLLECTION. GIVEN IN HIS MEMORY BY KATHERINE AMES SPALDING AND PHILIP SPALDING, OAKES AMES SPALDING, HOBART AMES SPALDING 42.224

23 Communion Cup, 1700

H..7⅝ in.; D. of base 4⁵⁄₁₆ in.; D. of lip 4⅜ in. (uneven); Wt. 9 oz., 17 dwt.

MARKS: *a* on side (below crack), at left of engraving, and on foot.

Bowl has very slight flare at rim, straight sides, lower part spirally gadrooned with chased dots and curves outlining upper edge of gadrooning. Base plain beyond applied disc with smaller disc at junction of turned stem, two spool forms (lower obviously seamed) above pear-shaped baluster, cast rayed collar below, the scallops of which extend beyond small dome of flat foot with moulded edge, incised reeds on step, and flange with added strengthening rim. Edge of bowl cracked.

Engraved *Ex dono/Mr. Joshua &/Mrs. Hanna/Bangs/To The Church of Eastham/1700.*

HISTORY: Joshua Bangs (d. 1709/10), m. Hannah Scudder; to the Church of Eastham, Massachusetts; presumably when Eastham and Orleans became separate towns, the cup was returned to the Bangs' descendants, from a recent generation of whom it was bought.

NOTES: The earliest known communion cup in this form. A similar pear-form stem, but with visible seam, is found on Dummer's 1708 cups, First Church, Boston.

REFERENCES: K. C. Buhler, "A Communion Cup by Jeremiah Dummer," *MFA Bulletin*, XXXVI, no. 213 (1938), pp. 14-16; *Ensko 1948*, p. 14, illus.; *Phillips 1949*, p. 49; *Wenham 1949*, pl. IV; *Buhler 1950*, pp. 22-23, fig. 15.

EXHIBITIONS: *Johns Hopkins 1940*, no. 18, illus., *Chicago 1949*, no. 162, illus. p. 111; *Minneapolis 1956*, no. 213, fig. 34; *Richmond 1960*, no. 46; *ESU 1960*, no. 5, pl. 5.

ANONYMOUS GIFT 37.1172

23

24

24 Church Cup or Beaker, c. 1700

H. 4½in.; D. of base 2½ in.; D. of lip 3⁹⁄₁₆ in.; Wt. 6 oz., 11 dwt.

MARK: *a* on side.

Slightly flaring lip, cylindrical sides, vertical gadrooning on curved section above very slightly stepped base encircled by molded baseband. Center point on bottom, between initials.

Engraved on bottom *the: gifft*/of/·E·B·/—lower-case letters semiscript, block initials.

HISTORY: Unknown (see *Notes*).

NOTES: The long held idea that Edward Boylston was the donor is untenable in view of his not having joined the Church in Brattle Square until 1720. A logical donor would have been Edward Brattle (1670-1719), brother of Thomas Brattle, whose name is first on the list of founders. The church records indicate that silver was owned in 1700, and this is the only piece known now which could have then been in the possession of the church. A matching beaker was made by William Cowell for the church (Cat. no. 101); one by John Dixwell with taller gadroons for the Congregational Church, Exeter, New Hampshire; many others were made by Dummer, some with narrow reeding on the sides (*MFA 1956*, no. 54).

REFERENCES: *Jones 1913*, p. 67, pl. XXVII; *Paull 1913*, pp. 23-24, illus.; *Avery 1930*, pp. 63, pl. VI; C. L. Avery, "The Beginnings of American Silver," *Antiques*, XVIII, no. 2 (1930), p. 122, fig. 3; *Clarke-Dummer 1935*, no. 11, pl. III; *Ensko 1948*, p. 31, illus.; *McLanathan 1956*, p. 56, fig. 9.

EXHIBITIONS: *MFA 1906*, no. 97; *MFA 1911*, no. 362; *An Introduction to Silver*, The Newark Museum, Oct. 1953-May 1954, no. 86, illus.; *Minneapolis 1956*, no. 214, fig. 48; *Buffalo 1965*, no. 103.

GIFT OF THE BENEVOLENT FRATERNITY OF CHURCHES
SILVER OF THE CHURCH IN BRATTLE SQUARE 13.400

25 Spoon, c. 1700

L. 6⅞ in.; Wt. 1 oz., 8½ dwt.

MARKS: *a* on back of stem and in bowl (both away from bowl).
Rectangular in section, handle is very thin at wavy end which is bent forward. Bowl has molded and rounded drop in grooved rattail flanked by leafy scroll design—apparently the Dummer stamp most common in survival. The spoon's position in the swage gives it a longer drop and causes the first scroll to be slightly further from the edge than on other spoons.
Engraved *MW* on back of handle.

HISTORY: Unknown.

NOTES: *Clarke-Dummer 1935* records seven other spoons on which the same bowl stamp appears (Cat. nos. 64, 65, 66, 68, 69, 70, 73).

GIFT OF MISS ESTHER JACKSON AND MRS. PERCY O. DALEY *59.1001*

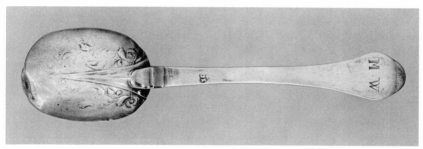

25

TIMOTHY DWIGHT
1664–1692

TIMOTHY DWIGHT was the grandson of John (d. 1661), one of the first settlers of Dedham, Massachusetts and son of Captain Timothy (b. 1630), and the second of his six wives, Sarah, daughter of Michael Powell, whom he married in 1653. His third wife, whom he married in 1665, was Anna Flint of Braintree, whose cousin was the wife of John Hull. Their ten children included Nathaniel, ancestor of Timothy Dwight, president of Yale College.

Timothy was baptized in the First Church in Dedham "1d 8 m 1654" by the old calendar, and undoubtedly served his apprenticeship with his stepmother's cousin and his partner. In 1676 Hull's son-in-law, Samuel Sewall, made the first of several entries in his diary about Tim Dwight. In 1678 Dwight was listed among Medfield's Contributors to Harvard College for the sum of ten shillings; and in that year Hull recorded his illness with smallpox. Dwight, as "Goldsmith," penned his will on December 9, 1691 "visited by the hands of ye Just & Almighty God with a sore and languishing sickness" and left to his "dear wife Elizabeth all my Estate Personal & Real except one Gun." The latter was "a Musquet with a German lock" for his brother Michael. He left "house & land scituated in Boston with all the privileges & appurtenances thereto" as well as land in Roxbury and a farm at Marlborough. His inventory included: "to Several Goldsmiths tools of all sorts £20-10-; household stuff and wearing apparel £44-18-6."

Sewall recorded the bearers at his funeral: "Cousin Dummer, Capt Jno Walley, Capt. Wing., Rowse, Thos. Savage, Goldsmith, Robt. Saunderson." The last would have been the son of his former master. Rowse, too, was a goldsmith, the emigrating "Willem Ros, from Wesel" (1639-1704/5).

Dwight's mark (a), on the two pieces known of his fashioning, shows his initials, a pellet between, over six grouped pellets in a heart-shaped punch.

a

26

26 Salver, c. 1680–1690

H. 3³⁄₁₆ in.; D. of base 3¹¹⁄₁₆ in.; D. of dish 11⅝₆ in.; Wt. 18 oz., 18 dwt.

MARKS: *a* stamped three times (flanking and at right of unicorn's head) on rim, opposite prickwork.

Circular stepped flat dish, almost horizontal broad brim, its edge scribed or lightly molded, center point on top. Trumpet foot, a quarter-round at upper joining, splayed stepped base with narrow horizontal flange. A trefoil prickwork design on the rim is partly covered by engraving, and the original pricked initials, a *T* at the top, are covered by engraved ones.

Engraved TBM; *RP* has been added in large script letters under rim.

HISTORY: Early history unknown; Thomas and Mary Barton, m. 1710; for subsequent history see Cat. no. 39.

NOTES: The decorative engraving was probably done by John Coney. On the brim between four branches of leaves, each with a carnation toward the rim and three with pendent tulip blossoms, the fourth a bud, are figures of animals: a unicorn and a lion, both prancing; an elephant with turreted howdah on his back; and an animal with horns, a hump, and a long tail (described as a gazelle and as a camel). The flowers, leaves, and feet of the animals extend into the step of the dish, in contrast to the engraving on his own plate (see Cat. no. 36). The only other piece by Timothy Dwight known today is a tankard, its lid reminiscent of his master's tankard (Cat. no. 1) engraved with flowers that are in a scroll-handled vase at the lion thumbpiece, which is unique in published American silver (*MFA 1956*, no. 57, illus.).

REFERENCES: *Bigelow 1917*, pp. 237-238, fig. 144; *Jones 1928*, p. 38; *Avery 1930*, pp. 49, 69; *Morison 1930*, illus. opp. p. 156; *Clark [Buhler] 1931*,

p. 46, illus.; K. C. Buhler, "Three Early American Salvers," *MFA Bulletin*, XXXIII, No. 198 (1935), pp. 52-54, illus.; *Buhler 1947*, p. 39, fig. 13; *Wenham 1949*, p. 38; *Phillips, Antiques*, no. 6 (1948), p. 416; *Phillips 1949*, p. 34; *Buhler 1950*, p. 23, fig. 16; *Buhler 1955*, p. 457, fig. 4; *Ellis 1961*, pp. 19, 21, fig. 1.

EXHIBITIONS: *Yale 1939*, no. 85; *Chicago 1949*, no. 165, illus. p. 110; *Minneapolis 1956*, no. 217; *MFA 1956*, no. 57; *Richmond 1960*, no. 51, illus.; *R.I. 1965*, no. 67, fig. 31.

GIFT OF MR. AND MRS. DUDLEY LEAVITT PICKMAN 31.227

26

27

27 Toys, c. 1685

Unknown Maker

Caster: H. 2 in.; D. of base 13⁄16 in.; Wt. 9½ dwt.
Caudle cup: H. 1⅜ in. (inc. finial); D. of base 1 in.; D. of lip 13⁄16 in.;
Wt. 13 dwt.
Plate: D. 211⁄16 in.; Wt. 6½ dwt.

Mark: Illegible, on caster below slot for fastener.
Caster: seamed, cylindrical; molding at base, rim (bezel broken), and bottom
of cover. Bayonet fastening. Turned finial with quatrefoil-shaped cut-card
design below (see that on fig. 37 in catalogue of *A Loan Exhibition of Antique
English Silver Miniatures,* New York, 1941). *Covered Caudle cup:* bottom
soldered on (probably a repair since it has a center point), curved sides,
straight neck, strap scroll handles, one broken. Low domed cover with turned
finial (bent). Considerably dented. *BS* scratched on edge. *Plate:* silver washed
on copper, circular with slightly domed center; wide rim embossed with
rather coarse floral design, dots near edges.

History: Bethiah Shrimpton (1681-1713), whose nuncupative will stated that
her "silver baby things" should go to her sister Hunt's children; descended
in the family to be owned in 1946 by Mr. and Mrs. Francis S. Dane.

Notes: Other pieces of the same set are in the Yale University Art Gallery,
Garvan Collection; matching caster, caudle cup, tankard, and lighting set
descended from the youngest of sister Hunt's children.

Reference: A. Winchester, "Silver Toys," *Antiques,* XXXVII, no. 6 (1940),
p. 287.

Theodora Wilbour Fund in memory of Charlotte Beebe Wilbour
63.957-959

EDWARD WEBB
died 1718

EDWARD WEBB is believed to have been trained in England; the date of his arrival in Boston is not in the published records. His death occurred on October 21, 1718. His will, recorded in the Suffolk Probate Court, was written when he was "of Boston Goldsmith being sick and weak"; Daniel Oliver was sole executor. The *Boston News-Letter* in November 17/24, 1718, reported that "having no poor friends in England that wanted, and getting his money here, he bequeathed Two Hundred Pounds . . . for the use of the poor of Boston." His inventory included "2 tests with plaine and flower'd Spoon Swages."

The same Boston paper in 1739 reported stolen spoons with makers' marks WEBB and COWELL, whereby he appears to be the earliest Boston goldsmith to use his surname as a mark. The mark used on the silver in this collection is that of his initials in a rectangle *(a)*.

a

28 Porringer, 1690–1700

H. 2 in.; D. of lip 5¼ in. (uneven); L. of handle 2⅞ in.; Wt. 7 oz., 16½ dwt.

MARKS: *a* on bowl and on back of handle.

Everted rim, curved sides, slight step to domed bottom. Center point in bowl. Cast handle pierced with two quatrefoils and circle graduated to tip, flanked by three circles each side, double-arched cuttings at bowl and sides.

Engraved *IB* on handle, earlier initials (erased) were also away from bowl. On bottom: *Johanna Butler ye : 16th : 9 mo : 1708.*

HISTORY: Early history unknown. Johanna Buttler, m. Joseph Woods in January, 1729; bought by donor about 1928 in New Bedford.

NOTES: Very similar handle on porringer by Webb privately owned (exhibited *ESU 1960*, no. 17). It too has initials of a later owner (Rufus and Katherine Greene).

REFERENCES: *Hipkiss 1943*, p. 24, illus.; *Buhler 1957*, p. 38.

THE PHILIP LEFFINGWELL SPALDING COLLECTION. GIVEN IN HIS MEMORY BY KATHERINE AMES SPALDING AND PHILIP SPALDING, OAKES AMES SPALDING, HOBART AMES SPALDING 42.259

28

29

29 Porringer, c. 1700

H. $1^{15}/_{16}$ in.; D. of lip $4^5/_8$ in.; L. of handle $2^1/_2$ in.; Wt. 6 oz., 10 dwt.

MARK: *a* in bowl near center point.

Slightly everted rim, curved sides, stepped and very slightly domed bottom. Handle cutting of heart in graduated circles, shaped cuttings flank initials, circles flank double-arched hole at bowl. Handle very neatly soldered in angle.

Engraved initials *MI* or *IW* on handle; on bottom: *EI;* inside rim at handle: *ALJ* and *OWH*.

HISTORY: Mary Jackson, daughter of Edward Jackson (d. 1757), m. Oliver Wendell; her great niece, Amelia Lee Jackson, m. Oliver Wendell Holmes.

NOTES: It is uncertain whether the first initials should be read away from the bowl (*MI* for Mary Jackson) or toward the bowl (*IW* for Jacob Wendell, father of Oliver). The handle design is similar to that on New York porringers which Miss V. Isabelle Miller considered the earliest New York cutting (*New York Silversmiths of the Seventeenth Century,* Museum of the City of New York, 1962-1963).

THE EDWARD JACKSON HOLMES COLLECTION. BEQUEST OF MRS. EDWARD JACKSON HOLMES *65.386*

30 Tankard, c. 1700

H. 6 in. (with thumbpiece); D. of base $4^1/_8$ in.; D. of lip $3^1/_2$-$3^5/_8$ in. (uneven); Wt. 16 oz., $15^1/_2$ dwt.

MARKS: *a* at left of handle and on cover.

Straight tapering sides, incised lines at rim, and applied baseband which is finely reeded above a torus molding. Stepped and rather high flat cover with wide flange serrated at front and back, the edge scribed. Dolphin and mask thumbpiece, wavy line on molded hinge plates, five-part hinge. Hollow scroll handle grooved on curve with slight curl below; long rattail body drop, disc at lower joining, notched shield-shaped handle tip. No center point visible, perhaps removed by later engraving.

30

Engraved on bottom ITE and later (in script) *S. Carter;* weight scratched on bottom *16-18.*

HISTORY: Unknown.

EXHIBITION: *MFA 1956,* no. 140.

BEQUEST OF ANNIE BOLTON MATTHEWS BRYANT 34.32

31 Tankard, c. 1715

H. 6½ in. (inc. thumbpiece); D. of base 4⁹⁄₁₆ in.; D. of lip 3¾ in.; Wt. 22 oz., 2 dwt.

MARKS: *a* upside down at left of handle and across the flat edge of the cover, the *E* side at the angle of the dome struck before the thumbpiece was in its present position.

Straight tapering sides, everted rim with two incised lines below, center point on bottom. Applied baseband as on preceding, with applied bead slightly above disc of lower handle joining. Molded and stepped cover, the top hammered into a slight dome; flange lightly grooved, serrated at front with a slight jog each side of hinge plate, under which the extended flange is soldered with a blister (bezel missing). Double spiral thumbpiece grooved above tapering support. Molded hinge plates with meander wire (inner one repaired) for five-part hinge (with loose pin). Outer plate molded and rounded

31

on scroll handle with long rattail at upper joining, the flat surface stopping below curve, and a (bent) curl beginning the lower surface, the tip finished with a slanted disc with very little overhang of the curve. The vent hole is a slot. The cover was perhaps originally similar to Cat. no. 30.

Engraved *IM* below a letter worn by thumbpiece on handle; *IMW* (in script) on side might be a repetition of the original engraving.

HISTORY: Unknown.

NOTES: A midband appears on the tankard by John Coney which was bequeathed by Samuel More to the First Church of Boston in 1716. The same base molding appears on Cat. no. 30 and on a tankard by Webb in the City Art Museum of St. Louis, which has the plain handle with curl and disc tip and a domed cover, but the thumbpiece is a later scroll type.

REFERENCE: *Buhler 1939*, pp. 114-115, illus.

GIFT OF ARTHUR D. FOSS 39.4

JOHN CONEY
1655/6–1722

JOHN CONEY was, to judge by his surviving work, the most versatile and productive goldsmith of his generation, and the MFA has the greatest single aggregate of his work. The first piece given to this museum was the Anna Quincy sugar box (Cat. no. 33), which was one of his most ambitious works; the excellence of his heraldic engraving is represented on the Spalding tankard (Cat. no. 43); and his engraved plate (Cat. no. 36) thus far has no peer.

Coney was born on January 5, 1655/6 to John Coney, cooper, emigrant at the age of six years, and his wife Mary, daughter of Robert Nash. In 1670 he was legally of age to be apprenticed, and various factors suggest the partners Sanderson and Hull as his masters. He was married to Sarah of unknown surname, by whom he had two children in 1678 and 1679 who died in infancy; about 1683 he married Sarah Blackman, who bore him four children, of whom only Sarah survived her father. In 1694 he married Mary (Atwater), widow of Captain John Clark, and of their six daughters, four lived to maturity. Mary was the sister of Hannah Atwater, who had married Jeremiah Dummer in 1672. In 1688 Coney was a neighbor of diarist Samuel Sewall on Court Street; at the turn of the century he was located near the Town Dock; and in 1717 he moved to Ann Street. He served as constable, "hogg reeve," and tithingman. He engraved paper money for the colony and cut a seal for Harvard College. As recorded in its account books, the First Church in Charlestown, Massachusetts, "13 March 1711/12 sold the brass mony [from the contribution box] to Mr Conye the gooldsmith for six shillings." He died in 1722, leaving an apprentice and carefully inventoried tools to show that his activities had continued into his sixties.

Coney used the following marks to identify his work: *(a)* IC with annulet between and fleur-de-lis below in heart-shaped stamp; *(b)* IC with fleur-de-lis below in heart; *(c)* IC in small rectangle; and *(d)* IC crowned, with coney below, in shield. A fifth mark of his initials, in an ellipse, is not represented in the MFA; it appears alone and on bezels of pieces with his coney mark.

a   *b*   *c*   *d*

32

32 Pair of Spoons, c. 1680

42.231: L. 7⅝ in.; Wt. 1 oz., 16½ dwt.; *42.232:* L. 7⁹⁄₁₆ in.; Wt. 1 oz., 14 dwt.

MARKS: *a* on back of stem and in bowl of each.

Each with trifid tip bent forward, curved and tapering to stem rectangular in section and quite thick above short V-drop with incised bar on back of elliptical bowl.

Engraved *KP* over italic date *1742* on back of each. 42.231 has script *KA.P.* on front; 42.232 has script *GPT* in another cutting on front.

HISTORY: Probably Katherine Brackenburg, m. Samuel Phipps; their daughter Katherine, m. John Blaney, Charlestown; second marriage, 1718, to Benjamin Andrews (d. 1739); third marriage 1743, to Joseph White; her son John Andrews (b. 1719), m. Margaret Davis; their daughter Katherine (b. 1750); descended in the family to Katherine Andrews Pond (b. c. 1885), from whom the spoons were bought.

NOTES: Katherine Pond thought that her grandmother had added the script initials for her but could not identify the others. The history given above cannot be absolutely proved but is convincing. The only published trifid-handled spoons by identified American makers with the short V-drop of the earlier slip and Puritan spoons are these, in a set of four (one owned by The Metropolitan Museum of Art in New York and one by Yale University Art Gallery, Garvan Collection).

REFERENCES: *Hipkiss 1943*, p. 30, illus.; *Buhler 1957*, p. 45.

THE PHILIP LEFFINGWELL SPALDING COLLECTION. GIVEN IN HIS MEMORY BY KATHERINE AMES SPALDING AND PHILIP SPALDING, OAKES AMES SPALDING, HOBART AMES SPALDING 42.231-232

33

33 Sugar Box, 1680–1690

H. 4¹³⁄₁₆ in. (inc. handle); W. at rim 6 in; L. at rim 7²⁵⁄₃₂ in.; Wt. 28 oz., 10 dwt.

MARKS: *a* once on bottom and twice in matting of top, indistinctly
on molding of rim.

Raised, elliptical, with convex sides, horizontal rim, and almost flat bottom.
Sides embossed with twelve lobes divided by granulated or matted designs
around flutings with leaf tips above and chased small scallops outlining
top and bottom of the matting. Cast paneled legs affixed equidistant below
four flutes with pad joinings and double spiral feet. Applied bar at back
holds short ends of three-part hinge for lid. Cover has molded flange with
narrow applied molding at edge, its domed surface has border of sixteen
bosses divided by short flutes with shaped tips surrounding matting for oak
leaves which ray from an elliptical laurel wreath across which lies the handle.
Stems with small veined trefoil tips extend from oak leaves to fill sides.
The cast handle is a snake twice coiled in central upright loops, whose tapering tail extends in many loops lengthwise on box almost to the tip of
the oak leaf ellipse; the less coiled neck ends in a modeled head with
forked tongue. The head and the tail are equidistant from the center. There
is no sign of a bezel, and the hinge, in three equal parts for the hasp at the
front, would seem not to permit one. The curved hasp, triangular with
finely scalloped edge, has two decorative holes at the sides and one near the
tip to fit over the staple soldered through the front boss.

Engraved in slightly curved semiscript on bottom: *The gift of Grandmother
Norton to Anna Quincy born 1719.* Added after 1837: *Joanna Quincy
(Thaxter) Loring/Sophia (Loring) Whittemore/Anna Quincy (Thaxter)
Cushing/Mary (Cushing) Churchill. 1900.*

HISTORY: First owner conjectured as John Norton; his widow, Mary (Mason)
Norton, to Anna Quincy (1719-1799), daughter of John Quincy (Harvard
1708) and Elizabeth (Norton). Anna married John Thaxter 1744; their
daughter Joanna Quincy (1757-1856), m. Thomas Loring; their daughter
Sophia, m. Nathaniel Whittemore; the eldest daughter of her cousin Susan
Joy Thaxter, Anna Quincy Thaxter, m. Benjamin Cushing; their daughter
Mary, m. Joseph Richmond Churchill.

NOTES: The donor's daughter, Anna Quincy Churchill, M.D., agreed to the gift to the museum of this sugar box, which by family tradition had passed to the eldest daughter. The first John Norton in the Colony was minister of the First Church, Boston (d. 1661). His widow, Mary (d. 1678), left to his nephew, Rev. John Norton of Hingham (d. 1716), twenty pounds and her husband's library; this nephew's wife, Mary (daughter of Arthur and Joanna Parker Mason), is the "Grandmother Norton" of the engraved semi-script on the bottom: John Marshall Phillips in *Phillips 1949* compared this piece to the London example of 1676 illustrated in C. J. Jackson's *History of English Plate* (London, 1911, p. 832). In *Antiques, 1949-1950*, he included it with the 1700-1725 group, but acknowledged that it was probably from the seventeenth century.

REFERENCES: *Bigelow 1917*, pp. 398-399, fig. 287; Stephen G. C. Ensko, *American Silversmiths and Their Marks*, New York, 1927, illus. frontispiece; *Jones 1928*, p. 28, pl. VI, no. 1; *Avery 1930*, p. 49, C. Louise Avery, "The Beginnings of American Silver," *Antiques*, XVIII, no. 2 (1930), pp. 122-125, fig. 4; *Bell 1930*, p. 210, pl. V; *Buhler 1932*, pp. 45-47, illus. p. 46; *Clarke-Coney 1932*, no. 84 and pl. XXIV; *Buhler 1934*, p. 49; T. H. Ormsbee, "Trends in Collecting," *Antiques*, XLI, no. 1 (1942), pp. 24-26, fig. 3; *Buhler 1947*, pp. 36-37, fig. 5; *Ensko 1948*, p. 121, illus.; *Wenham 1949*, pp. 34, 196, fig. 43; *Phillips, Antiques*, no. 2 (1949), p. 117; *Buhler 1950*, pp. 19-20, illus. cover and fig. 11; *McLanathan 1956*, p. 54, fig. 6; *Comstock 1958*, p. 80, fig. 2; K. C. Buhler, "The Nine Colonial Sugar Boxes," *Antiques*, LXXXV, no. 1 (1964), pp. 88-89, fig. 1.

EXHIBITIONS: *MFA 1911*, no. 238, pl. 7; *MFA 1932*, no. 1; *Harvard 1936*, no. 95; *Harvard 1939; Yale 1939*, no. 50, fig. 18; *MMA 1941; Chicago 1949*, no. 156, illus. p. 111; *Kansas 1950; Presentation Silver 1955*, illus.; *MFA 1956*, no. 23; *Richmond 1960*, no. 28, illus. frontispiece.

GIFT OF MRS. JOSEPH RICHMOND CHURCHILL 13.421

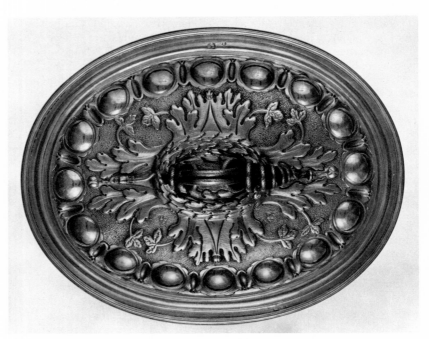

33

34

34

34 Caudle Cup, c. 1690

H. 5⅝ in. (inc. handle); D. of base 5⅛ in.; D. of lip 5¾ in.;
Wt. 26 oz., 17½ dwt.

MARKS: *a* on neck and not quite centered on bottom.

Bulbous body of heavy gauge, curved neck with scribed molding, short
lengths of graduated punches form border of embossed sides, narrowly
stepped bottom very slightly domed. Embossment of running design of
flowers centering on a demiboy, issuing from a scalloped or petaled design,
is all executed with very short or dotted punches; the lad's position is
different on each side. Cast caryatid handles affixed over rim and in curve of
neck with freestanding scroll; lower joining forked with scroll tips, one fixed
and lower curving freely; modeled bosses on sides repeated as woman's
headdress of handle grip.

Engraved on bottom IMM; the weight is scratched *27-1-7;* added on neck in script: *Oliver Wendell Holmes* (on side opposite mark).

HISTORY: John and Mary (Brattle) Mico, m. 1689; her heirs, Jacob and Sarah (Oliver) Wendell, m. 1714; their son Oliver, m. Mary Jackson 1762; their daughter Sarah, m. Rev. Abiel Holmes 1801; their son Oliver Wendell, m. Amelia Lee Jackson 1840; their son Oliver Wendell, m. Fanny Dixwell 1861; his nephew, Edward Jackson Holmes.

NOTES: Mate to this with added engraving of the Holyoke coat of arms is owned by Harvard University and is known to have belonged to Edward Holyoke and probably his father, Elizur, who died 1711/12 leaving "168¼ ounces of plate at 8/." It was justly published by Mr. Phillips as one of the masterpieces in colonial silversmithing.

REFERENCES: Oliver Wendell Holmes, *Poems by Oliver Wendell Holmes*, "On Lending a Punch Bowl," Boston, 1851; *Avery 1930*, p. 293, pl. LII; *Clarke-Coney 1932*, no. 21; *Phillips 1949*, p. 33 and pl. 8b; *Buhler 1950*, p. 61; K. C. Buhler, "Important Silver from the Edward Jackson Holmes Collection," *MFA Bulletin*, LXV, no. 340 (1967) pp. 61-65, figs. 1-3.

EXHIBITIONS: *MFA 1932*, no. 30; *Harvard 1936*, no. 97; *Yale 1939*, no. 34, fig. 9.

THE EDWARD JACKSON HOLMES COLLECTION. BEQUEST OF MRS. EDWARD JACKSON HOLMES 65.388

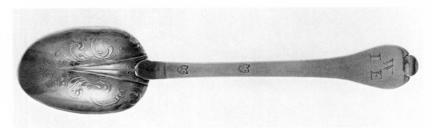

35

35 Spoon, c. 1690

L. 7¹¹⁄₁₆ in.; Wt. 1 oz., 18 dwt.

MARKS: *a* twice on back of stem and in bowl toward handle.

Trifid end handle, the tip forward bent, curves to a stem rectangular in section and quite thick at rounded drop on almost elliptical bowl stamped with outline of raised dots grouped in groove of the tapering rattail and flanked by dotted leafy scrolls terminating in a flower tip. A very faint line on edge at front of handle.

Engraved IᵂE on back of handle; added in script on front of handle horizontally: *1st Ch. T. by S. Winslow 1790.*

HISTORY: Early history unknown; Joshua and Elizabeth (Savage) Winslow, m. 1720; 1790 given to First Church in Tyngsboro, Massachusetts by Sarah Tyng (b. 1720), daughter of Col. Eleazer and Sarah (Alford) Tyng, m. John Winslow (Joshua's brother), Sept. 4, 1760.

NOTES: John and Joshua Winslow were sons of the goldsmith Edward. The only other recorded stamped spoons by Coney are those made for Mary Shrimpton (Yale University Art Gallery, Garvan Collection, and privately owned) which are from a different swage and marked only on the back. Coney's inventory included "9 Spoon punches."

REFERENCES: *Jones 1913*, pp. 471-472; *Bigelow 1917*, p. 265, fig. 165;

Clarke-Coney 1932, no. 75, pl. XXV; *Buhler 1932*, pp. 48-49, illus. p. 45.
EXHIBITIONS: *MFA 1911*, no. 246, pl. 14; *MFA 1932*, no. 3; *Towle 1954*.
THE JOHN WHEELOCK ELLIOT FUND 24.444

36

36 Plate, 1680–1700

D. 11³⁄₁₆ in.; Wt. 17 oz., 7½ dwt.

MARK: *a* on rim midway between two cherubs' heads.

Circular plate has horizontal broad brim with scribed edge, the center
slightly stepped. Center point in dish. Engraved within the area of the brim
are three bibbed (?) cherubs' heads encircled by scrolled wings between wide-
spreading floral sprays of tulips and carnations; within a fourth floral
spray are initials in a plumed cartouche, a partial mask in its foliate base.

Engraved CRE in plumed cartouche. Scratched weight 17=½ and added in
script *RP* (Rachel Pickman) on bottom.

HISTORY: Early history unknown; possibly owned by family of Love Rawlins,
wife of Benjamin Pickman (1707/8-1773); his sister, Rachel Pickman; Love's
son Benjamin (1740-1819); for subsequent history see Cat. no. 39.

NOTES: Indian printed cottons or Stuart embroideries seem possible
sources for the design of the engraving on this outstanding piece. Benjamin
Pickman's inventory (1819, taken on scales unaligned with ours) lists this
as "1 dish 17=5 at 1.10 18.97." A dish in New College, Oxford, by TH,
London, 1665, has a similar design embossed. Other plates by Coney: one,
D. 9⅛ in., engraved *SE* for Sarah Eliot (*Antiques*, LXV, no. 1 [1954], p. 49);

36

one with very broad brim engraved with Eyre arms (Minneapolis
Institute of Arts).

REFERENCES: *Bigelow 1917*, p. 238; *Avery 1930*, pp. 48, 55, and pl. III; *Bell
1930*, p. 210, pl. VI; *Morison 1930*, illus. opp. p. 164; *Clark [Buhler] 1931*,
pp. 48-49, illus., p. 46; *Clarke-Coney 1932*, no. 59 and pl. XXI; *Buhler,
Antiques*, no. 5 (1945), p. 269, fig. 5; *Phillips 1949*, p. 34, and pl. 4b; *Phillips
Antiques*, no. 6 (1948), p. 415; *Wenham 1949*, p. 200, fig. 49; *Buhler 1955*,
p. 458, illus. p. 457; *McLanathan 1956*, p. 59, fig. 15; *Ellis 1961*, p. 23
and fig. 2.

EXHIBITIONS: *MFA 1932*, no. 8; *Yale 1939*, fig. 7; *MMA 1941*; *Minneapolis
1956*, no. 198, fig. 40; *MFA 1956*, no. 25; *Richmond 1960*, no. 34.

GIFT OF MR. AND MRS. DUDLEY LEAVITT PICKMAN 31.226

37   37

37 Miniature Caudle Cup, 1680–1700

Attributed to JOHN CONEY

H. 1¼ in. (uneven); D. of base 1¼ in.; D. of lip 1⅝ in.; Wt. 11½ dwt.

MARKS: None.

Bulbous body on stepped flat base, almost straight rim, lower part chased
and divided into four panels horizontally by a row of dots above curve
and at step, vertically by paired bands with matting between. In each matted
panel is a stylized leaf form similar to the leaf pattern on the base; the

vein is a matted triangle. The wire handles are in scroll form, their tips free-standing and upcurved. The pattern on the base is more elaborate; the long vein of the leaf is cross-hatched; three loops at each side and a broad one across the top have lines of dots inside and a single dot in the angles. There is no visible center point.

HISTORY: Bought by Mrs. Patterson together with a less well made cup, marked by Coney's apprentice, Paul Revere I (see Cat. no. 145).

EXHIBITION: *MFA 1956,* no. 43, figs. 42, 42a.

BEQUEST OF MRS. F. GORDON PATTERSON *56.117*

38

38 Beaker, c. 1695

H. 4¹⁄₁₆ in.; D. of base 2¹⁵⁄₁₆ in.; D. of lip 3½ in.; Wt. 6 oz., 11 dwt.

MARKS: *a,* very worn, at left of handle and in center of bottom over center point.

Straight sides with slightly flaring lip taper to applied molded baseband, the edge perhaps slightly cut. Crude strap handle (added) with incised lines at edges, poorly soldered at rim, where body is cracked, and slightly above baseband, has curled tip. Hole in body at upper part of the engraved *R* has been repaired.

Engraved *HNR* on front, added in large script monogram.

HISTORY: Unknown before 1928, when lent by the donor.

NOTES: See Coney beakers of 1693 (First Congregational Church, Bristol,

Rhode Island) and that of Ipswich Church, gift of Thomas Knowlton, now owned by Yale University Art Gallery, Garvan Collection. Beakers dated 1713 (First Congregational Church, Hampton, N.H.) had no baseband.

REFERENCES: *Hipkiss 1943*, p. 27, illus.; *Buhler 1957*, p. 45.

EXHIBITION: *MFA 1932*, no. 40.

THE PHILIP-LEFFINGWELL SPALDING COLLECTION. GIVEN IN HIS MEMORY BY KATHERINE AMES SPALDING AND PHILIP SPALDING, OAKES AMES SPALDING, HOBART AMES SPALDING 42.236

39   40

39 Cup, 1690–1700

H. 3⅞6 in.; D. of base 1¹¹⁄₁₆ in.; D. of lip 2⁵⁄₁₆ in.; Wt. 3 oz., 2½ dwt.

MARKS: *b* at left of handle and on bottom.

Globular body contracted for cylindrical neck with molded rim, the curved base very slightly domed in the center, on narrow molded footring. No center point. Narrow band of reeding on neck is stopped for upper joining of cast scroll handle, which has angled upper surface, slight grip with graduated beading below, scroll tips, lower one with tiny elliptical disc applied; slight scroll midway inside and outside above lower joining. Larger band of reeding on shoulder, vertical gadrooning rising from footring.

Engraved *MW* on bottom just below mark; added on front (between gadrooning and reeding) large script monogram *SPL*.

HISTORY: Mary Willoughby (b. Salem 1676), granddaughter of Francis Willoughby (deputy governor of Massachusetts, 1665-1671), m. Thomas Barton, 1710; their daughter Mary, m. Dr. Bezaleel Toppan; their daughter Mary (1744-1817), m. Benjamin Pickman IV (1740-1819) 1762; their son Thomas (1773-1817), m. second Sophia Palmer (1786-1862); their daughter Mary Toppan (1816-1878), m. Dr. George Bailey Loring, 1851; their daughter Sally Pickman Loring (1859-1913), m. Theodore F. Dwight; their son Lawrence (1896-1918), cousin of the donor.

NOTES: Thomas Barton in 1758 bequeathed unto his "dearly beloved wife . . . All her Maiden Plate as a Tanckard Spoons etc. and as much more as she may want to be useful for her and all my Gold Rings had at funerals saving what may be made use of for my own funeral." In the inventory of the estate of their granddaughter's husband, Benjamin Pickman IV (1740-1819), are to be found many of the pieces in the Pickman Collection. Lawrence Dwight, an only child, was killed in the First World War. Descended in another branch of the family is Cat. no. 40; a differently proportioned similar cup by Coney is in a private collection; one by Edward Winslow is owned by the Minneapolis Institute of Arts, its small molding on the rim a recent addition for strength. The form of the cup may be traced to stoneware jugs of the sixteenth century.

REFERENCES: *Bigelow 1917*, p. 170, fig. 91; *Avery 1930*, pp. 66, 314, and pl. IX; *Clark [Buhler] 1931*, p. 44, illus.; *Clarke-Coney 1932*, no. 42, pl. XVIII, mark in error; *Ensko 1948*, illus. p. 32; *Wenham 1949*, p. 188, fig. 20; *Buhler 1950*, p. 36, fig. 29; *Ellis 1961*, p. 23, fig. 3.

EXHIBITIONS: *MFA 1932*, no. 5; *Chicago 1949*, no. 155, illus. p. 109; *MFA 1956*, no. 29; *Richmond 1960*, no. 23.

GIFT OF MR. AND MRS. DUDLEY LEAVITT PICKMAN *31.218*

40 Cup, 1690–1700

H. of body 3⅜ in.; D. of lip 2²⁷⁄₃₂ in.; Wt. 3 oz., 1 dwt.

MARKS: *b* on neck at left of handle and on bottom.

Mate to Cat. no. 39.

Engraved *MW* on bottom. Added in thin dotted script on front: *MP/to/FWP*.

HISTORY: Mary Willoughby, m. Thomas Barton, 1710; their granddaughter Mary Toppan (1744-1817), m. Benjamin Pickman IV (1740-1819); their son Benjamin (1763-1843), whose youngest son was Francis Willoughby Pickman; Martha (Codman) Karolik, his great-niece.

REFERENCES: *Clarke-Coney 1932*, no. 43, mark in error; *Hipkiss 1941*, p. 212, no. 143, illus.; Hipkiss, *MFA Bulletin*, no. 236 (1941), illus. p. 86.

EXHIBITIONS: *MFA 1932*, no. 33; *Minneapolis 1956*, no. 193, *MFA 1956*, no. 29; *R.I. 1965*, no. 48, fig. 10.

M. AND M. KAROLIK COLLECTION. *39.227*

41

41 Tankard, 1690–1700

H. 6⅛ in. (inc. thumbpiece); D. of base 4¾ in.; D. of lip 4⅛ in.;
Wt. 28 oz., 9½ dwt.

MARKS: *a* on cover, at left of handle, and on bottom.

Tapering sides, incised lines below rim, very simply molded applied base-band. Flat stepped cover with molded flange serrated at front and at either side of hinge plate. Molded hinge plates, the inner notched, the outer with shaped applique on scroll handle with rattail body drop; double spiral thumb-piece with modeled support. Handle tip missing.

Engraved *MA* on bottom. Allen arms and crest in helmeted acanthus cartouche on front. Scratched weight *28-9½* on bottom.

HISTORY: Unknown.

NOTES: Tankard on renewable loan to the Henry Ford Museum and Greenfield Village, Dearborn, Michigan.

REFERENCES: *Buhler 1934*, p. 49, illus.; *Clarke-Coney 1932*, no. 90.

EXHIBITION: *MFA 1932*, no. 43.

BEQUEST OF CHARLES HITCHCOCK TYLER 32.372

42 Tankard, 1690–1700

H. 6⅞ in. (inc. thumbpiece); D. of base 5⁵⁄₁₆ in.; D. of lip 4½ in.; Wt. 26 oz.

MARKS: *a* on cover, at left of handle, and on bottom.

Tapering sides, molded rim with incised lines below, applied baseband (solder scraped and lumpy). Center points on bottom and in lid. Flat stepped cover with molded edge serrated at front and flanking extension under hinge plate; narrow bezel. Five-part hinge, meander wire in molded hinge plates, the outer shaped. Scroll handle with rattail body drop, double spiral thumbpiece, shield tip with overhang at base, vent hole a slot at handle tip. Dent from thumbpiece below hinge. Added spout and engraving of crest and old English *P* on cover removed in 1941. A hole at right of engraving previously patched.

Engraved in script on side: *Love Rawlins Pickman./to her great niece./ Martha Pickman Codman./1864.* Seemingly no trace of earlier engraving.

HISTORY: Captain John Rawlins of England and Boston married as his second wife the widow Love (Prout) English (1677-1743), whose inventory included "A Tankard 24 oz. 16 dwt." which, allowing for differences in scales, might have been this one; their daughter Love (b. 1709), m. Benjamin Pickman of Salem, 1731, whose son Benjamin (1740-1819), m. Mary Toppan (1744-1817) (his inventory [1819] included "2 tanckards" 29-10, 24-10, one of which was probably the present piece); their youngest child, Love Rawlins Pickman

42

(b. 1786, d. unmarried, 1863); her brother Benjamin (1763-1843), m. in 1789 Anstiss Derby (1769-1836); their daughter Anstiss Derby Pickman (1793-1856), m. John W. Rogers in 1815; their daughter Martha Pickman Rogers (1829-1905), m. June 1, 1850 John Amory Codman(1824-1886), their daughter Martha Catherine (b. July 24, 1858), m. February 2, 1928 Maxim Karolik.

REFERENCES: *Clarke-Coney 1932*, no. 92; *Hipkiss 1941*, p. 228, no. 154, illus.; Hipkiss, *MFA Bulletin*, no. 236 (1941), illus. p. 86.

EXHIBITION: *MFA 1932*, no. 32.

M. AND M. KAROLIK COLLECTION *39.186*

43 Tankard, 1690–1700

H. 7⅞ in. (inc. thumbpiece); D. of base 5⅞ in.; D. of lip 5 in.; Wt. 39 oz., 10 dwt.

MARKS: *a* on cover, at left of handle, and on bottom.

Straight tapering sides, incised lines at rim, applied molded baseband. Flat stepped cover, molded flange serrated front and back. Cast dolphin and mask thumbpiece, scroll handle with broad rattail on body, cast cherub's head tip; five-part hinge with wavy lines in molded hinge plates, the outer shaped.

Engraved with Browne arms and crest in acanthus scroll cartouche on front; *MB* on bottom.

HISTORY: Mary Browne (1679-1753), daughter of William Browne (d. 1716), m. Benjamin Lynde (Harvard 1686) 1699; their son Benjamin (b. 1700) (Harvard 1718), m. Mary, daughter of Major John Bowle and widow of Captain Walter Goodridge; their daughter Mary, m. Andrew Oliver (Harvard 1749); descended in the family to Dr. E. Lawrence Oliver.

NOTES: Although Dr. Bowditch (see *References*) believed it to have been bequeathed by William Browne (d. 1687) to his daughter Mary (Browne) Winthrop, the style of the engraving is no earlier than that on the Shrimpton tankard, made for Mary, married 1692 (Yale University Art Gallery, Garvan Collection), and is very similar to that on the privately owned Foster tankard, c. 1700, which also has the dolphin and mask thumbpiece. (See also tankard owned by William Clarke [d. 1710] in the North Church in Salem). Dr. Bowditch's belief that a tankard would not have been made for a lady can be many times disproved, and it seems that this one was made for Mary (Browne) Lynde. Andrew Oliver's inventory included this "2 quart tankard," which was not specified in his will.

REFERENCES: *Hipkiss 1942*, illus. p. 85; *Hipkiss 1943*, pp. 25-26, illus.; *Buhler, Antiques*, no. 5 (1945), p. 269, fig. 8; Harold Bowditch, "Heraldry and the American Collector," *Antiques*, LX, no. 6 (1951), p. 538-541, fig. 4; *Buhler 1955*, illus. p. 459; *McLanathan 1956*, p. 65, figs. 27a, 27b.

EXHIBITIONS: *MFA 1932*, no. 38; *Chicago 1949*, no. 157.

THE PHILIP LEFFINGWELL SPALDING COLLECTION. GIVEN IN HIS MEMORY BY KATHERINE AMES SPALDING AND PHILIP SPALDING, OAKES AMES SPALDING, HOBART AMES SPALDING *42.242*

43

43

44

44 Wrought Candlestick, 1690–1700

H. 6³⁄₁₆ in.; D. of base 3¹⁵⁄₁₆ in.; Wt. 5 oz., 3½ dwt.

MARKS: *c* on candle socket and above gadroon of foot.

Deep cylindrical candle socket has applied flange with half-round gadroon and at bottom a narrower scallop-edged flange above the turned section. Baluster stem, turned and splayed at junction of flat disc (hole in center beneath), which has flange of quarter-round gadroon with narrow horizontal edge. Under this is soldered, at inner line of gadroon, an almost straight foot splaying to another quarter-round gadroon with narrow horizontal rim above concave section with molded edge and applied strengthening band beneath.

Engraved *RA* above gadroon on foot.

HISTORY: Probably made for a member of the Angier family, since Mary Toppan, who married Benjamin Pickman, was the granddaughter of Sarah (Angier) Toppan; for subsequent ownership see Cat. no. 39.

NOTES: Benjamin Pickman's inventory in 1819 listed "3 candlesticks wt. 26 oz. 5." This and the cast pair (Cat. no. 57) now total 26 oz., 4 dwt. The baluster stem of this is similar to that of the cup by F. Terry, London, 1626, owned by the First Church in Boston, of which Coney once was a member. Insofar as we know, this single candlestick is unique; other early wrought candlesticks are the pair by Jeremiah Dummer (Yale University Art Gallery, Garvan Collection), and those by John Noyes (Cat. no. 90).

REFERENCES: *Bigelow 1917*, pp. 285-287, fig. 188; *Jones 1928*, p. 40; *Avery 1930*, p. 350 and pl. IX; *Bell 1930*, p. 210, pl. VI; Edward Wenham, "Candlesticks and Snuffers by American Silversmiths," *Antiques*, XVIII, no. 6 (1930), pp. 491-493, fig. 7; *Clark [Buhler] 1931*, p. 45; *Clarke-Coney 1932*, no. 11 and pl. VI; *Ensko 1948*, p. 92; *Phillips 1949*, p. 58; *Wenham 1949*, p. 199, fig. 46a; *Buhler 1950*, pp. 36-37, fig. 30; *McLanathan 1956*, p. 58, fig. 14; *Comstock 1958*, p. 79, fig. 1; *Ellis 1961*, p. 27, illus. p. 25, fig. 6.

EXHIBITIONS: *MFA 1932*, no. 86; *Yale 1939*, no. 28; *MMA 1941*; *Chicago 1949*, no. 148, illus. p. 109; *Minneapolis 1956*, no. 197; *Richmond 1960*, no. 37.

GIFT OF MR. AND MRS. DUDLEY LEAVITT PICKMAN 31.217

45

45 Trencher Salt, 1690–1700

H. 2⅛ in.; D. of base 3⁵⁄₁₆ in.; Wt. 2 oz., 8 dwt.

MARK: *a* inside bowl.

Circular with convex molding and tiny flange at base, slightly concave sides with gadrooning on shoulder below molded rim of shallow well for salt.

Engraved *SM* flanked by short dashes on the side.

HISTORY: Sarah (Winslow) Standish Payne (1639-1726), third marriage 1672 to Richard Middlecott; their daughter Sarah (b. 1678), m. Louis Boucher 1702; their daughter Sarah (b. 1705), m. John Foye; their daughter Elizabeth (b. 1735), m. David Munroe of Lexington, Massachusetts; their daughter Abigail (b. 1771), m. Willard Brigham of Marlborough, Massachusetts; their daughter Abigail (b. May 22, 1807) married at Rindge, New York, October 12, 1836, to Joseph Hill, West Cambridge, Massachusetts; parents of the donor.

NOTES: Long thought to have been a mate to the one made by Edward Winslow (*MFA 1956*, no. 144), the slight differences led to a closer study of their histories. The present piece appears as "1 salt" in the inventory of its owner, Sarah (Winslow) Middlecott (1639-1726). The Winslow salt was made for her daughter, Sarah Middlecott. Similar salts by Jacobus Vander Spiegel (1668-1708) of New York, and Jacob Gerritse Lansing of Albany (1681-1767), and a second one by Edward Winslow are known today. Jones (1928) cites an English salt dated 1693 in the Manchester (England) Art Gallery as being similar but for the gadrooning at the base. In 1687 William Fitzhugh of Virginia ordered from his agent in England "half a dozen Trencher salts."

REFERENCES: *Bigelow 1917*, p. 255, fig. 157; *Jones 1928*, p. 29 and pl. IX, no. 1; *Avery 1930*, pp. 68, 344; *Clarke-Coney 1932*, no. 112 and pl. XXX; *Buhler 1932*, p. 47, illus. p. 46; *Wenham 1949*, p. 197; *Buhler 1950*, p. 27.

EXHIBITIONS: *MFA 1932*, no. 2; *Yale 1939*, no. 47; *MFA 1956*, no. 31; *Richmond 1960*, no. 29.

GIFT OF MISS HARRIET A. HILL IN MEMORY OF HER MOTHER, ABIGAIL BRIGHAM HILL *15.912*

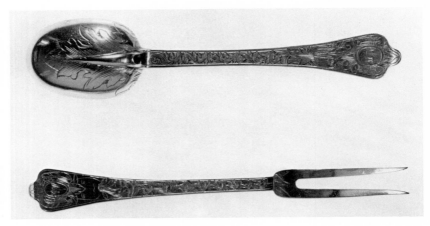

46

46

46 Miniature Fork and Spoon, c. 1700

L. of spoon 4½ in.; L. of fork 4⅚₆ in.; Wt. together 13 dwt.

MARKS: *c* in medallion on front of each handle.

The flat handles of the fork and spoon are rectangular in section, thinner as they broaden to a wavy end, the tip bent forward; fork has narrower stem but same tip and two tines (square in section) tapering to pointed tips. The elliptical spoon bowl has a long rattail flanked by chased and engraved leaf forms in a triangle at the tip.

Engraved *MW* in medallion on back of each handle. Decorative engraving, tighter on the spoon, of scrolls and leaves issuing from the mouth of a mask; at tips are medallions in line-scrolled cartouches, the center motif forming the mask's forehead.

HISTORY: Mary Willoughby, m. Thomas Barton, 1710; for subsequent history see Cat. no. 39.

NOTES: Perhaps the prototypes were the London forks and spoons owned by Mary Browne (see Cat. no. 43) in the Oliver Collection, Massachusetts Historical Society.

REFERENCES: *Bigelow 1917*, p. 281 and fig. 185; *Avery 1930*, p. 358; *Clark [Buhler] 1931*, p. 44, illus. p. 44; *Clarke-Coney 1932*, no. 82, and pl. XXV; *Wenham 1949*, p. 145, figs. 178f, 181c; *Ellis 1961*, p. 25, illus. p. 23, fig. 4.

EXHIBITIONS: *MFA 1932*, no. 87; *Chicago 1949*, no. 152, illus. p. 108; *Richmond 1960*, no. 21.

GIFT OF MR. AND MRS. DUDLEY LEAVITT PICKMAN 31.222-223

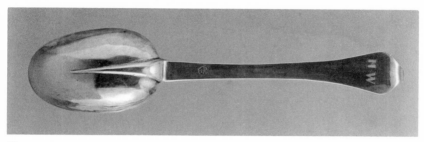

47

47 Spoon, c. 1700

L. 7¹⁵⁄₁₆ in.; Wt. 1 oz., 17 dwt.

MARK: *b* on back of handle toward bowl.

Stem rectangular in section, thin as it broadens for wavy end with tip bent forward. Very slight rounded drop on long rattail on back of elliptical bowl. Engraved *MW* on back of handle.

HISTORY: Mary Willoughby, m. Thomas Barton, 1710; for his bequest and subsequent history see Cat. no. 39.

REFERENCES: *Bigelow 1917*, pp. 266-267, fig. 167; *Clark [Buhler] 1931*, pp. 43-44, illus. p. 43; *Clarke-Coney 1932*, no. 78, mark in error.

EXHIBITION: *MFA 1932*, no. 6.

GIFT OF MR. AND MRS. DUDLEY LEAVITT PICKMAN 31.221

48

48 Sugar Box, c. 1700

H. 5½ in. (inc. handle); W. at rim 6⁹⁄₁₆ in.; L. at rim 8 in.; Wt. 22 oz., 17½ dwt.

MARKS: *a* on bottom of box and twice on flange of cover, flanking and above hasp hinge.

Elliptical body with angle between straight flaring rim and curved sides ornamented with sixteen bosses in tangent reeded frames, the angles filled with trefoil forms; slightly curved base. Four cast paneled legs broad at joinings have flat pad feet, incised rays on inner curve, modeled rays on outer. Applied molded bar with meander wire at back of body and below five-part hinge for lid, which has flat flange, narrow applied molding on edge. Cover stepped with band of embossed reeding in molding around domed center and gadrooned ellipse around slight depression in center for handle, a coiled serpent whose tongue and tail are tangent to the gadrooning. Thinner and less worked, the serpent's head is the same length as that on Cat. no. 33. Three-part hinge at front for shaped hasp with fleur-de-lis cutting in center, three scrolls at each side and circular hole (off center) for staple through front boss. Edge of cover repaired. Very small center point on bottom.

Engraved *SG* on clasp.

HISTORY: Samuel Gardner of Salem (1648-1724); the inventory of his grandson of the same name (1712-1769) listed "1 Sugar box wt 23 oz"; subsequent history unknown.

NOTES: Somewhat similar feet are on a sugar box attributed to Daniel Greenough owned by The Metropolitan Museum of Art, New York.

REFERENCES: *Avery 1930*, p. 50; *Clarke-Coney 1932*, no. 85; *Buhler 1934*, p. 49, illus. p. 48; *Phillips 1949*, p. 64; K. C. Buhler, "The Nine Colonial Sugar Boxes," *Antiques*, LXXXV, no. 1 (1964), pp. 88-89, fig. 3.

EXHIBITIONS: *MFA 1932*, no. 42; *American Furniture and Decorative Arts*, Milwaukee Art Center, June 30-July 31, 1960.

BEQUEST OF CHARLES HITCHCOCK TYLER 32.270

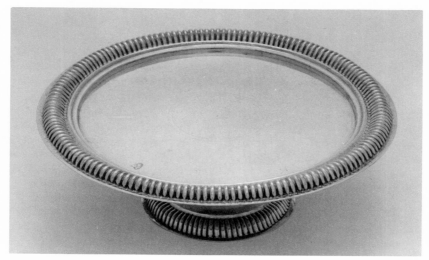

49

49 Salver, c. 1700

H. 2 in.; D. of base 2⅞ in.; D. of dish 6⁵⁄₁₆ in.; Wt. 5 oz., 11 dwt.

MARK: *b* near rim.

Circular plate with sharp narrow step for molding and half-round reeded border with narrow flange, affixed by very thin narrow flange to trumpet foot splaying to quarter-round reeding with narrow flange. Two concentric circles scratched (or lightly engraved) on plate. Center point on top and bottom of plate.

Engraved *SW* under rim. *RP* added in same script as on Cat. no. 36.

HISTORY: Initials suggest this was probably made for a member of the Willoughby family (see Cat. no. 39).

NOTES: See Cat. no. 51.

REFERENCES: *Clark [Buhler] 1931*, p. 44; *Clarke-Coney 1932*, no. 53, mark in error; *Ellis 1961*, p. 25.

EXHIBITION: *MFA 1932*, no. 7.

GIFT OF MR. AND MRS. DUDLEY LEAVITT PICKMAN 31.225

50 Chocolate Pot, 1701

H. 8¹⁄₁₆ in. (inc. finial); D. of base 3⅝ in.; D. of lip 3½ in.; Wt. 18 oz., 13½ dwt.

MARKS: *b* on bottom, on shoulder between spout and handle, and (partially) at back of hole in cover; *c* below and at each side of partial mark.

Raised in form of oriental vase with curved shoulder, incised lines around joining of finely molded cylindrical neck (no visible vertical seam), applied molded baseband seamed opposite handle (very neat soldering but one area pitted). Cover has deep bezel, incised lines on flange, step to molded top with domed center open and fitted with cylindrical neck having two narrow molded bands. Turned ball finial with rounded tip soldered to slightly domed disc with deep bezel which closes the necessary hole for a stirring rod, differentiating a chocolate pot from a coffee pot. A curved spout, broad at the base over three rows of quite large, shaped strainer holes, is soldered below shoulder and curves to mouth, with seam on upper surface next to which runs

50

a row of graduated beads from molded applique at tip, which once held
hinged cover for straight mouth. Beads also tapering upward from base of
handle almost as high as joining. At right angle to spout is curved upper socket
affixed with slight flange for pinned wooden scroll handle with slight grip;
lower socket tapers to body with decorative cut-card joining (slight repairs).

Engraved in semiscript on bottom within guidelines: *The gift of Wm
Stoughton Esquire / To Mrs Sarah Tailer : 701.*

HISTORY: Lt. Governor William Stoughton's will, executed July 6, 1701:
"Unto my niece Mrs Sarah Tailer I give as a particular remembrance of me
twelve pounds to buy a piece of Plate"; Sarah (d. 1708), daughter of Nathaniel
Byfield, Newbury, Massachusetts, m. March 2, 1698/9 William Tailer, later
Lt. Governor of Massachusetts, who married second in 1711 Madam Abigail
(Gillam) Dudley, widow of Thomas; subsequent ownership unknown until
the seller, Frederick S. Whitwell, who believed it had come to him through
his Story-Bradstreet ancestry.

NOTES: One other chocolate pot by Coney (privately owned) is known, and
one teapot (The Metropolitan Museum of Art, New York). Coney is the
earliest New England goldsmith known to have made pots for chocolate
and tea.

REFERENCES: *Avery 1930,* pp. 72-73, 322, pl. X; *Bell 1930,* p. 209, pl. V;
E. J. Hipkiss, "A Chocolate Pot," *MFA Bulletin,* XXVIII, no. 165 (1930), p. 4;
Morison 1930, opp. p. 164; *Clarke-Coney 1932,* no. 18 and pl. III (marks
described as *b* above, in error; G. Norman-Wilcox, "Cut-Card Ornament,"
Antiques, XXIV, no. 5 (1933), p. 175, fig. 7b; G. Norman-Wilcox, "Shining
Examples of Craftsmanship," *Antiques,* XXXVI, no. 5 (1939), p. 241; *Ensko*

1948, p. 41; *Phillips 1949*, p. 57; *Phillips, Antiques*, no. 2 (1949), p. 118; *Wenham 1949*, p. 63 and fig. 85; *Buhler 1950*, pp. 41-42, fig. 34; *McLanathan 1956*, fig. 11.

EXHIBITIONS: *MFA 1932*, no. 4; *Harvard 1936*, no. 102; *Harvard 1939*; *Yale 1939*, no. 33; *MMA 1941*; Currier Gallery of Art, Manchester, New Hampshire, 1956; *Minneapolis 1956*, no. 195; *Richmond 1960*, no. 27.

GIFT OF EDWARD JACKSON HOLMES 29.1091

51 Salver, c. 1705

H. 2¹⁄₁₆ in.; D. of base 3⁵⁄₁₆ in.; D. of dish 9 in.; Wt. 9 oz., 19½ dwt.

MARK: *d* on dish near rim.

Circular plate with sharp narrow step for molding and half-round reeded border with narrow flange, affixed by very thin and narrow flange to trumpet foot splaying to quarter-round reeding with narrow flange, center point on base.

Engraved *MW* on bottom; *RP* added in script on bottom.

HISTORY: Mary Willoughby, m. Thomas Barton, 1710; for subsequent history see Cat. no. 39.

NOTES: Whereas the *RP* on the plate (Cat. no. 36) could stand for Benjamin Pickman's aunt, Rachel; this and the Dwight salver (see Cat. no. 26) were among the pieces brought into the Pickman family by Benjamin's wife, Mary Toppan, and presumably did not, therefore, belong to Rachel. This is probably the "1 salver, wt 11 oz 10" in Benjamin Pickman's inventory.

Other salvers by Coney are Cat. no. 49; one with Checkley arms (Harrington Collection, Dartmouth College); with Dudley arms (Minneapolis Institute of Arts); with gadrooned borders and Lowell arms in nineteenth-century engraving (The Metropolitan Museum of Art, New York); and a recently discovered one (Heritage Foundation, Deerfield, Massachusetts).

REFERENCES: *Avery 1930*, pp. 69-70, pl. IX; *Clark [Buhler] 1931*, p. 44, illus. p. 45; *Clarke-Coney 1932*, no. 54; *Ellis 1961*, p. 25, illus. p. 29, fig. 10.

EXHIBITION: *MFA 1932*, no. 49.

GIFT OF MR. AND MRS. DUDLEY LEAVITT PICKMAN 31.224

51

52

52 Tankard, c. 1705

H. 5⅞ in. (inc. thumbpiece); D. of base 4⅜-4½ in. (uneven); D. of lip 3¾ in.;
Wt. 15 oz., 10½ dwt.

MARKS: *d* on cover, at left of handle, and on bottom.

Straight tapering sides, incised lines below everted rim, applied molded baseband. No center point but mark is in center of bottom; center point on lid.
Flat cover (the step is a band of reeding), scribed lines on rim serrated at front
and flanking molded hinge plate with wavy lines, quite thick bezel; chased
cusped thumbpiece, its support soldered to reeding. Five-part hinge plate on
hollow scroll handle slightly shaped; rattail at upper joining, lower probably
resoldered; vent hole under tip of cherub's head without wings.

Engraved *MW* on handle below hinge plate. Large script *SPL* on front;
scratched on cover, rather indistinctly, *James / Faben* (?).

HISTORY: Mary Willoughby, m. Thomas Barton 1710; this was her "maiden
. . . tanckard" specified in Thomas' will to be for her; for subsequent history,
see Cat. no. 39.

NOTES: Large added spout removed in 1932. This tankard is unusually small,
although smaller ones, not miniatures, are known.

REFERENCES: *Clark [Buhler] 1931*, pp. 44-45; *Clarke-Coney 1932*, no. 100;
Ellis 1961, pp. 24-25.

EXHIBITION: *MFA 1932*, no. 48.

GIFT OF MR. AND MRS. DUDLEY LEAVITT PICKMAN *31.220*

53

53 Caster, c. 1705

H. 5½ in.; D. of base 2½ in.; Wt. 5 oz., 1 dwt.

MARK: *d* on side opposite engraving; cover unmarked.

Cylindrical seamed sides with convex molding slightly above applied, molded, splayed baseband with strengthening strap under edge; applied molding on body, applied bead forms bezel, open opposite seam for bayonet fastenings. High seamed cover has applied, stepped, and flattened dome through which the turned ball finial is doweled or soldered. Sides cut in clusters of heart and scroll forms, tiny flange over vertical molding to which bayonet fasteners are affixed.

Engraved IFD; added: *to / I + R + D* on body.

HISTORY: Unknown.

NOTES: Two other cylindrical casters by Coney are known; one in the MFA (see *Addenda*); one owned by the Newark Museum Association, New Jersey. Both have Coney's earlier mark, but each one is quite different from the other.

REFERENCES: *Avery 1930,* p. 346, pl. XII; *Hipkiss 1943,* p. 28; *Wenham 1949,* fig. 50; *Buhler 1957,* p. 46.

EXHIBITION: *MFA 1932,* no. 81.

THE PHILIP LEFFINGWELL SPALDING COLLECTION. GIVEN IN HIS MEMORY BY KATHERINE AMES SPALDING AND PHILIP SPALDING, OAKES AMES SPALDING, HOBART AMES SPALDING 42.233

54

54 Porringer, c. 1710

H. 1⁹⁄₁₆ in.; D. of lip 5³⁄₁₆-5¼ in. (uneven); L. of handle 2¹³⁄₁₆ in.; Wt. 8½ oz.

MARK: *d* on bowl at left of handle.

Curved sides, almost straight rim, stepped and domed bottom. Center points top and bottom. Cast handle in geometric design, open circles at sides, the tip a circle above trefoil over quartrefoil; double-arched opening at body and shaped side holes.

Engraved ᴛʙᴍ on handle away from bowl.

HISTORY: Thomas and Mary (Willoughby) Barton, m. 1710; for subsequent history see Cat. no. 39.

NOTES: Four porringers were listed in Benjamin Pickman's inventory in 1819 with a total weight of 30 oz., 10 dwt.; the MFA's three (this, Cat. nos. 84 and 97) total 18 oz., 5 dwt., which suggests that his largest is unknown today. Coney used this handle on many of his porringers.

REFERENCES: *Bigelow 1917*, pp. 309-310, fig. 212; *Avery 1930*, p. 46; *Bell 1930*, pl. VII; *Clark [Buhler] 1931*, pp. 44-45, illus.; *Clarke-Coney 1932*, no. 68; *Ellis 1961*, p. 25, illus. p. 23, fig. 5.

EXHIBITION: *MFA 1932*, no. 47.

GIFT OF MR. AND MRS. DUDLEY LEAVITT PICKMAN 31.219

55 Pair of Casters, c. 1710

42.234: H. 4¹⁵⁄₁₆ in.; D. of base 1⁹⁄₁₆ in.; Wt. 4 oz., 5 dwt. *42.235:* H. 5 in.; D. of base 1⁹⁄₁₆ in.; Wt. 4 oz., 8½ dwt.

MARKS: *d* on side and bottom of each, the latter obliterating center points, if any.

Raised baluster form, curved bottom, on cast concave and molded footband. High domed cover, molded disc applied for turned ball finial, splayed rim and heavy applied molding for bayonet fasteners. 42.234 pierced in daisy(?) pattern and horizontally chased; 42.235 similar but the piercing only simulated.

HISTORY: According to Avery (see *References)* the pieces formerly belonged to the Gibb family.

NOTES: Other baluster casters by Coney: the Lowell caster (Cat. no. 56); a pair with Hutchinson arms owned by descendants of William Hutchinson; one engraved IGL, privately owned (*Exhibition of Early American Silver,* Wadsworth Atheneum, Hartford, Conn., January 1-28, 1945, no. 44).

REFERENCES: *Avery 1930,* p. 347 and pl. XII; *Hipkiss 1942,* p. 83, illus.; *Hipkiss 1943,* p. 29, illus.; *Wenham 1949,* pp. 54-55, fig. 71; *Buhler 1957,* p. 45; *Comstock 1958,* pl. 45a.

EXHIBITION: *MFA 1932,* no. 82.

THE PHILIP LEFFINGWELL SPALDING COLLECTION. GIVEN IN HIS MEMORY BY KATHERINE AMES SPALDING AND PHILIP SPALDING, OAKES AMES SPALDING, HOBART AMES SPALDING 42.234-235

55

56

56 Sugar Caster, c. 1710

H. 6¾ in.; D. of base 2⅜ in.; Wt. 7 oz., 4 dwt.

MARKS: *d* in center of base obliterating center point (if any) and very worn mark near rim.

Raised baluster form on very neatly soldered molded cast splayed foot. Small bead near lip open for bayonet fastening. Domed cover with applied molded edge and band of vertical molding below for bayonet fasteners, slightly molded top and turned ball finial through low dome (finial bent). Simple oval piercings with punched dots.
Engraved WPE on bottom.

HISTORY: Probably William and Eunice (Orne) Pickering; her sister (?) Esther Orne m. Samuel Gardner; their granddaughter m. Francis Cabot Lowell, Jr., grandfather of Guy Lowell, architect of the MFA.

NOTES: Casters were made in sets of three. William Fitzhugh of Virginia had ordered from London in 1688 "a sett of Castors that is to say for Sugar, Pepper & Mustard"; and in the inventory of Isaac Smith of Boston in 1787 a set was still designated "3 casters viz. Sugar Mustard & pepper 12 oz. 8 dwt."

REFERENCES: *Clarke-Coney 1932*, no. 14; *Comstock 1958*, pl. 45a.
EXHIBITION: *MFA 1932*, no. 77.
GIFT OF MARY SARGENT POTTER IN MEMORY OF HER SISTER, MRS. GUY
LOWELL 53.2208

57

57 Pair of Cast Candlesticks, C. 1710

31.215: H. 6⅞₆ in.; D. of base 3¹⁵⁄₁₆ in.; Wt. 10 oz., 11½ dwt.; *31.216:* H. 6¼ in.; D. of base 3¹⁵⁄₁₆ in.; Wt. 10 oz., 9 dwt.

MARK: *d* on quarter-round of base of each candlestick.

Turned molded socket and baluster stem are in two parts vertically; a vent hole in disc at base above a splayed molded foot with strengthening band (almost square in section at, and overlapping, edge). In 31.216 lower parts of socket are filled; in 31.215 a hole is in the socket.

HISTORY: See Cat. no. 39.

NOTES: Listed (with Cat. no. 44) in the inventory of Benjamin Pickman, 1819. Coney's inventory included two candlestick molds. This pair and the faceted pair made for tutor Henry Flynt (now in the Deerfield Collection, Massachusetts) are known. Candlesticks by American goldsmiths are extremely rare.

REFERENCES: *Bigelow 1917*, pp. 287-288, fig. 189; *Jones 1928*, p. 40; *Avery 1930*, pp. 48, 68, 350, pl. IX; *Morison 1930*, illus. opp. p. 164; E. Wenham, "Candlesticks and Snuffers by American Silversmiths," *Antiques,* XVIII, no. 6 (1930), pp. 492-493, fig. 6; *Clark [Buhler] 1931*, illus. p. 45; *Phillips 1949*, p. 82; *Wenham 1949*, p. 35, fig. 46b; *Buhler 1950*, p. 37, fig. 30; *Ellis 1961*, p. 27, illus. p. 25, fig. 6.
EXHIBITION: *MFA 1932*, no. 46.
GIFT OF MR. AND MRS. DUDLEY LEAVITT PICKMAN 31.215-216

58

58

58 Chafing Dish, c. 1710

H. 3½-3¹¹⁄₁₆ in. (inc. supports); D. of lip 6 in.; L. 12¼ in. (inc. handle);
Wt. 18 oz., 11½ dwt.

MARK: *d* on body at left of handle.

Raised circular curved sides, splayed for band of guilloche piercing, framed
by applied molding below and molded rim. Bottom cut out and concave band
of piercing applied at edge, and soldered beneath it a flat dish with up-curving
rim. Pierced grill, perhaps cut from center (same diameter as hole), has applied
slightly overhanging molded edge and screw through center secured with

shaped nut. Three cast supports have scroll tips affixed over rim, pad lower joinings, and angled leg for claw feet (three toes forward, one back as in Cat. no. 60) with screws deeply countersunk into wooden balls. Turned socket affixed below scroll on one support for turned wooden handle.

Engraved IFS on bottom.

HISTORY: Sarah (b. 1672), daughter of Simon and Hannah (Newgate) Lynde, m. Nov. 16, 1699 John Foye; descended in the family to Mrs. Richard Saltonstall Pattee, from whom it was bought.

NOTES: Other, similar chafing dishes by Coney are a single one in the Garvan Collection, Yale University Art Gallery, and a pair privately owned.

J. H. AND E. A. PAYNE FUND 57.701

59 Mug, 1705–1715

H. of body 4³⁄₁₆ in.; D. of base 3¾ in.; D. of lip 3⅛ in.; Wt. 8 oz., 18 dwt.

MARKS: *d* at left of handle and on center bottom.

Straight tapering sides, molded rim with applied molding below, and quite wide baseband. Hollow scroll handle with flat outer surface, slight grip on shoulder, pointed tip and small vent hole, disc on body tangent to baseband for lower joining. Large added spout was removed.

Engraved SIR on bottom; the *S* and *I* perhaps over earlier initials.

HISTORY: Unknown.

NOTES: Coney's bill (*R.I. 1965*, no. 49) dated 1713 and charging for "a silvʳ mug wᵗʰ a holow handle" suggests a new form for him in the hollow handle and is the reason for this dating.

REFERENCES: *Clarke-Coney 1932*, no. 45; *Buhler 1932*, pp. 45-49, illus. p. 47.

EXHIBITION: *MFA 1932*, no. 44.

CHARLES T. AND SUSAN P. BAKER BY BEQUEST OF THE LATTER 21.1256

59

60

60 Pair of Chafing Dishes, 1705–1720

H. 3⅞-4 in. (inc. supports); D. of rim 5⁵⁄₁₆ in.; Wt. of 31.213, 13 oz., 18 dwt.; Wt. of 31.214, 13 oz., 16 dwt.

MARKS: *d* on grate and on body.

Raised with vertical step from flat base to curved everted rim, very slightly flaring sides, incised lines beneath edge of rim. Sides cut in band of scrolls, leaves, and other forms. Applied vertical molding at edge above step of base; row of shaped holes cut in sides below an applied molded band on outside, plain band (or flange) inside which supports grate. Circular grate, slightly domed at point where screw fastens underneath, pierced in two circles, the inner a leaf design, the outer a fleur-de-lis, each separated by a leaf (?). Three cast curved supports with flat inner surfaces are affixed at rim and below molded band; short legs, square in section, taper to claw feet, three outer and one back toe, all too sharp not to have grasped wooden balls originally. The supports rise and fork to double spiral tips for dish. One support, at left of mark, indicates the dish once had a socket for a handle.

Engraved WPE on bottom.

HISTORY: Inventoried in Benjamin Pickman's estate, 1819 (see *Notes*); for subsequent history see Cat. no. 39.

NOTES: The engraved initials probably for William and Eunice Pickering, who were married in 1724, or for William and his second wife, also named Eunice (Orne), widow of Josiah Neal, whom he married in 1738. (Was Sarah Orne who married Clark Gayton Pickman in 1770 her niece?) They died childless and in his brother's, Benjamin Pickman's, inventory of 1819, the weight of the pair was given as 25 oz., 10 dwt., suggesting, although the scales were unaligned with ours, that they were already without handles. No other American chafing dish with these straight sides has been published.

REFERENCES: *Bigelow 1917*, p. 326, figs. 229-230; *Jones 1928*, p. 27; *Avery 1930*, pp. 69, 334 and pl. IX; *Bell 1930*, p. 210, pl. VI; *Morison 1930*, illus. opp. p. 164; *Clark [Buhler] 1931*, p. 47; *Clarke-Coney 1932*, no. 15, pl. XIII; *Phillips 1949*, p. 58; *Wenham 1949*, fig. 91; *McLanathan 1956*, p. 58, fig. 12; *Ellis 1961*, p. 27, illus. p. 25, fig. 7.

EXHIBITION: *MFA 1932*, no. 45.

GIFT OF MR. AND MRS. DUDLEY LEAVITT PICKMAN 31.213-214

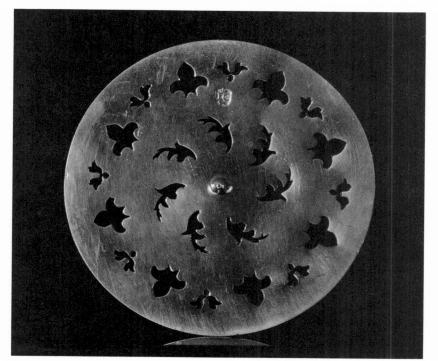

60

61 Pepper Box, 1710–1720

H. 3¼ in.; D. of base 2⁄₁₆ in.; Wt. 2 oz., 16 dwt.

MARK: *d* on bottom.

Octagonal in section, straight slightly tapering sides seamed under handle
have grooved band to form bezel and two grooved bands above splaying
curved foot; the base forms one step and an applied strengthening strap forms
another. Cover stepped and domed has seamed sides which reverse outline
of base. Plain piercing in concentric circles on dome of lid. Two cracks in
edge of cover. Thin double scroll handle affixed at upper band has slight grip
and is grooved to lapped curl affixed over lower bands with sharply upcurved
scroll tip.

Engraved *PA* on bottom; Appleton crest (a pineapple) on torse above *M=A*
on front panel.

HISTORY: Probably Priscilla Appleton (d. 1724), m. Rev. Robert Ward 1722;
her brother Rev. Nathaniel Appleton (1693-1784) of Cambridge, m. 1719
Margaret, daughter of Rev. Henry and Mercy (Greenough) Gibbs of Watertown; their daughter Margaret, m. Rev. Joshua Prentiss of Holliston; their
great-granddaughter, the donor.

NOTES: Tiny stampings on cover and body (above engraving) indicate proper
closing. The inventory of Coney's tools included "2 pepper box punches."
Mr. Clarke records two other pepper boxes cylindrical in section.

REFERENCES: *Clarke-Coney 1932*, no. 56 and pl. VII; Norman-Wilcox,
Antiques, part 2, (1944), p. 81, no. 6.

EXHIBITIONS: *MFA 1932*, no. 64; *MFA 1956*, no. 41; *Richmond 1960*, no. 35.

GIFT OF MRS. D. EDWARD BEEDE 42.88

61

62

62 Caster, 1710–1720

H. 6¼ in.; W. of base 1⁵⁄₁₆ in. (edges of foot and panels of body alternately measure 1 and 1½ in.); Wt. 5 oz., 11 dwt.

MARK: *d* on bottom.

Hexagonal baluster form, probably seamed on one angle; molding and convex section above flat bottom, on cast splayed molded footband; applied flange below bezel. Domed cover with wide area of molding above rim, sides indented midway, cast angular finial with disc holding scroll-pierced panels at top. Tiny hole at angle in body at foot.

Engraved on front with Charnock arms in cartouche as on dated Flynt cup of 1718 in R. W. Norton Art Gallery, Shreveport, Louisiana.

HISTORY: John Charnock, Boston (d. 1723); his second wife and widow Hannah (Holyoke), m. 1727 Theophilus Burrill, Lynn, Massachusetts (see Cat. nos. 180-181); Charnock's son by first marriage to Mary (King) was John (b. 1701), m. Emma, sister of the goldsmith John Blowers; their son John (born 1726); his adopted daughter, Polly (d. 1840), m. Nathan Dane (1752-

1835), uncle of Francis S. Dane, from whom the piece was bought.

NOTES: The last-named John Charnock and his wife were the parents by adoption of "Polly Charnock," thus known in the Dane family, although her marriage to Nathan Dane is recorded by her family name of Brown. Polly Dane, widow in 1840, left "2 Silver pepper boxes $6." The second box is not known today and this one is unique in all published silver. The inventory of Coney's tools included "6 Caster punches 14/6."

REFERENCES: K. C. Buhler, "Two Angular New Englanders," *Antiques*, LI, no. 3 (1947), p. 195, illus.; *Buhler 1950*, p. 38; "Some Recent Acquisitions," *MFA Bulletin*, LXI, no. 325 (1963), pp. 116-117, illus.; *Antiques*, LXXXV, no. 6 (1964), p. 704, illus.

EXHIBITIONS: *MFA 1956*, no. 42, fig. 24; *Richmond 1960*, no. 31, illus.

MARION E. DAVIS FUND 63.956

63 Cann, 1715–1720

H. of body 4⅛ in.; D. of base 2¾ in.; D. of lip 2¹¹⁄₁₆ in.; Wt. 8 oz., 1 dwt.

MARKS: *d* at left of handle and on center bottom.

Straight sides taper to everted rim with double incised lines below and curve at base where the molded and splayed cast foot has been banged into body so that one side is cracked. No center point. Cast hollow scroll handle, scroll grip at shoulder, grooves on sides of slightly curved surface reach to slight scroll above tightly scrolled tip; a disc at lower joining.

Engraved IWE on handle. Stoddard crest, (a demihorse issuing from a ducal crown) on front.

HISTORY: Probably the Winchester, West, or Wheeler families.

REFERENCES: *Clarke-Coney 1932*, no. 10, pl. XIX; *Buhler 1932*, p. 49, illus. p. 48.

EXHIBITIONS: *MFA 1911*, no. 269, pl. 7; *MFA 1932*, no. 50.

BEQUEST OF HENRY W. CUNNINGHAM 31.419

63

63

HENRY HURST
1665–1717

HENRY HURST (or Hendrick Husst) of Boston is said to have been a "Sweed" who came from London in 1699, but he is not listed in Sir Ambrose Heal's *London Goldsmiths*. He was married in Boston by Mr. Thomas Cheever to Mary Bill on August 31, 1704. Their daughter Mary was born the following year; in 1707 and again in 1709 a daughter was born named Mehitable, but of his family only "Mary Hurst my beloved daughter" was mentioned in his will when he was "sick & weak of body" The inventory of the estate of "Henry Hurst late of Boston Goldsmith" was filed February 8, 1717; the executors were John Comer, pewterer, and Samuel Gardner, tailor. Everything was to be sold for his daughter's benefit, but if she died, the Old North and New North Churches in Boston were each to have a "Silver Flaggon of thirty pounds price" and the executors were to share the estate. Thomas Milner and John Dixwell were appraisers for the plate; each was paid for the debts of the deceased. Two pounds and fourteen shillings was paid for rings for the executors, but to what goldsmith is not recorded. "Hurst the goldsmith for Rings" had been paid £5 4s. by the executors of Frances Lanyon's estate in 1712. Hurst's shop tools were valued at £23, his 165 ounces of plate at 10s. 6d. ounce.

Hurst is known by only one mark *(a)*, his initials in an ellipse, the outer bars of initials forming sides of the punch.

a

64 Tankard, c. 1700

H. 7 in. (inc. thumbpiece); D. of base 5³⁄₁₆ in.; D. of lip 4⅜ in.; Wt. 26 oz., 5 dwt.

MARKS: *a* twice on cover within border and twice at right of handle.

Straight tapering sides, incised lines at and below everted rim, applied molded baseband. Flat cover, the wide scribed flange serrated at front and at sides of extension under hinge plate, has reeding on upper two-thirds of step with vertical edge at flat top, narrow bezel (some repairs and one hole in step of lid). Wide band of flat chasing in floral design on cover not quite at edge. Center point on cover, but obliterated from base, or perhaps the body was forged. Dolphin and mask thumbpiece, meander wire above rectangular support soldered to step of cover; meander wire in molded hinge plates; five-part hinge, lower plate slightly shaped and not symmetrical above em-

64

64

bossed fruit and foliage on curve of scroll handle, its upper joining broad and incurved for rattail drop; embossing finished with punched curved rays. Cast cherub's-mask terminal set high on handle end with elaborate outline and pendant scroll and flower tip almost aligned with base.

Engraved *AL* on base; partially erased TTK; in script below *Came into the possession of / Dudley Leavitt Pickman / 1908.*

HISTORY: Triangular initials unidentified; Abigail Lindall, daughter of Timothy and Mary (Verin) Lindall, m. in 1704, as his second wife, Benjamin Pickman II; their grandson William (1747/8-1815) m. Elizabeth Leavitt; their son, the first Dudley Leavitt Pickman, grandfather of the donor.

NOTES: The handle is, insofar as we know, unique for a New England tankard; the other known piece by Hurst is another tankard, characteristically New England with stepped flat lid, similar dolphin and mask thumbpiece, and cherub tip for a plain handle (owned by the First Church in Medford).

REFERENCES: *Bigelow 1917*, p. 134, fig. 65; *Jones 1928*, pl. II, no. 4; *Avery 1930*, pp. 45, 302; *Morison 1930*, illus. opp. p. 156; *Clark [Buhler] 1931*, p. 49, illus. p. 47; *Ensko 1948*, p. 21; *Phillips, Antiques*, no. 2 (1949), p. 116; *McLanathan 1956*, illus. cover; *Ellis 1961*, p. 27, illus. p. 29, fig. 8.

EXHIBITIONS: *MFA 1911*, no. 684, pl. 22; *Yale 1939*, no. 137; *MFA 1956*, no. 103.

GIFT OF MR. AND MRS. DUDLEY LEAVITT PICKMAN 31.228

EDWARD WINSLOW
1669–1753

EDWARD WINSLOW, son of Edward and Elizabeth (Hutchinson) Winslow, was born in Boston on November 1, 1669 and probably learned his craft from Jeremiah Dummer. Owing to the great richness of his four known sugar boxes, it was at one time thought that he had served his apprenticeship in London. He held so many positions in the colony that one wonders how he had time to fashion the silver known to be from his forge.

He was an active member of the Old South Church, Boston, of which, with his wife Hannah, daughter of Rev. Joshua Moody, he became a member in 1692. He was listed as a communicant of the Brattle Street Church in 1741. He married second in 1712 the widow Elizabeth (Dixie) Pemberton; his third wife, Susanna (Farnum) Lyman, survived him. His three dishes for the Second Church in Boston, made in 1711, are unique in all published silver; and his baptismal basin, the gift of Adam Winthrop to the same church in 1706, is the earliest New England one made for this purpose (Dummer's and Coney's were domestic originally).

Samuel Sewall records purchasing in 1713/14 six silver spoons from Captain Winslow "cost about 21s. a piece" and "January 16, 1721/22 I went to his Excellency and presented him with a Ring wt 3p and 3 grains cost 35s. and 3d. with this Motto Post tenebras Lucem Jan 7 1721/22: respecting the Darkness of the Small Pocks, and our Divisions; which his Excellency received very graciously in Mr. Sergeant's Counting Room. Capt. Winslow made it". In 1736 the estate of Mary Mico paid him £37 8s. for eighteen rings, indicating prolonged activity.

Although he decreed that his household plate be sold to meet legacies and expenses of his estate, a sugar box and a tankard of his fashioning, the latter with his coat of arms, descended in the family until this generation and are now owned respectively by the Yale University Art Gallery, Garvan Collection, and Phillips Academy, Addison Gallery of American Art in Andover, Massachusetts.

Winslow's early mark (a) is of his initials over a device (usually called a fleur-de-lis) in a shield. A reported mark shows similar initials and punch but without the device. A later mark (b) shows his initials in double, or fused, circles.

a   b

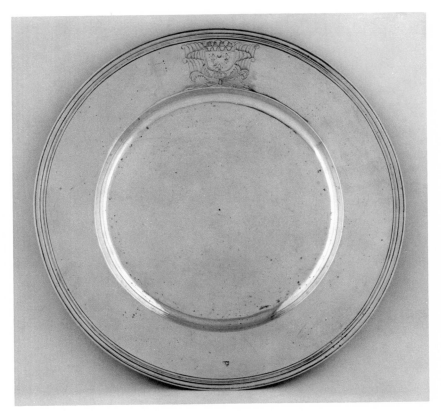

65

65 Plate, c. 1690

D. 10¾-10¹³⁄₁₆ in. (uneven); Wt. 14 oz., 18½ dwt.

MARK: *a* on rim opposite arms.

Circular, almost horizontal flange with scribed rim, step to flat base. Center point on face.

Engraved with Palmes coat of arms on rim in feather cartouche surprisingly similar to that on the MFA's Elizabethan wine cups from Boston in Lincolnshire made in London in 1582.

HISTORY: Edward Palmes, d. March 21, 1714/15 in New London; subsequent history unknown.

NOTES: Plates are rare in American silver. Those published are a small one by Dummer (Cat. no. 19); three by Coney (Cat. no. 36, one engraved for Sarah Eliot, and one with Eyre arms [see *Notes,* Cat. no. 36]); one in King's Chapel by Dummer; a pair by Winslow with Foster arms (one in the Clearwater Collection, The Metropolitan Museum of Art, New York, and one in the R. W. Norton Art Gallery, Shreveport, Louisiana). It is known from Suffolk probate records that James Lloyd in 1693 had "3 Trencher plates"; Rev. John Oxenbridge in 1674 had "one wrought plate with my own and her mother's arms." David Mason in 1725 had one, and Tutor Flynt had two of 15 oz. and 14 oz., 7 dwt. respectively. Joseph West in 1693 left "two silver plates" to Rebekah Foster.

REFERENCES: "The Almanac," *Antiques,* XXXIII, no. 6 (1938), p. 333; *Buhler, Antiques,* no. 5 (1945), p. 269, fig. 6; *McLanathan 1956,* p. 63, fig. 21.

EXHIBITIONS: *Yale 1939,* no. 196; *Lyman Allyn Museum 1946; Hartford 1947; R.I. 1965,* no. 208, fig. 19.

GIFT OF DR. FRANKLIN S. NEWELL 38.63

66 Spoon, c. 1690

L. 7⅝ in.; Wt. 1 oz., 18 dwt.

MARK: *a* on back of stem.

Stem, rectangular in section, tapers in thickness and broadens to forward bent trifid tip. Rounded drop on elliptical bowl has beads through center of rattail, which is flanked by dotted and scrolled foliate design terminating in flower form.

Engraved R$\overset{M}{*}$s on back of handle tip.

HISTORY: Richard and Sarah (Winslow) Middlecott, m. 1672; for subsequent history see Cat. no. 45.

REFERENCE: *Buhler 1950*, p. 17, fig. 9.

EXHIBITION: *Chicago 1949*, no. 222.

GIFT OF MISS HARRIET A. HILL IN MEMORY OF HER MOTHER, ABIGAIL BRIGHAM HILL *15.913*

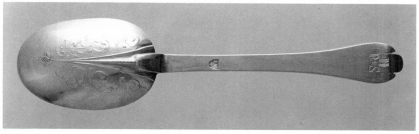

66

67 Standing Salt, c. 1690–1700

H. 5½ in. (inc. scrolls); W. of base 4¹⁵⁄₁₆ in.; Wt. 9 oz., 1 dwt.

MARK: *a* in well.

Fashioned like the Dummer salt (Cat. no. 20) except that there is only one band of ornament, gadrooning at the base of the spool. The well is smaller with no center point in the curved bottom; its torus molded rim has a tiny edge. The octagonal top is in two steps and the four supports, set in the upper flat step, are square in section, their points in the angles of the octagon. Their scroll tips are thinner than those on the Dummer salt. Support at right of initials is crudely repaired, slight repair on curved step at left of initials. There are holes at five points in the base at joining line and in two angles of the step.

Engraved with Edes crest, a leopard's head, opposite initials IEM.

HISTORY: John (b. March 31, 1651) and Mary (Tufts) Edes, m. October 15, 1674; subsequent history unknown.

NOTES: The similarity of craftsmanship between this and the Dummer salt corroborates the belief that Winslow was Dummer's apprentice.

REFERENCES: *Halsey 1925*, pl. 16; *Jones 1928*, p. 28; *Morison 1930*, illus. opp. p. 164; *Avery 1930*, pp. 39, 341-342, pl. V; *Bell 1930*, pl. VIII; *Currier 1938*, in "From the Author's 'Note Book' "; "The Almanac," *Antiques*, XXXIV, no. 5, p. 263; E. J. Hipkiss, "An Early American Salt," *MFA Bulletin*, XXXVI, no. 216 (1938), pp. 46-47, illus. cover; *Hipkiss 1942*, p. 86, illus. p. 83; *Antiques*, XLIII, no. 1 (1943), pp. 35-36; *Hipkiss 1943*, pp. 34-35; *Phillips 1949*, p. 51; *Buhler 1950*, p. 25, illus. opp. p. 14, pl. 1; *McLanathan 1956*,

p. 63, fig. 22; *Buhler 1957*, fig. 1.
The Philip Leffingwell Spalding Collection. Gift of
Philip L. Spalding 38.64

67

67

Massachusetts: WINSLOW

68

68 Salver, c. 1700

H. 1⅝ in.; D. of foot 2¾ in.; D. of dish 5¾ in.; Wt. 4 oz., 9½ dwt.

MARK: *a,* somewhat worn, on face.

Dish has circular, raised, everted, and molded edge with reeding on curved rim to tiny horizontal flange. Trumpet foot affixed by tiny flange has quarter-round reeding and molded edge as on dish. Center point on top and bottom.

Engraved *RB* to *M·V* in contemporary block letters underneath dish on guideline near edge.

HISTORY: Unknown.

GIFT OF MELVILLE WESTON IN MEMORY OF ANSTISS WESTON *58.333*

69 Sugar Box, c. 1700

H. 5¾ in. (inc. handle); W. at rim 6¹¹⁄₁₆ in.; L. at rim 8½ in.; Wt. 22 oz., 15½ dwt.

MARKS: *a* twice on rim of body flanking back boss (would have flanked lost hinge) and twice on flange of cover above lost hasp.

Raised elliptical body, the bottom stepped and slightly domed with narrow reeding below curved sides; almost straight rim. Sides have four bosses within raying gadroons, a triangular acanthus design on matted ground at corners. Cast scroll legs with slight trefoil pads affixed to edge of reed and inner edge of step. Molded and domed cover (originally hinged at back), straight bezel set unevenly under flange, probably after hinge was off, has applied punched molding on edge of flange, reeding in midmolding, and leafy scroll design on matted ground around raised ribbon-crossed wreath enclosing simple scrolls. Cast handle has a small modeled ring atop flowing curves which divide to form a centered scroll-tipped loop fastened on the cover. At the point of division, leaf forms protrude and are repeated beneath the upright modeled and scrolled ends. These leaves are also tangent to the central groove of the lid. That a hinged hasp was once on the front of the lid is clear from the staple soldered through the front circle. Repairs at back and cracks near front in angles of cover molding. No center points.

Engraved GSM on front boss above staple. The initials of the original owners would have been on the hasp or on the bottom.

HISTORY: Original owners unknown; Gurdon and Mary (Whittingham or

Withington) Saltonstall of Boston and New London, Connecticut, m. Nov. 13, 1712; subsequent history unknown.

NOTES: Not mentioned in the will of Mary Saltonstall, but in her inventory among "Sundry pieces of plate . . . 1 sugar box & spoon." Only the Middlecott box by Winslow (*MFA 1956*, no. 143) has the snake handle of Coney's boxes; the other three have slight variants of this. The MFA's is the simplest of all the boxes and might therefore be the earliest; each of the others is dated 1702.

REFERENCES: *Avery 1930*, p. 50; *Hipkiss 1942*, pp. 84, 86; illus. p. 84; *Antiques*, XLIII, no. 1 (1943), pp. 35-36; *Phillips 1949*, pp. 54, 57; *Wenham 1949*, fig. 44; *Buhler 1957*, fig. 6; K. C. Buhler, "The Nine Colonial Sugar Boxes," *Antiques*, LXXXV, no. 1 (1964), pp. 88-89, fig. 9.

EXHIBITIONS: *Harvard 1936*, no. 111, pl. 19; *Harvard Memorial Society 1939; Hartford 1947.*

THE PHILIP LEFFINGWELL SPALDING COLLECTION. GIVEN IN HIS MEMORY BY KATHERINE AMES SPALDING AND PHILIP SPALDING, OAKES AMES SPALDING, HOBART AMES SPALDING 42.251

69

70

70 Mug, c. 1710

H. of body 3½ in.; D. of base 3 in. (uneven); D. of lip 2⅜ in.; Wt. 6 oz., 10½ dwt.

MARK: *b* at left of handle.

Straight tapering sides, applied (?) narrow rim, band semicircular in section two inches below, and molded baseband. Center point on bottom. Hollow scroll handle, flat outer surface, slight grip, upper joining (which is probably repaired) almost flush with rim; disc at lower joining, rounded upcurved tip (vent hole a slit).

Engraved on base in modern script *Edward Hutchinson/1678-1752.*
E almost obliterated from handle at left below grip.

HISTORY: Edward Hutchinson (1678-1752), m. Lydia Foster 1705; descended in the family by 1906 to Mrs. Estes Howe, mother of the donor.

EXHIBITION: *MFA 1906*, no. 331, illus. pl. V.

BEQUEST OF MISS LOIS LILLEY HOWE 64.2046

71 Flagon, 1713

H. 12⁵⁄₁₆ in. (inc. finial); D. of base 6³⁄₈ in.; D. of lip 4¼ in.; Wt. 50 oz., 5 dwt.

MARKS: *a* on cover and at left of handle.

Raised tapering sides, applied everted rim and molded bead below; the rounded bottom seemingly inset and concealed by a raised molded reverse curve baseband (heavy solder underneath), a molded bead at joining, and thick bead at edge. Cover with applied rim is molded and stepped to flat top with turned finial broad at base and pinned through; no bezel. Meander wire in molding of outer shaped hinge plate, five-part hinge, long curved molded inner plate, slight modeling in upright support for double cusped thumbpiece, its sides in a scroll. Hollow scroll handle with curled free-standing pointed tip affixed at and below upper bead and with disc above lower bead, its tip slightly angled and rounded (vent hole rather large).

Engraved on the front in a foliate wreath: *This belongs to/the Church in/*

Brattle Street/1713. Scratched weight on bottom: *51 oz., 19 dwt.*

HISTORY: See *Notes.*

NOTES: Flagons first came to New England as royal gifts to King's Chapel in 1694. They are one form of plate used in colonial churches which was not also fashioned for domestic use, although English ones were. The possible source of these flagons is suggested in the records of Benjamin Colman, who was called from England in 1699 to be the first minister of the Church in Brattle Square (as it was also called): "On October the 12th 1711. The old Meeting house being burnt down, with a great part of yᵉ Town, Our Chh. invited the Pastors of yᵉ said first Chh. who were wont to meet there, to preach with us in turn every Sabbath, & to joyn in the Administration of all Ordinances; to which they with their Church consented, & continued with us unto May the fourth 1713. When they took leave of us with a very grateful letter, read publicly by me to our Congregation, & went into their new House."

The four flagons are as alike as if they had been made by one man; but the makers' marks and the dates differentiate them. Those by John Noyes (Cat. no. 93) and Nathaniel Morse (Cat. no. 106) are both dated 1711. The third, dated 1712, is by John Edwards (Cat. no. 82). This fourth flagon, by Winslow, is dated 1713. It seems likely that the flagons were made as a gift by the First Church during the years when its members were sharing the Brattle Street Church.

REFERENCES: *Jones 1913,* p. 68; *Paull 1913,* p. 23, illus. p. 24; *Bigelow 1917,* p. 155; *Avery 1930,* p. 66; *Ensko 1948,* illus. p. 14; *Phillips, Antiques,* no. 4 (1949), p. 283; *Buhler 1950,* p. 27; *Buhler 1955,* illus. p. 458; *McLanathan 1956,* fig. 9.

EXHIBITIONS: *Jamestown 1907,* no. 473; *Towle 1954; Art Treasures 1955; Dallas 1958,* no. 134, illus.; *Buffalo 1965,* no. 107.

GIFT OF THE BENEVOLENT FRATERNITY OF CHURCHES
SILVER OF THE CHURCH IN BRATTLE SQUARE *13.405*

72 Cann, c. 1715

H. of body 4⅞ in.; D. of base 3⅛ in.; D. of lip 3⅛-3¼ in. (uneven);
Wt. 11 oz., 2 dwt.

MARK: *b* at left of handle.

Molded rim, tapering sides curving above almost flat bottom, on cast splayed footband with incised lines near vertical edge (bent). Center point on bottom. Hollow scroll cast handle, curved outer surface, scroll at upper joining extends to form slight grip and has turned V-shaped drop below; disc at lower joining, short scroll tip, vent hole in seam.

Engraved with Hutchinson arms in circle within scroll and foliate cartouche; helmet supports torse and crest. Stamped square under foot.

HISTORY: Same as Cat. no. 70.

NOTES: Bigelow, in writing of the chocolate pot with Hutchinson arms by Winslow in The Metropolitan Museum of Art, Clearwater Collection, states that the Winslow and Hutchinson families were closely related. The Clearwater Collection also has a tankard by Winslow with Hutchinson arms. Edward and Thomas Hutchinson gave two of the three unique armorial dishes made by Winslow to the Second Church in Boston; an armorial pair of cast candlesticks (privately owned) are by Winslow, and privately owned is a cann by Paul Revere II with Hutchinson arms.

EXHIBITIONS: *MFA 1906,* no. 326, illus. group pls. V and XV.

BEQUEST OF MISS LOIS LILLEY HOWE *64.2047*

72

73

73 Pepper Box, c. 1710–1730

H. 3⁷⁄₁₆ in. (inc. finial); D. of base 1⁷⁄₈ in.; Wt. 2 oz., 15 dwt.

MARK: *a* on bottom.

Cylindrical body seamed under molded strap handle, both tips curled, applied molding flush with flat bottom; small bead below rim forms bezel (broken). Low domed cover with slight flange and curved step, simple circular piercings, tiny turned finial, molded vertical band almost at edge of flange to fit over bezel.

Engraved MGR on front; no trace of earlier initials.

HISTORY: Early history unknown; Moses Gill (1733-1800) and his second wife, Rebecca Boylston, m. 1773; found in 1955 in the possession of the late Mrs. William R. Jennison, Fitchburg, Massachusetts, from whose estate it was bought.

NOTES: Other examples by Winslow are two pepper boxes with beaded handles and quite different lids (Yale University Art Gallery, Garvan Collection).

EXHIBITION: *R.I. 1965,* no. 207.

CHARLES HITCHCOCK TYLER FUND 55.8

DAVID JESSE
c. 1670–1705/6

DAVID JESSE was born in Hartford, Connecticut, a town then without goldsmiths. He could well have been an apprentice of John Coney from the similarity of their work. He married in Hartford, Mary, daughter of Phineas Wilson, a prosperous merchant from Dublin. Their son David was baptized in the Brattle Street Church in Boston in 1700; Mary, Phineas, and Elizabeth were born shortly thereafter; the youngest child, Susanna, may not have known her father. In 1704 Jesse was chosen constable to serve in John Noyes' stead and he is said to have belonged to the Artillery Company. The scarcity of his work is explained by the shortness of his life. The *Boston News-Letter* January 13, 1705/06 carried the notice of his death. His inventory mentioned "The Chamber over the Shop" where there were "Some Pictures and things on the Mantle tree" and "Working Tools in the Shop and Cellar".

Jesse used an annulet above, pellet below, his initials in a circle *(a)*, and perhaps had his mark in two sizes.

a

74 Tankard, 1690–1700

H. 5⅞ in. (inc. thumbpiece); D. of base 4³⁄₁₆-4¼ in. (uneven); D. of lip 3⅝ in.; Wt. 17 oz., 19 dwt.

MARKS: *a* twice at left of handle and twice on lid.

Tapering sides with paired incised lines below everted rim; applied molded baseband. Center point on bottom and in lid. Stepped flat cover with very narrow bezel, scribed flange, shaped at front and flanking curve under five-part hinge, double spiral thumbpiece, meander wire in molded hinge plates, outer one shaped on shoulder of scroll handle with a short V-shaped body drop and rounded tip with slot vent.

Engraved RGK on handle, long serif on *R* and upper part worn by thumb-piece. No evidence of earlier initials.

HISTORY: Early history unknown; Rufus and Katharine (Stanbridge) Greene, m. 1728; their daughter Katharine (b. November 22, 1731; d. London, April 11, 1777), m. January 16, 1757, John (b. August 29, 1728; d. 1803), son of Thomas (1682-1728) and Rebecca (Holmes) Amory; their son, John Amory, Jr. (b. June 21, 1759), m. November 23, 1791, Katharine, daughter of Levi and Catharine (Chandler) Willard; their daughter Catharine Willard Amory (1796-1850), m. Henry Codman (1789-1853); their son John Amory Codman (1824-1886), m. Martha Pickman Rogers (1829-1905) 1850; their daughter

74

Martha Catherine (Codman) Karolik.

NOTES: See Rufus Greene's biography (p. 255); his inventory included only the one tankard.

REFERENCES: *Hipkiss 1941*, pp. 230-231, no. 157; Edwin J. Hipkiss, "American Arts of the Eighteenth Century," *MFA Bulletin*, no. 236 (1941), illus. p. 86.

EXHIBITION: *R.I. 1965*, no. 120, fig. 7.

M. AND M. KAROLIK COLLECTION *39.185*

JOHN ALLEN
1671/2–1760

JOHN ALLEN's baptism appears in the records of the First Church, Boston, for 1671/2: "sonne of our Teacher Baptized the 3rd day of the first month." His father was the Reverend James Allen, whose first wife was Hannah, sister of Jeremiah Dummer. John's mother was Elizabeth (Houchin), widow of John Endicott II. An apprenticeship under Dummer seems reasonable; he would undoubtedly have served with his partner John Edwards. Allen, "weak in body," wrote his will in 1736, but it was not probated until 1760.

Allen was once credited with two beakers (Yale University Art Gallery, Garvan Collection) bearing the mark of initials *I A* in an inverted heart. This attribution was repudiated by the late John M. Phillips. Allen used his initials in a quatrefoil in the days of his partnership with John Edwards. The mark *(a)* of a barred *I* with an angled open crossbar on the *A,* a pellet between, in a rectangle, was long assigned to Josiah Austin, who was too young to have made these pieces. Present attribution to Allen is based upon the same mark being on an early teapot with the arms of Dudley (*MFA 1956,* no. 1), a family for whom he is known to have made silver.

a

75

75 Creampot, c. 1740

Attributed to JOHN ALLEN

H. 3½ in.; D. of base 1⅞ in.; Wt. 2 oz., 18½ dwt.

MARKS: *a* at left of handle and at center point on bottom.

Bulbous body with molded rim, on molded splayed foot. Rim cut for applied small triangular spout with body drop and high, curved lip. Cast scroll handle with slight grip, long upper joining with drop, very slight jog above lower joining, scroll and pointed tip.

Engraved MHB/*1878* on front (see Rufus Greene casters, Cat. no. 217).

HISTORY: Early history unknown; probably Benjamin Hall, Jr. in 1807 (see Cat. no. 217); descended to the donor.

NOTES: The creampot by John Edwards (*MFA 1956*, no. 61, fig. 35) and the one by Paul Revere I (Cat. no. 150) are similar in form.

REFERENCES: *Bigelow 1917*, p. 408, fig. 298; *Ensko 1948*, p. 91 (published in both as by Josiah Austin).

EXHIBITION: *MFA 1911*, no. 27, pl. 3 (as by Josiah Austin).

BEQUEST OF HENRY W. CUNNINGHAM *31.416*

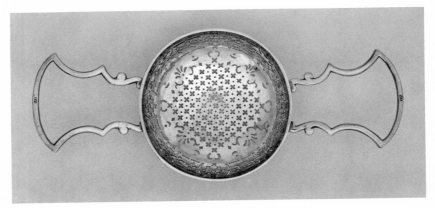

76

76 Punch Strainer, c. 1740

Attributed to JOHN ALLEN

H. 1¼ in.; D. of bowl 3⅝ in.; L. 8⅝ in.; Wt. 3 oz., 9 dwt.

MARKS: *a* on end curve of each handle.

Circular bowl, sides curving to slightly rounded bottom, applied molding
at lip. Two flat, cast handles have scroll joining at molding, slight scroll on a
short curve, and a longer curve splaying to a wide, curved end. Sides pierced
with a band formed of parallel spaced slits, divided front and sides by
grouped X's within brackets, and between each group of curved and flower
(?) forms. The center is pierced with a square of X's divided by dots; frame
of scrolls and fan forms at each side.

Engraved CRM at front above one group of X's.

HISTORY: Unknown until Ricketson family of New Bedford; Clark and Mary
(Wood) Ricketson (1776-1826) m. 1795; descended in family to the donors.

EXHIBITION: *MFA 1906*, no. 3, pl. XIX (as by Josiah Austin).

GIFT OF MR. AND MRS. HENRY HERBET EDES 36.43

JOHN EDWARDS
1671–1746

JOHN EDWARDS was the son of a "chirurgeon" who came to Boston from England c. 1685, when the boy was of age to start his apprenticeship, probably with Jeremiah Dummer. John's brief partnership with John Allen at the turn of the century has been noted most often in the standing salt of their fashioning, the third American one known and still in private possession. The goldsmith married Sybil Newman (stepdaughter of Zerubabel Endicott) in 1694. His first son and namesake became a bookseller. His sons Thomas and Samuel followed their father's craft; Joseph became a stationer and had a son and namesake who carried on the goldsmithing tradition. His daughter, Mary, married Ebenezer Storer, and many pieces made for them have been preserved in subsequent generations. John Edwards served in many public offices, frequently in the company of other goldsmiths: John Dixwell, John Noyes, and Andrew Tyler. In 1740 he married his son Samuel's mother-in-law, Abigail (Fowle) Smith, who survived him. He died in 1746 leaving a total estate of £4,840 8s. and "A parcell Tools £336-5-9 / Goods in the shop £1042-10-5," indicating that he was still active at the time of his death. One of the appraisers of his estate was Jacob Hurd.

Edwards used his initials (a) in a quatrefoil and (b) in a notched quatrefoil. Apparently later he crowned his initials (c) and placed a device (in clear marks seemingly a fleur-de-lis) below them in a conforming shield punch. A simple rectangular mark of his initials is not represented in the MFA. The quatrefoil mark (a) appears on dated pieces by Edwards from 1699 to 1708; the notched quatrefoil (b) on the flagon of 1712 (Cat. no. 82) is on the Hatfield beaker of 1713 (error in *Jones 1913*), and the baptismal basin of 1714 in the First Church of Christ, Portsmouth, New Hampshire. The crowned initials mark (c) appears on the beakers in the First Parish, Plymouth, Massachusetts, bequeathed in 1710 to be made within two years of the bequest. However, from 1715 on this was Edwards' commonly used large mark.

a   b   c

77

77 Miniature Caudle Cup, c. 1695

Attributed to JOHN EDWARDS by tradition

H. 1 in. (inc. handles); D. of base ⅞ in.; D. of lip 1½-1⁹⁄₁₆ in. (uneven);
Wt. 13 dwt.

MARK: None.

Straight sides curve to rounded bottom with rope foot rim. Center point on
bottom. Four panels formed on sides by horizontal row of dots near rim
and at foot rim and by vertical dots between chased, paired lines at handles
and midway between. Each panel has three dotted flower forms on stems
from base, the outer ones curving. Scroll handles of rope design with
free-standing tips affixed at rim and at start of curve.

Engraved *ES* on bottom; *1770* added later.

HISTORY: The initials for the granddaughter of the goldsmith, Elizabeth
Storer (1726-1786), m. Isaac Smith; the date, the birth of their sixth child
(and third of the name) Elizabeth (1770-1849), who married but died without
issue; her great-niece Elizabeth (b. 1843, d. unmarried); her great-nieces,
the donors.

EXHIBITION: *MFA 1956*, no. 60, fig. 36.

GIFT OF THE MISSES ROSE AND ELIZABETH TOWNSEND 56.669

78 Spoon, c. 1695

L. 7³⁄₁₆ in.; Wt. 1 oz., 5½ dwt.

MARK: *a* on back of stem.

Rather thin, rectangular stem flattening and broadening to sharply upturned trifid tip. Rounded drop and grooved rattail stamped in swage of delicate beaded scrolls with flowers (?) enclosed in each scroll, and star at tip on elliptical bowl.

Engraved *M·P* in block letters on back of handle.

HISTORY: Unknown.

NOTES: Other spoons stamped in same swage: one with trifid end and quatrefoil mark in the Henry Francis du Pont Winterthur Museum, Delaware; a pair with same mark but wavy end engraved OTC for The Old Church, in the First Church, Boston.

REFERENCES: *Halsey 1925,* pl. 16; *Hipkiss 1943,* pp. 39-40; *Buhler 1957,* p. 48.

THE PHILIP LEFFINGWELL SPALDING COLLECTION. GIVEN IN HIS MEMORY BY KATHERINE AMES SPALDING AND PHILIP SPALDING, OAKES AMES SPALDING, HOBART AMES SPALDING 42.230

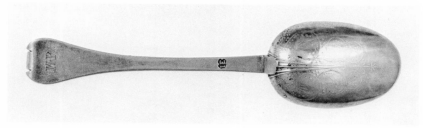

78

79 Mug, c. 1695–1700

H. of body 4¼ in.; D. of base 4³⁄₁₆ in.; D. of lip 3⁷⁄₁₆-3⅝ in. (uneven);
Wt. 12 oz., 12 dwt.

MARK: *a* at left of handle.

Straight tapering sides; incised lines below everted rim; wide, applied,
molded midband; baseband matching upper half of midband. No center point.
Hollow, scroll handle affixed at rim and above baseband, vent hole in
groove under mask tip (handle has hole at left side below mask).

Engraved on handle in semiscript *S*Russell;* original initials almost erased
from bottom with scratchings of later initials; scratched weight on
bottom *12-16*.

HISTORY: Unknown.

NOTES: The mask insofar as we know is unique and the proportions
are particularly successful.

REFERENCES: Hollis French, *Art in America,* VII, no. 3 (1919), pp. 138-142;
Halsey 1925, pl. 16; *Hipkiss 1943,* pp. 38-39, illus.; *Buhler 1951,* pp. 288-289,
fig. 2; *Buhler 1957,* p. 48.

EXHIBITIONS: *Chicago 1949,* no. 67, illus. no. 113; *Richmond 1960,* no. 53;
ESU 1960, no. 24, pl. 26.

THE PHILIP LEFFINGWELL SPALDING COLLECTION. GIVEN IN HIS MEMORY
BY KATHERINE AMES SPALDING AND PHILIP SPALDING, OAKES AMES SPALDING,
HOBART AMES SPALDING 42.532

79

80

80 Cup, 1700–1710

H. 3¼ in. (inc. handle); D. of base 2½ in.; D. of lip 2¹⁵⁄₁₆ in.; Wt. 4 oz., 9 dwt.

MARK: *b* on bottom.

Heavy gauge, almost straight sides with flaring lip; applied, molded base-band very neatly soldered. No center point. Molded strap handle; raised ridge in center; rounded tips; soldered at curve of lip and slightly bent at joining above baseband.

Engraved on front: *S LINDALL 1708/LOVE RAWLINS PICKMAN/1788/ MARY PICKMAN LORING/1857*. None of the engraving appears to be contemporary with the cup; the first two names are in the same lettering.

HISTORY: Sarah Lindall, spinster; her sister Abigail Lindall, m. Benjamin Pickman II (1672-1719) as his second wife (she was mother of his surviving children); Love Rawlins (1709-1786), wife of Benjamin Pickman III (1708-1773); their daughter Love Rawlins Pickman; their great-great granddaughter Mary Pickman Loring (1857-1864), a cousin of the donor.

REFERENCES: *Clark [Buhler] 1931*, p. 50, illus. p. 48; *Ellis 1961*, p. 27.

GIFT OF MR. AND MRS. DUDLEY LEAVITT PICKMAN 31.229

81 Porringer, 1700–1710

H. 1⁹⁄₁₆ in.; D. of lip 4 in.; L. of handle 2 in.; Wt. 3 oz., 9½ dwt.

MARK: *b* at left of handle.

Curved sides, everted rim, stepped and domed bottom (strange hammer marks around base). Center point in bowl. Geometric handle with circular piercings at sides and in tip over heart; quite wide, double-arched opening at bowl flanked by circles, shaped holes, and scroll tips at sides.

Engraved B⟨C⟩P on handle away from bowl.

HISTORY: Traditionally Benjamin and Priscilla Collins of Lynn, whose descendants sold it in 1946 to Mrs. Dorothy Draper Hamlen, from whom it was bought.

NOTES: This is the size of a child's porringer but has married owners' initials. A very similar handle (*Bigelow 1917*, p. 313) is on a John Edwards porringer in the Yale University Art Gallery, Garvan Collection, with added engraving for M. Storer. It lacks the second hole at the tip, and the arched opening is smaller.

GIFT OF GUY WARREN WALKER, JR. 64.1600

81

82

82 Flagon, 1712

H. 11¾ in. (inc. finial); D. of base 6³⁄₁₆ in.; D. of lip 4³⁄₁₆ in.; Wt. 48 oz., 3 dwt.

MARKS: *b* on cover and at left of handle.

Construction similar to flagon by Edward Winslow (Cat. no. 71); lip of cover more rounded (no bezel); both hinge plates have meander wire, the inner shorter than Winslow's, the outer curving to point. Small vent hole, no disc at lower joining. One bad dent on right side.

Engraved on front in foliate wreath *This belongs to/the Church in/Brattle Street / 1712.* Scratched weight, *49-8,* on bottom.

HISTORY: The Brattle Street Church; see Cat. no. 71.

NOTES: Part of a set of four flagons including those of Winslow (Cat. no. 71), Noyes (Cat. no. 93), and Morse (Cat. no. 106). Although this appears to have an added bottom, the one made by Edwards for the First Church,

Boston appears to be in one piece, as does the one by Noyes (Cat. no. 93).

REFERENCES: *Jones 1913*, p. 68, pl. XXVII; *Paull 1913*, p. 23, illus. p. 24; *Bigelow 1917*, p. 155; *Avery 1930*, pp. 66, 311; *Buhler 1950*, p. 27; *Buhler 1951*, p. 288, fig. 1; *Buhler 1955*, illus. p. 458; *McLanathan 1956*, p. 56, fig. 9.

EXHIBITIONS: *MFA 1906*, no. 108, pls. XVI, XXVII; *MFA 1911*, no. 389, pl. 11; *Chicago 1949*, no. 166, illus. p. 108; *Towle 1954*; *Art Treasures 1955*; *Minneapolis 1956*, no. 219, fig. 48; *Dallas 1958*, no. 134, illus.; *ESU 1960*, no. 25, pl. 6; *Buffalo 1965*.

GIFT OF THE BENEVOLENT FRATERNITY OF CHURCHES
SILVER OF THE CHURCH IN BRATTLE SQUARE 13.402

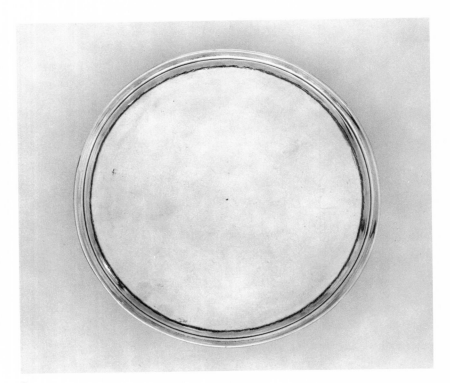

83

83 Salver, 1710–1715

D. of dish 5¹³⁄₁₆ in.; Wt. 3 oz., 15½ dwt.

MARK: *b* near rim on dish.

Heavy gauge, circular dish with raised and everted molded rim. Center point on top and bottom. Center area top and bottom shows circle (not visible in illustration), doubtless from trumpet-style foot (missing).

Engraved ICA near rim on bottom.

HISTORY: Unknown.

EXHIBITION: *MFA 1911*, no. 392, pl. 11.

GIFT OF MISS ELIZABETH L. DALTON IN MEMORY OF HER BROTHER,
HENRY R. DALTON 47.1345

84

84 Porringer, 1710–1720

H. 1¾ in.; D. of lip 4⅞ in.; L. of handle 2⁵⁄₁₆ in.; Wt. 6 oz. 3 dwt.

MARK: *c* in center of bowl.

Everted rim, curved sides, stepped flat bottom domed at center. Center point on base. Roughly cast handle of three shaped cuttings each side of initial area, circle over teardrop holes in bell-form tip, scroll edges, crude soldering at angle of rim.

Engraved TᴮM on handle away from bowl.

HISTORY: Thomas and Mary (Willoughby) Barton, m. 1710 (see Cat. no. 39).

NOTES: An almost identical handle is on a porringer by John Potwine (see *Addenda*).

REFERENCES: *Bigelow 1917,* p. 313, fig. 217; *Avery 1930,* p. 332; *Bell 1930,* pl. VII; *Clark [Buhler] 1931,* p. 44, illus. p. 45; *Ellis 1961,* p. 27, illus. p. 23, fig. 5.

EXHIBITION: *Minneapolis 1956,* no. 218.

GIFT OF MR. AND MRS. DUDLEY LEAVITT PICKMAN 31.230

85 Beaker, 1720

H. 5⅝ in.; D. of base 3 in.; D. of lip 3¾ in.; Wt. 7 oz.; 13 dwt.

MARKS: *c* above inscription at back.

Straight sides, flaring lip, applied molded baseband, no center point.

Engraved in one line and in semiscript: *The Gift of M.ʳ Nich.º Boone Bookseller, to the Church on Church Green in Boston. 1720.*

HISTORY: See *Notes.*

NOTES: The Church on Church Green was also called the New South Church and was founded in 1715 with forty-four members and completed in January, 1717. The donor, one of the founders, had been a member of the Third or South Church, later the Old South Church (Hamilton A. Hill, *History of the Old South Church,* Cambridge [Mass.], 1890). Boone was the first publisher of the *Boston News-Letter,* New England's first newspaper.

REFERENCES: F. V. Paull, "Communion Silver of the New South Church, Boston," *MFA Bulletin,* X, no. 59 (1912), p. 37, illus. p. 38; *Jones 1913,* p. 71, pl. XXVIII.

EXHIBITIONS: *MFA 1906,* no. 106, pl. XII; *MFA 1911,* no. 410.

GIFT OF THE NEW SOUTH CHURCH SOCIETY 12.397

85

86

86 Mug, c. 1720

H. of body 4⅛ in.; D. of base 3³⁄₁₆ in.; D. of lip 3¹⁄₁₆ in.; Wt. 7 oz., 16 dwt.

MARK: *c* at left of handle.

Tapering sides; molded rim; finely drawn, applied baseband. Very worn center point on bottom. Hollow, scroll handle with slight grip; flat surface; broad, rounded tip (bent up) with vent hole a slit. Both joinings crudely repaired.

Engraved IWS, very worn, on battered bottom.

HISTORY: Jacob Wendell and Sarah Oliver, m. August 12, 1714; descended in family to Edward Jackson Holmes (see Cat. no. 34 for descent).

THE EDWARD JACKSON HOLMES COLLECTION, BEQUEST OF MRS. EDWARD JACKSON HOLMES 65.262

87 Communion Cup, 1732

H. 8 in.; D. of base 3⅞ in.; D. of lip 4 in.; Wt. 10 oz., 11½ dwt.

MARK: *c* near lip opposite engraving.

Bell-shaped cup with slightly flaring rim; disc on bottom at joining of cast, baluster stem; raised foot domed and splaying to molded edge and applied rim. Center point in bowl.

Engraved within feather cartouche with angel's head between upper curls, mask (?) within straight lines with leaf ornament between lower scrolls, one cross-hatched and one plain, in semiscript: *The Legacy/of Stephen Minot Esqr / to the Church / in Brattle-street / 1732.* Weight scratched under foot, *11-1* and also *14-8.*

HISTORY: See *Notes.*

NOTES: Once fitted with domed cover (probably made by Joseph Foster; see Cat. no. 452), bezel within straight rim; turned, acorn (?) finial soldered on. One of a pair given to the Church; the other is in the Worcester Art Museum. Minot was admitted to the Brattle Street Church in 1700.

REFERENCES: *Jones 1913,* p. 67, pl. XXVII; *Paull 1913,* p. 23, illus. p. 24; *Avery 1930,* pp. 67, 286, pl. XLVII; *McLanathan 1956,* p. 56, fig. 9; *Wenham 1949,* p. 9.

EXHIBITIONS: *MFA 1906,* no. 101, pls. 26, 27; *MFA 1911,* no. 421 or 422, pl. 11 (pair); *Cranbrook 1952,* no. 11; *Towle 1954; Art Treasures 1955; Minneapolis 1956,* no. 220, pl. 48, *Dallas 1958,* no. 134, illus.; *Buffalo 1965,* no. 101.

GIFT OF THE BENEVOLENT FRATERNITY OF CHURCHES
SILVER OF THE CHURCH IN BRATTLE SQUARE 13.397

87

88

88 Communion Cup, c. 1737

H. 8¼ in.; D. of base 4 in.; D. of lip 4⅛ in.; Wt. 12 oz., 2½ dwt.

MARK: *c* partly obliterated by cartouche containing arms.
Same form as Cat. no. 87.

Engraved in semiscript in cartouche of foliate scrolls and pendent bellflowers: *A Gift/To the Church/in Lynde Street/BOSTON*. Added opposite,
in similar but more boldly cut cartouche, by Samuel Edwards, the arms of
the donor Hugh Hall.

HISTORY: Made for The West Church, founded in 1737. Records of the
church show that the coat of arms of the donor, Hugh Hall, was engraved by
Samuel Edwards. See Cat. no. 200.

NOTES: Fitted with domed cover with acorn finial, probably made by Lewis
Cary, c. 1824.

REFERENCES: *Buck 1903*, illus. opp. p. 225; *Jones 1913*, p. 87, pl. XXXIII;
Avery 1930, pp. 67, 286, pl. XLVII; *Buhler, Antiques*, no. 5 (1945), p. 270,
figs. 13, 14; *Wenham 1949*, p. 9; *McLanathan 1956*, p. 49, fig. 1.

EXHIBITION: MFA 1911, no. 423, pl. 11.

GIFT OF THE WEST BOSTON SOCIETY, "WEST CHURCH" 92.2848

88

Gift of Mr. John Clough to the Church of Ch...
...Street of which the Rev.: Mr. Samuel Checkley is...

1744

89

89 Beaker, 1744

H. 5¾ in.; D. of base 3½ in.; D. of lip 3⅞ in.; Wt. 10 oz., 8 dwt.

MARK: *c* near rim, above date.

Straight sides, slightly flaring lip, applied molded baseband. Center point on bottom.

Engraved in semiscript with flourishes: *The Gift of M.ʳ John Clough to the Church of Christ in / Summer Street of which the Revᵈ Mˢ Samuel Checkley is Pastor/1744.*

HISTORY: See *Notes.*

NOTES: The donor was one of the forty-four persons, many of them from the Third or South Church, who founded the New South Church (the former then became the Old South Church). Samuel Checkley, Harvard class of 1715, was ordained April 15, 1719 by the Mathers, Benjamin Wadsworth, Benjamin Colman, and Joseph Sewall. He opened his pulpit to George Whitefield in 1740.

REFERENCES: F. V. Paull, "Communion Silver of the New South Church, Boston," *MFA Bulletin,* X, no. 59 (1912), p. 37, illus. p. 38; *Jones 1913,* p. 72, pl. XXVIII; *Buhler 1951,* p. 288, fig. 3.

EXHIBITIONS: *MFA 1906,* no. 105, pls. XII, XXVI; *MFA 1911,* no. 411, pl. 11; *Columbus 1947.*

GIFT OF THE NEW SOUTH CHURCH SOCIETY *12.396*

JOHN NOYES
1674–1749

JOHN NOYES was the elder son of the fourth son of the emigrant, the Reverend James Noyes, who settled in Newbury, Massachusetts in 1634/5 with his wife Sarah (Brown). He became the first Teacher of the church there, for which his grandson later made beakers. The first John Noyes, one of many of the name, was born in Newbury in 1645 and is believed to have been a cooper. He married Sarah, daughter of Peter Oliver; their first-born was Sarah in 1671, and their son John was born in Boston in 1674. The father died in 1678 according to Samuel Sewall's diary. It is probable that Noyes was apprenticed to Jeremiah Dummer; in March 1699 he married Susanna Edwards, sister of John Edwards (q.v.). Although the marriage was performed by the Reverend Samuel Willard of the Third, later the Old South, Church, John Noyes appears among the founders of the Church in Brattle Square in December of that year. He was Fourth Sergeant of the Artillery Company in 1699, and is mentioned as "Ensign Noyes" in Sewall's diary in 1702 when he was given a silver cup for his marksmanship. He declined to serve as constable in 1704 and paid his fine. Five daughters are recorded to John and Susanna Noyes, the first in 1701 and the fourth named Sarah. The latter, born in 1712, was granted administration of her father's estate when he died intestate.

Two marks are assigned to Noyes: *(a)* initials in an ellipse and *(b)* initials with cross-crosslet below in shield, each seemingly with good reason. A third, small, cartouche-shaped mark of his initials on an unpublished spoon (privately owned) was assigned to him by an early nineteenth-century owner.

a   *b*

90

90 Pair of Candlesticks, 1695–1700

H. 9¼ in. (each); W. of base 6⅜ in. (each); Wt. of *54.594*, 20 oz.; of *54.595*, 20 oz. 4 dwt.

MARK: *a* on lowest part of foot.

Removable drip-pan or bobeche fashioned of two thin cut-cornered squares, originally joined but half-open now; very deep bezel; circle of reeding midway on upper surface, the lower has molding of same diameter in two steps, incurved at bezel. Applied (bent) molded rim above stop-fluted, hollow column. Incised line on band at base above hollow octagonal flange in two horizontal parts; reeding on upper curved step; angular tapering step beneath, free-standing at stem where inner disc joins base (wider than column) splaying to circular, narrow reeding in cut-cornered square. To this is soldered a molded splayed rim with band of reeding and strengthening strap extending beyond the edge to form an additional slight step. (Bezel broken on 54.595 but top firm.)

Engraved with Bowdoin crest in buckled circle with motto in corner on edge of step. 54.594 has engraved weight *19-10* on edge of foot; 54.595, *20-3* also on edge of foot.

HISTORY: Pierre Baudouin, who emigrated from La Rochelle, France, to Casco Bay in 1687; in Boston 1690 (d. 1706); his son James (d. 1747); his son James (1726-1790), after whom Bowdoin College was named, m. Elizabeth Erving; their son James (Harvard 1771), died childless, 1811; his sister Elizabeth, m. Sir John Temple Bt.; their daughter, m. Thomas Lindall Winthrop, grandfather of the donor.

NOTES: In the *MFA Bulletin* mentioned below, it was stated erroneously that James Bowdoin was a delegate to the Continental Congress. He had been elected but did not attend.

REFERENCES: *Phillips 1949*, p. 58; K. C. Buhler, "A Pair of Candlesticks by John Noyes, 1695-1700," *MFA Bulletin*, LIII, no. 292 (1955), pp. 25-29, illus.

EXHIBITIONS: *MFA 1956*, no. 107; Bowdoin College, Walker Art Gallery, 1959; *Richmond 1960*, no. 97, illus.; *R.I. 1965*, no. 146, fig. 4.
GIFT OF MISS CLARA BOWDOIN WINTHROP 54.594-595

91

91 Tankard, c. 1700

H. 6¾ in. (inc. thumbpiece); D. of base 4⅞ in.; D. of lip 4¹⁵⁄₁₆ in.; Wt. 27 oz., 5½ dwt.

MARKS: *a* on cover, on body at left of handle, and on bottom.

Tapering sides; incised lines below molded rim; applied, molded baseband joined under handle, very neatly soldered. Center point on lid, but none on body (rim cracked in many places). Stepped, flat cover has wide flange with paired, incised lines, shaped at front and at sides of extension to five-part hinge; meander wire in molded hinge plates, outer shaped on shoulder of hollow scroll handle; rattail at upper joining; scalloped shield tip affixed with even overhang (circular vent hole in slit). Dolphin and mask thumbpiece, worn by contact with dented handle.

Engraved IBS on handle.

HISTORY: John Barnard, m. Sarah Martyn, September, 1715 (conjectured; see *Notes*); subsequent history unknown.

NOTES: The Brattle Street Church in 1700, "Ordered that Deacon Barnard be presented with a piece of plate of ye value of Twelve pounds & that T. Brattle do speak to Mr. Noyse to make a silver tankard of that value." Nowhere in the records of the Church is the Deacon's first name given; Dr. Richard D. Pierce, historian of the First Church, Boston, identified him as Deacon John Barnard and suggested that "he may have gotten his title from the Second Church." A portrait attributed to Peter Pelham, dated 1727, of Deacon John Barnard of the Second Church is in the Heritage Foundation, Deerfield; and the Boston town records contain the marriage of John Barnard and Sarah Martyn in September 1715. Their initials could have been added; the style of the tankard is nearer 1700, the date of the church gift.

REFERENCES: *Hipkiss 1943*, pp. 40-41; *Buhler 1957*, p. 48.

THE PHILIP LEFFINGWELL SPALDING COLLECTION. GIVEN IN HIS MEMORY BY KATHERINE AMES SPALDING AND PHILIP SPALDING, OAKES AMES SPALDING, HOBART AMES SPALDING 42.245

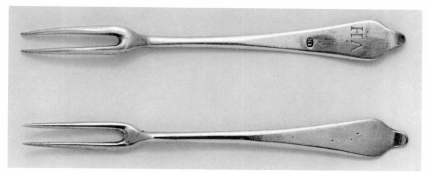

92

92 Pair of Forks, c. 1710

L. 7⁹⁄₁₆ in.; Wt. of pair, 2 oz., 18 dwt.

MARKS: *a* quite high on back of handles.
Heavy handle semicircular in section, broadened and flattened at wavy end with forward tip; two heavy tines from slight shoulder taper to points.
Engraved *HA* on back of handles.

HISTORY: Hannah Arnold m. Samuel Welles, September 15, 1719; descended in the family to the donor.

NOTES: Traditionally a part of Hannah Arnold's wedding silver, but the style and mark indicate earlier ownership.

REFERENCES: *Paull 1913*, p. 23, illus.; Walter A. Dyer, *Early American Craftsmen*, New York, 1915, illus. opp. p. 242; *Eberlein and McClure 1927*, p. 135; *Bigelow 1917*, pp. 281-282, fig. 186; *Avery 1930*, p. 358; *Wenham 1949*, p. 146, fig. 181b; *Buhler 1950*, p. 28.

EXHIBITIONS: *Jamestown 1907*, no. 106; *MFA 1911*, no. 798; *Knife/Fork/Spoon*, Walker Art Center, Minneapolis, and the Towle Silver Company, January 21, 1951-January 14, 1953, no. 64. *Richmond 1960*, no. 95.

GIFT OF WINTHROP SARGENT 13.406-407

93

93 Flagon, 1711

H. 11¹³⁄₁₆ in. (inc. finial); D. of base 6³⁄₁₆ in.; D. of lip 4⅜ in.; Wt. 48 oz., 3 dwt.

MARKS: *b* on lid and at left of handle.

The straight sides and curved bottom apparently in one piece, the effect that of the other three flagons (Cat. nos. 71, 82, 106). A faint center point on bottom. No disc at lower joining. Handle tip angled and the vent a slot, inner hinge plate almost as long as that on Winslow's flagon (Cat. no. 71) (both plates have wire), the molded outer plate ends in a curve. Upper joining tangent to rim, above and below bead (as on Morse's flagon, Cat. no. 106), perhaps resoldered. Both handle tips are cracked at edge.

Engraved on front in foliate wreath: *This belongs to/the Church in/Brattle Street / 1711*. On bottom, the weight: 49 oz = 10 dwt.

HISTORY: See *Notes* for Cat. no. 71.

REFERENCES: *Jones 1913,* p. 68, pl. XXVII; *Paull 1913,* p. 23, illus. p. 24; *Bigelow 1917,* p. 155; *Avery 1930,* pp. 66, 311, pl. LV; Clarice Lorenz Aiken. "Silver of New England Churches," *Antiquarian,* XV, no. 1 (1930), p. 58, illus.; *Buhler 1950,* p. 27, illus. p. 28, fig. 21; *Buhler 1955,* pp. 456-460, illus. p. 458; *McLanathan 1956,* p. 56, fig. 9.

EXHIBITIONS: *MFA 1906,* no. 210; *MFA 1911,* no. 796, pl. 4; *London 1954; Art Treasures 1955; Minneapolis 1956,* no. 263, fig. 48; *Dallas 1958,* no. 134, illus.; *ESU 1960,* no. 29, pl. 6; *Buffalo 1965,* no. 104, illus.

GIFT OF THE BENEVOLENT FRATERNITY OF CHURCHES
SILVER OF THE CHURCH IN BRATTLE SQUARE *13.404*

JOHN DIXWELL
1680–1725

JOHN DIXWELL, son of the regicide and his second wife, Bathsheba, was born at New Haven, Connecticut, on March 6, 1680/1. On July 11, 1705 he was in Boston; according to Samuel Sewall's *Diary*, "Her Majestie's Letter of the Third of May 1705 from St. James's, is read at the Board, wherin a new seal is ordered, and the old one to be defac'd; John Dixwell, the Goldsmith, being sent for, cut it in two in the middle, with a Chisel. . . ." In 1708 he married Mary Prout; four daughters are recorded to them in the Boston birth records. Their son Basil (1711-1746) followed his father's craft, but he died at Louisburg. A son John was recorded as "a considerable dealer in the Ironmongery way, a young gentleman exceedingly beloved and esteemed for his many good Qualities by all his Acquaintances" when he died at the age of thirty-one. Mary (Prout) Dixwell died in 1721, aged thirty-five; and in April of the next year the goldsmith married Martha Bowes, who died October 3, 1722. His third wife was Abigail (Walker) Bridgham, widow of Henry Bridgham. They were married April 18, 1723, by Peter Thacher, second minister of the New North Church, to which in 1717 Dixwell had presented a cup of his fashioning similar to that he made for Madam Knight (Cat. no. 96). Jeremiah Bumstead's diary noted: "1725 April 21 Mr. Dixwell, Elder of ye New North Church dyed of a feaver, which much seazed his head—lay about a week—aged 44 years; & buryed on ye 23 day." His death is attributed to smallpox inoculation. His widow was administratrix of his estate; John Edwards was one of the appraisers. The sale of his household goods, which had included "Images and Glasses on the Mantle Tree," was held at his house on Union Street, Boston, and was advertised in the *Boston News-Letter* early in June. In his shop among his tools were "2 belly pott anvills," presumably for canns, and "397 oz 5 Silver at 15/16."

Dixwell used two marks of his initials in an oval (*a*) and (*b*), differentiated only by their size.

a　　　　　*b*

94

94 Church Cup, 1710–1720

H. 4½ in.; D. of base 2¹¹⁄₁₆ in.; D. of lip 4 in.; Wt. 7 oz., 12 dwt.

MARK: *a* on side opposite engraving.

Flaring lip; almost straight sides curve to flattened base on heavy, molded footband. Center point on bottom. Hammer marks on curve of lip; three dents on curve below mark, several slight ones below engraving.

Engraved on side in two lines: *Harwich: Chh: / Cup:*

HISTORY: The North Parish in the Town of Harwich (founded 1700), which became the First Parish (Unitarian) Church of Brewster.

NOTES: Two pairs of cups were owned by the church and the MFA has one of each (see Cat. no. 95). The mate to this cup is privately owned.

REFERENCES: *Jones 1913*, pp. 91–92; *Hipkiss 1943*, pp. 43–44.

GIFT OF THE FIRST PARISH (UNITARIAN), BREWSTER, MASSACHUSETTS 13.583

95

95 Church Cup, 1710–1720

H. 4¹¹⁄₁₆ in.; D. of base 2⁵⁄₁₆-2³⁄₈ in. (uneven); D. of lip 3¹¹⁄₁₆ in.; W. 5 oz., 7 dwt.

MARKS: *b* twice on side.

Slimmer, lighter, on smaller foot than Cat. no. 94 and with the bottom curved. Center point on bottom.

Engraved in one line: *Harwich Chh Cup.*

HISTORY: The North Parish Church in Harwich (see Cat. no. 94).

REFERENCES: *Jones 1913*, pp. 91-92; *Hipkiss 1943*, pp. 43-44, illus.; *Buhler 1957*, p. 49.

EXHIBITIONS: *MFA 1911*, no. 332 or 333, pl. 9; *Park Square 1925*, no. 295.

THE PHILIP LEFFINGWELL SPALDING COLLECTION. GIVEN IN HIS MEMORY BY KATHERINE AMES SPALDING AND PHILIP SPALDING, OAKES AMES SPALDING, HOBART AMES SPALDING 42.214

96 Two-Handled Cup, 1722

H. 5¼ in. (inc. handles); D. of base 2⅜ in.; D. of lip 4 in.; Wt. 8 oz., 4½ dwt.

MARK: *b* on side near handle.

Flaring lip, almost straight sides curving to rounded base on molded footband. Center point on bottom. Two strap scroll handles, edges molded, affixed below rim and above curve, have rounded, free standing tips, the lower curved upward.

Engraved in semiscript on front: *The gift of Sarah Knight to the / Chh of Christ in Norwich / Apr 20:1722.*

HISTORY: Sarah, daughter of Thomas and Elizabeth Kemble, m. Richard Knight, carver; gift from her in 1722 to the Church of Christ, Norwich, Connecticut (became First Congregational Church); by 1919 George S. Palmer, from whom it was bought by the donor.

NOTES: Sarah Knight (1666-1727) kept a journal of her horseback ride, *Journey from Boston to New York in the Year 1704,* which was first published in New York in 1827. She opened a school in Boston in 1706; among her pupils were Benjamin Franklin and Benjamin Mather.

Similar cups by Dixwell were made for the New North Church, Boston (now in King's Chapel) and for the First Congregational churches of Deerfield, Milford, Hadley, and Charlestown, Massachusetts; the last now owned by Yale University Art Gallery, Garvan Collection.

The earliest New England baptismal basins had been made for domestic use wherein such "great basons" soon went out of style. Flagons were exclusively ecclesiastic in the colonies, although beakers and cups are found domestically. These two-handled cups, which John M. Phillips noted as the earliest evidence of Queen Anne styles following Dixwell's visit to Europe in 1710, seem, with the exception of one at Yale, to have been strictly for church use. The first of them known today was made by Dixwell in 1714.

REFERENCES: *Jones 1913,* p. 359, illus.; *Bigelow 1917,* pp. 90-91, fig. 36; *Avery 1930,* pp. 63, 281-282, pl. XI; *Hipkiss 1942,* p. 86, illus. frontispiece; *Hipkiss 1943,* p. 42; "The Almanac," *Antiques,* XLIII, no. 1 (1943), pp. 35-36; *Buhler 1957,* p. 49.

96

EXHIBITIONS: *The Early Plate in Connecticut Churches Prior to 1850,* The Connecticut Society of Colonial Dames of America, Wadsworth Atheneum, Hartford, May, 1919, catalogue by Florence Paull Berger, no. 166; *Hartford 1947; ESU 1960,* no. 30, pl. 29; *Craftsmen and Artists of Norwich,* Norwich, Connecticut, September 12-October 3, 1965, no. 139, illus.

THE PHILIP LEFFINGWELL SPALDING COLLECTION. GIVEN IN HIS MEMORY BY KATHERINE AMES SPALDING AND PHILIP SPALDING, OAKES AMES SPALDING, HOBART AMES SPALDING 42.215

PETER OLIVER
1682–1712

The great-grandfather of the goldsmith was Thomas Oliver, "chirurgeon," who arrived in America in 1632 and had, among his sons, John and Peter, names which recur in subsequent generations. His grandson John married Susannah Sweet; their youngest son, Peter, was born two years before his father's death. Similarities in Peter's work to that of Dummer and of Winslow have been noted. He married Jerusha, daughter of Increase Mather, in March 1709/10; she died December 20, 1710. On March 1, 1711/12, he married Hopestill Wensley, for whose mother he had made a flagon, presented to the Second Church of Christ in Boston in 1711. "Sick and weak," he wrote his will on April 24, 1712; Sarah Knight (see Cat. no. 96) was a witness. Samuel Sewall's diary notes: "April 29, 1712. Went to the funeral of Mr. Peter Oliver." His will was probated May 8, 1712, but no inventory was taken. His brothers were to share with the widow unless she had a child by him.

Quite reasonably, because of his short life, very little silver by him has been recorded; the outstanding piece is the above-mentioned flagon, its antithesis a miniature tankard of great charm owned by the Worcester Art Museum. A chocolate pot similar to Winslow's is known (*MFA 1956*, no. 111, fig. 45), and a fine tankard with a dolphin and mask thumbpiece (Phillips Academy, Addison Gallery of American Art, Andover).

Oliver is known only by pieces marked with his initials in a heart *(a)*.

a

97 Porringer, c. 1710

H. 1⅝ in.; D. of lip 4³⁄₁₆ in.; L. of handle 2⅛ in.; Wt. 3 oz., 12 dwt.

MARK: *a* on curve of bowl at left of handle; on the back of the handle there is probably an irregularity in the casting, not a punch mark.

Slightly everted rim; sides curve to domed bottom; center point in bowl. Trefoil handle with open holes at sides, round tip, three half-moon cuttings, the upper notched, an uneven quatrefoil cutting in the center (handle quite thickly soldered in angle of rim).

Engraved TBM on handle toward bowl.

HISTORY: Thomas and Mary Barton, m. 1710; for subsequent history see Cat. no. 39.

NOTES: This is the size of a child's porrringer but has adults' initials. Similar examples of this unusual handle were made by Jeremiah Dummer, a porringer for William Brattle, privately owned; William Cowell, one with oval mark (*Antiques,* XXIX, no. 5 [1936], p. 195), one with crowned mark and an unmarked one, both at Yale University Art Gallery, Garvan Collection; and one by Thomas Savage (privately owned).

REFERENCES: *Bigelow 1917,* p. 306, fig. 206; *Clark [Buhler] 1931,* p. 44, illus. p. 45; *Ellis 1961,* p. 27, illus. p. 23, fig. 5

EXHIBITION: *Minneapolis 1956,* no. 264.

GIFT OF MR. AND MRS. DUDLEY LEAVITT PICKMAN 31.231

97

WILLIAM COWELL
1682/3–1736

WILLIAM COWELL was the last child born to John and Hannah (Hurd) Cowell on January 25, 1682/3 (Boston Commissioners' Reports). Edward in 1668 was the first; also listed are Mary, 1669; John, 1671; Hannah, 1672; John, 1674; Jeremiah, 1676; Hannah, 1677; and Mehitable, 1680. Mary, Hannah, Mehitable, and William were the only survivors at the blacksmith John Cowell's death in 1693. Hannah Cowell, his wife, was an aunt of Jacob Hurd. Her death in 1713 was noted by Samuel Sewall: "Nurse Hanah Cowell buried. Bearers Mr. Odlin, Thomas Walker; Deacons Maryon, Hobart; Brother Wheeler, Foreland. Was a very pious Woman, and a true Lover of the first Ways of New England. Col. Hutchinson, Sewall, Em Hutchinson, Townsend, Mr. Wadsworth, Colman, followed after the Mourners."

William was probably an apprentice of Jeremiah Dummer; almost as soon as he was free to practice his craft he was married by James Allen of the First Church, Boston to Elizabeth Kilby, May 13, 1706. On July 1, 1707, his son John was born; his daughter Hannah was born in 1709; his son William in 1711 was followed by a surviving William, July 19, 1713 (see *Appendix*); a daughter Mary, in 1717, Sarah in 1722; "Gemini Sons" Joseph and Christopher in 1725; Rebecca in 1727, and Benjamin in 1729 complete his recorded family. He held various town offices in Boston and became an innholder; his estate in 1736 referred to both occupations. Excerpts from the inventory, of which one appraiser was his cousin Jacob Hurd, reflect them both: "Sundry Tools in the Shop: £145-1-3; 159 oz 14 dwt Silver as Stock at 27/p oz: 206-2-0; 57 1/2 oz wrot Plate in the Family's use at 27/: 77-12-6; Stock of Liquors Sugr & Sundrys in the Shop: 194-0."

Cowell's early mark *(a)* of his initials in an ellipse was once erroneously attributed to William Cross, a London-trained goldsmith who emigrated to America before 1695 and whose work is unknown today. A more elaborate mark *(b)* shows a mullet flanked by pellets over his initials with a pellet below in a conforming shield. His surname mark *(c)* preceded by initial and colon, in a cartouche, was also used by his son, but appears with *(b)* on a tankard of his fashioning owned by the First Church in Newton, Massachusetts, dated 1727.

a   b   c

98

98 Cup, c. 1705

H. 3⅛ in. (inc. handles); D. of lip 3⁷⁄₁₆ in.; Wt. 4 oz., 14 dwt.

MARK: *a* at left of handle above reeding.

Flaring lip above band of spiral reeding, straight sides above wide gadrooning which curves sharply to stepped flat bottom. Center point inside. Cast handle with scroll tip affixed above reeding; slight shaping on shoulder, inside below curve and outside above lower joining on gadroon; lower tip forked with small scroll.

Engraved TFW on bottom.

HISTORY: Unknown.

NOTES: The majority of published cups in this style are two-handled.

REFERENCES: *Bigelow 1917*, p. 171, fig. 93; *Hipkiss 1943*, pp. 31-32 (as by William Cross).

THE PHILIP LEFFINGWELL SPALDING COLLECTION. GIVEN IN HIS MEMORY BY KATHERINE AMES SPALDING AND PHILIP SPALDING, OAKES AMES SPALDING, HOBART AMES SPALDING 42.223

99 Spoon, c. 1709

L. 7⅝ in.; Wt. 1 oz., 10 dwt.

MARK: *a* on back of stem.

Wavy end with long tip, very worn beading in molded rattail drop on almost elliptical bowl.

Engraved *BW* on back of handle.

HISTORY: Bathsheba Walker, daughter of James and Bathsheba (Brooks) Walker of Taunton, Massachusetts, m. Richard Godfrey, Jr. 1709; descended in the family to the donor.

GIFT OF MISS RUTH F. TINKHAM 53.1039

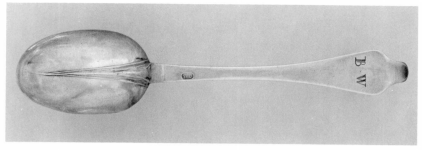

99

100 Baptismal Basin, 1716

H. 2¾-3 in. (uneven); D. 13 in.; Wt. 30 oz., 2 dwt.

MARK: *a* on rim opposite engraving.

Broad everted rim with slightly molded edge; deep bowl with domed center. Center point in bowl.

Engraved in semiscript within scroll and foliate partial frame *The gift of Mr Benjm Edmond, / late of London, Marchant, to / the Church in Brattle / Street, Boston N. E. / 1716.*

HISTORY: See inscription.

NOTES: In Boston records, two entries for Benjamin Edmunds may record two men or two marriages for one: Benjamin Edmunds and Rebecca Weeden married by Cotton Mather, May 29, 1711; Benjamin Edmonds and Rebekah Green married by Timothy Cutler, November 5, 1733. There is only one Benjamin Edmunds recorded in Suffolk Probate, a mariner, his will dated May 2, 1735 when he was "bound on a voyage to sea," was probated April 7, 1736, his wife Rebecca named. Although E. Alfred Jones considered the above mariner to be the donor, it is difficult to understand the self-designation of *merchant*.

REFERENCES: *Paull 1913*, p. 23, illus. p. 24; *Jones 1913*, p. 68, pl. XXVII; *Ensko 1948*, p. 132; *Phillips, Antiques*, no. 4 (1949), p. 284; *Buhler 1955*, illus. p. 458; *McLanathan 1956*, p. 56, fig. 9.

EXHIBITIONS: *MFA 1906*, no. 76, pl. V; *Jamestown 1907*, no. 474; *MFA 1911*, no. 291, pl. 8; *Chicago 1949*, no. 158, illus. 114; *Art Treasures 1955*; *Minneapolis 1956*, no. 205, fig. 48; *Dallas 1958*, no. 134; *ESU 1960*, no. 32, pl. 6; *Buffalo 1965*, no. 100.

GIFT OF THE BENEVOLENT FRATERNITY OF CHURCHES
SILVER OF THE CHURCH IN BRATTLE SQUARE 13.392

100

101

101 Church Cup, probably 1718

H. 4½ in.; D. of base 2½ in.; D. of lip 3⅝ in.; Wt. 5 oz., 19 dwt.

MARK: *b* on side.

Slightly flaring lip; cylindrical sides; vertical gadrooning on curved section above very slightly stepped base encircled by molded baseband. Center point on bottom.

Scratched weight: 6 oz., 6 dwt.

HISTORY: Made to match cup by Jeremiah Dummer (Cat. no. 24) for the Brattle Street Church.

NOTES: From Brattle Street Church records of meeting March 8, 1718: "After much Discourse, it was voted That there be an equal Dividend of ye next Remains of ye Moneys collected at the Sacrament, after ye payment of the charges for the Holy Table; the one half to be distributed by the Deacons to ye poor; the other to be applied to ye further supply of ye Communion Table with plate; provided that ye Distribution to ye poor do not exceed ye Summ of ten pounds p annum."

REFERENCES: *Paull 1913*, p. 23, illus. p. 24; *Jones 1913*, p. 67, pl. XXVII; Clarice Lorenz Aiken, "Silver of New England Churches," *Antiquarian*, XV, no. 1 (1930), pp. 56-58, illus.; *McLanathan 1956*, p. 56, fig. 9.

102

102 Salver, c. 1720

H. 2 7/16 in.; D. of base 3 9/16 in.; D. of dish 10 in.; Wt. 15 oz., 17 1/2 dwt.

MARK: *c* near rim.

Circular, with raised and everted rim, single incised lines at inner edge; quarter-round flange for joining trumpet foot with molded edge (added strengthening band ?). Faintly cut circle enclosing compass-made daisy at center point on dish.

Engraved *P:D:I* over *M* by one hand under rim.

HISTORY: Unknown.

EXHIBITIONS: *MFA 1906*, no. 68, pls. VIII and IX; *MFA 1911*, no. 300; *MFA 1956*, no. 45.

GIFT OF MRS. ARTHUR WELLINGTON IN MEMORY OF HER HUSBAND *44.80*

103 Porringer, c. 1720

H. 1⅞ in.; D. of lip 5⁵⁄₁₆ in.; L. of handle 2⅝ in.; Wt. 7 oz., 12½ dwt.

MARKS: *b* in bowl and on curve at left of handle.

Everted lip, curved sides, stepped and domed bottom. Center point in bowl. Cast handle of six shaped piercings and three circles in bell form tip, neatly soldered in angle below rim. Bottom repaired and sides battered.

Engraved *WMc* over *S* (apparently original) on handle away from bowl.

HISTORY: Unknown. The initials on the handle are the same as those on the John Burt cann (Cat. no. 118).

REFERENCES: *Hipkiss 1943*, p. 45.

THE PHILIP LEFFINGWELL SPALDING COLLECTION. GIVEN IN HIS MEMORY BY KATHERINE AMES SPALDING AND PHILIP SPALDING, OAKES AMES SPALDING, HOBART AMES SPALDING 42.533

103

104

104 Pepper Box, 1725–1736

H. 3¹¹⁄₁₆ in. (inc. finial); D. of base 2 in.; Wt. 2 oz., 19 dwt.

MARK: *b* at left of handle.

Cylindrical, seamed under handle; thin, molded baseband seamed at left side and flush with flat bottom; semicircular bead below rim to form bezel, which is broken at back. Domed cover, random piercings above molded rim with small flange; vertical molding (broken at edge) applied below. Small turned finial soldered through dome (bent). Scroll handle, the tips small horizontal cylinders, affixed below bead and above base molding; slight curl above upturned tip, applied slight grip on shoulder with long segmented rattail.

Engraved *EC* on bottom.

HISTORY: Unknown.

REFERENCES: *Hipkiss 1942*, illus. p. 83; *Hipkiss 1943*, p. 44; *Norman-Wilcox, Antiques*, Part I (1944), p. 21, fig. 3b; *Norman-Wilcox, Antiques*, Part II (1944), p. 81, no. 9.

THE PHILIP LEFFINGWELL SPALDING COLLECTION. GIVEN IN HIS MEMORY BY KATHERINE AMES SPALDING AND PHILIP SPALDING, OAKES AMES SPALDING, HOBART AMES SPALDING 42.216

105

105 Cann, 1730–1735

H. of body 5⅛ in.; D. of base 3¼ in.; D. of lip 3 in.; Wt. 11 oz., 6 dwt.

MARK: *c* at left of handle.

Heavy gauge bulbous body, molded rim, on cast splayed molded baseband. Center point on base. Cast scroll handle has faceted upper surface with seam in center and segmented drop at upper joining, elliptical disc at lower, slight grip and scroll tip with flattened sides.

Engraved RCM on handle; illegible earlier initials.

HISTORY: Early history unknown; Ralph Cross, m. Miriam Atkinson, September 27, 1757; descended in the family to Charles R. Cross (see Cat. no. 155).

BEQUEST OF CHARLES R. CROSS 22.585

NATHANIEL MORSE
c. 1685–1748

NATHANIEL MORSE served his apprenticeship under John Coney, whose own skill with engraving tools is exemplified in our collections. Morse, Morss, or Mors, as the name was spelled, became an engraver of note and in 1731 engraved the now rare portrait of Matthew Henry, a nonconformist divine. His marriages are recorded in the Church in Brattle Street with the amount of his donation, which was paid by the majority but not all of the couples listed. He was first married to Sarah Draper on March 9, 1710 with a "marriage fee" of 10s. Ten children were baptized for them between 1710 and 1727. He was married to his second wife, with a doubled gift of £1, on July 31, 1740. The *Boston Gazette* reported on June 17, 1748 the death of "Nathaniel Morse, an ingenious Engraver." His widow was administratrix of his estate and presented an inventory of which Samuel Edwards was one appraiser. That his son Obadiah Mors had taken over his silversmithing is suggested by the paucity of his "2 old Copy Books & sundry small Tools £7-7." He died intestate, and a further accounting was rendered by "Sarah Dolbeare formerly Sarah Morse."

An interesting division of activities was divulged in a manuscript notebook kept by Samuel Sewall of the expenses of Madam Bridget Usher's funeral in 1723:

June 12 to Mr John Edwards, 23 Rings   £23-2-0
June 15 To Nathan^l Morse, Mad^m Grove's Ring
                  2 pwht 18 grains £1-13-0

Two variants of Morse's elaborate mark of crowned initials over a device are known: one on the MFA flagon *(a)*, the other on the flagon owned by The North Parish, North Andover. He also used a simple rectangle with italic capitals divided by a pellet *(b)*. Marks of N MORS and MORS in rounded rectangles are also known; the latter perhaps used by his son Obadiah.

a   *b*

106

106 Flagon, 1711

H. 11⅞ in. (inc. finial); D. of base 6⅛ in.; D. of lip 4¼ in.; Wt. 45 oz., 14 dwt.

MARKS: *a* on lid and twice at left of handle.

Construction similar to Edward Winslow's flagon (Cat. no. 71) but with no disc at lower handle joining. Upper handle joining (perhaps resoldered) is tangent to rim above and below the bead as on John Noyes' flagon (Cat. no. 93). Inner hinge plate very slightly shorter than John Edwards's (Cat. no. 82); outer hinge plate rounded. Handle tip, angled beneath, has vent slot. Very uneven solder, crack at lower bead and in midmolding of baseband.

Engraved on front in foliate wreath *This belongs to / the Church in / Brattle Street / 1711*. Engraved on bottom *46 oz = 12 dwt*.

HISTORY: See *Notes* for Cat. no. 71.

REFERENCES: *Buck 1903*, p. 218; *Jones 1913*, p. 68, pl. XXVII; *Paull 1913*, p. 23, illus. p. 24; *Bigelow 1917*, p. 155; *Avery 1930*, pp. 66, 311; Eberlein and McClure, *The Practical Book of American Antiques*, Philadelphia, 1927, p. 135; Buhler, *Antiques*, no. 5, 1945, p. 270, fig. 10; *Buhler 1955*, illus. p. 458; *McLanathan 1956*, p. 56, fig. 9.

EXHIBITIONS: *MFA 1906*, no. 207, pls. XXVI, XXVII; *Jamestown 1907*, no. 475; *MFA 1911*, no. 749, pl. 4; *Art Treasures 1955*; *Minneapolis 1956*, no. 257, fig. 48; *Dallas 1958*; *Buffalo 1965*, no. 105.
GIFT OF THE BENEVOLENT FRATERNITY OF CHURCHES
SILVER OF THE CHURCH IN BRATTLE SQUARE *13.403*

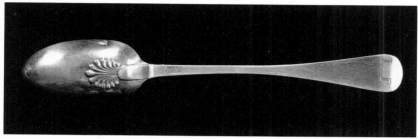

107

107 Teaspoon, c. 1732

L. 4½ in.; Wt. 6 dwt.

MARK: *b* on back of stem.

Rounded handle, ridge halfway on front, long rounded drop with shell below on almost elliptical bowl.

Engraved *LP* on back of stem.

HISTORY: Love Pickman (1732-1809) m. Peter Frye, 1751; presumably to her nephew Thomas (1773-1817); to his granddaughter Sally Pickman Dwight, from whose son's estate the donor, her cousin, acquired it.

NOTES: Spoon punches or spoon swages, appearing probably in every detailed inventory of tools were seldom specified as in Edward Webb's (q.v.) or in William Simpkins's. The latter left "stakes with a shell" which doubtless was one of the many variants of this spoon bowl design sometimes described (but not in this catalogue) as an anthemion. The only William Simpkins spoon recorded in the MFA is a rattail one, once on loan to the Museum, present whereabouts unknown. A more realistic shell is exemplified by Samuel Edwards's spoons (Cat. no. 206).

Attribution of this mark to Nathaniel Morse was made before 1920. It is very similar to a mark used by William Northey (c. 1734-1804) who would have been too young to have made this spoon.

REFERENCE: *Clark* [*Buhler*] *1931*, p. 50, illus. p. 49.

GIFT OF MR. AND MRS. DUDLEY LEAVITT PICKMAN *31.232*

BENJAMIN HILLER
born 1687/8

BENJAMIN HILLER, the third child of Joseph and Susannah Hiller, was born January 19, 1687/8. He is believed to have been apprenticed to John Coney; with Nathaniel Morse he witnessed a deed between Coney and William Taylor in 1708. His work, too, bears out the theory. On February 10, 1714, "Benjamin Hillier [sic]" was married to Elizabeth Russel by Rev. Dr. Cotton Mather of the Second Church. Her grandfather had been the second minister of the First Baptist Church, of which Hiller became a deacon in 1719. Four children are recorded born to the Hillers from 1717 to 1723.

Hiller made three handsome and stalwart mugs for the First Baptist Church, the first in 1714 engraved as a gift from his parents-in-law, the second from his mother-in-law. The third was a bequest of William Snell in 1727, although it is engraved as a gift. Snell made Hiller one of the beneficiaries of his estate and the church "Voted that the twelve ounces of plate [which Snell had left] should be made into a handsome Cup with his name upon it . . . But one Spoon be Reserved with his name upon for ye use of ye Lord's Table." The Snell mug is Hiller's last dated piece published. His outstanding work, the gallon-capacity tankard in the Henry Francis du Pont Winterthur Museum, Delaware, has a domed lid with a broad-based finial and on the handle a familiar cherub tip. A spout cup *(Jones 1928)* suggests that he was working in the mid-1730s. His octagonal caster, Yale University Art Gallery, Garvan Collection, is perhaps his most appealing piece and the rarest in form.

We know only one mark for Hiller: *(a)* his initials with addorsed crescents below in a shield of elaborate outline.

a

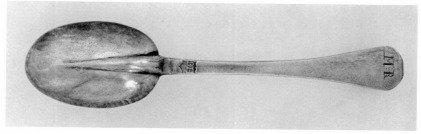

108

108 Porringer Spoon, c. 1710

L. 6⁷⁄₁₆ in.; Wt. 1 oz.

MARK: *a* on stem.

Handle, rectangular in section, thinning and broadening at wavy end; tip
bent sharply forward. Long, rather thick rattail on elliptical bowl (worn).
Engraved *MR* on back of handle.

GIFT OF MRS. CHESTER S. GODFREY *49.1141*

109

109 Tankard, 1710–1720

H. 6¹³⁄₁₆ in. (inc. thumbpiece); D. of base 4⅞ in.; D. of lip 4⅛ in. (both very uneven); Wt. 24 oz., 8 dwt.

MARKS: *a* on cover, at left of handle, and on bottom.

Tapering sides; everted rim with paired incised lines (broken at side and handle joining); applied, molded baseband (broken upper edge); repair to battered base. Molded and stepped flat cover; very narrow bezel; center point inside; flange grooved and serrated at front, slightly shaped at back where it completely backs hinge plate and loops to form inner parts of five-part hinge; dolphin and mask thumbpiece; hinge plates molded with meander wire, outer rounded and shaped on shoulder of scroll handle with thin rattail at upper joining. The end is bent sharply up and has cast cherub's-head tip with scant overhang at curve (round vent-hole in slot). Handle dented below left initials, rim and cover flange bent.

Engraved NP[?] on handle worn by thumbpiece.

HISTORY: Unknown.

NOTES: Yale University Art Gallery, Garvan Collection, has a Hiller tankard with double spiral thumbpiece.

REFERENCES: *Buhler 1955*, illus. p. 459; *Comstock 1958*, pl. 43b.

EXHIBITIONS: *London 1954*; *MFA 1956*, no. 79.

GIFT OF WALTER DEANE IN MEMORY OF HIS WIFE *19.35*

WILLIAM POLLARD
1690–1740

WILLIAM POLLARD was born to William and Margaret Pollard on April 2, 1690, the second son of the name. His grandmother was Anne Pollard, whose portrait at the age of 103 is owned by the Massachusetts Historical Society. His father appears to have died when he was very young, for his mother's first child by her second husband, Thomas Powell, was born in August, 1695. Since his uncle had married Mary, sister of Edward Winslow, in 1693, it is believed that he learned the craft from his uncle-in-law. In 1711 permission was granted "To Thomas Powell to Erect a Timber building for a Goldsmith Shop for his son of 15 foot long." He died in Charleston, South Carolina in 1740.

We know only one mark (a) for Pollard: his initials, with pellet between, in an oval or ellipse.

a

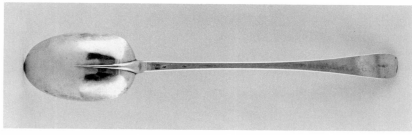

110

110 Serving Spoon, c. 1730

L. 15⅝ in.; Wt. 6 oz., 16 dwt.

MARKS: *a* twice on back of handle near bowl.

Long stem, semicircular in section, broadens to forward-bent, rounded tip with midridge extending almost half its length. Rather thin rattail extending halfway on bent elliptical bowl.

HISTORY: Unknown.

NOTES: A similar spoon (14½ in.) with shorter midrib by Winslow is in the Henry Francis du Pont Winterthur Museum (Delaware).

EXHIBITIONS: *MFA 1956*, no. 115; *ESU 1960*, no. 33, pl. 23.

GIFT OF MRS. HORATIO A. LAMB 41.223

III

III Tankard, 1730–1745

H. 8½ in. (inc. thumbpiece); D. of base 4¹³⁄₁₆ in.; D. of lip 4¼ in.;
Wt. 26 oz., 5½ dwt.

MARKS: *a* twice at left of handle.

Tapering sides; molded rim; applied, molded baseband. Later molded and
domed cover with turned, flame finial and tall scroll purchase; support, plain
at front, hits handle just above initials rather low on shoulder. Both cover and
purchase in the style of the later eighteenth century. Center point on
bottom of body and inside cover. Plain hinge plate for five-part hinge, molded
and shaped with drop on hollow scroll handle (broken vent hole); disc tip.
Added spout removed.

Engraved s§ᴛ on handle; faintly scratched *26-16* on bottom.

HISTORY: Unknown.

NOTES: A Pollard tankard with a similar body and original cover is in a
private collection.

GIFT OF MRS. DANIEL P. STANIFORD 41.703

112

112 Pair of Trencher Salts, 1715–1725

UNKNOWN MAKER

H. 1 in.; W. of base 2¾ in.; Wt. 3 oz., 13 dwt.

MARKS: None.

Deep elliptical bowl with flat flange, the outer edge shaped to conform to octagonal sides; sides, seamed at end, have concave center section with molding above and splayed molding below, an added strengthening band forming edge. No center points.

Engraved TAH on step of lower molding. On the base, other initials: wife's initial erased from one, husband's missing at small cut hole in other; together they would have been ABS (solder over A where tiny hole was cut, well repaired at seamed end of other).

HISTORY: Unknown.

NOTES: Similar salts in the MFA made by James Smith (London, 1732) are seamed at one corner and show solder at insertion of bowl (invisible on these). Another similar pair by John Coney (private collection) is not seamed and has longer bowls and plainer sides but the same initials, TAH, engraved inside the base.

REFERENCES: *Avery 1930*, p. 345; *Buhler 1934*, illus. p. 47; *Buhler 1950*, pp. 26-27, fig. 19.

BEQUEST OF CHARLES HITCHCOCK TYLER *32.366a* and *32.366b*.

113 Patch Box, 1722 (?)

UNKNOWN MAKER

H. ⅜ in.; L. 2 in.; Wt. 9½ dwt.

MARKS: None.

Elliptical with straight sides seamed, the flat base overlapping; solder inside. Flat cover, sides very slightly inset, solder in patches inside.

Engraved *L: Thayer* in capital initials and semiscript; scratched: *1722;* both on bottom. Lid has band of overlapping leaves (?) enclosing cupid with bow and arrow, heart pierced with arrow over background of buildings.

HISTORY: Lydia Thayer, m. Nehemiah Hayden, 1720; another Lydia Thayer, m. Josiah Carter, 1741.

NOTES: A box with similar border by John Edwards (privately owned) is dated 1721, giving credence to the scratched date of this. An identical box is in the Henry Francis du Pont Winterthur Museum, Delaware (see M. G. Fales, *American Silver in the Henry Francis du Pont Winterthur Museum, 1958,* no. 32).

EXHIBITION: *ESU 1960,* no. 80.

GIFT OF MR. AND MRS. HENRY HERBERT EDES 36.45

114 Patch Box, 1720–1750

UNKNOWN MAKER

H. ⁵⁄₁₆ in.; L. of base 1⅝ in.; Wt. 7½ dwt.

MARKS: None.

Heart-shaped with seam at point, shoulders not quite even; the loose lid and base overlapping the straight sides.

Engraved on cover with flower in center, the stem originating from cross-hatched point. Leaf design in curve of each shoulder.

HISTORY: Unknown.

NOTES: See *R.I. 1965,* fig. 28 for similar heart-shaped box with loose lid by William Whittemore (collection Rhode Island School of Design); and fig. 29 for similar flower on box by William Cowell (Currier Gallery, Manchester, New Hampshire). Other heart-shaped boxes at Henry Francis du Pont Winterthur Museum, Delaware, and Yale University Art Gallery, Garvan Collection, both with hinged lids.

EXHIBITION: *ESU 1960,* no. 80.

GIFT OF MRS. EDWARD JACKSON HOLMES 54.1131

113

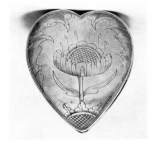

114

ANDREW TYLER
1692–1741

ANDREW TYLER was the son of Thomas, a mariner, and Miriam (Simpkins) Tyler. Although his birth is not in the public records, it is now accepted as having occurred in 1692. His older brothers were Thomas, born in 1685; John, born in 1687; and William, who became a brazier, born in 1688. A second John, born in 1695, became a pewterer. Andrew and William were both active in the settlement of John Coney's estate, and it was to Coney that Andrew was probably apprenticed. He married Miriam Pepperell of Kittery on January 12, 1714; their ten children were baptized in the Brattle Street Church.

Tyler served repeatedly as scavenger, assessor, and member of the committee on graves, and held various other public appointments. His name continues to appear in Boston records until 1741 in August, when his will was probated. He left £30 to the Workhouse and to his son Andrew "all or any such part of my Library as my wife shall please to give him." To each of his surviving children he left £5, and to the three overseers of his will, "William Pepperell Esqr, William Tyler Esqr, and Peleg Wiswall Gentm," he left gold rings.

Tyler's crowned initials marks (*a* and *b*) are variously described as having a bird or cat below in a shield; he also used his initial and surname with pellet between in an ellipse (*c*), his initials in a rectangle (*d*), and over a device in a heart (*e*).

a   *b*   *c*   *d*

e

115 Spout Cup, c. 1720

H. 4⁷⁄₁₆ in. (inc. finial); D. of base 1¹⁵⁄₁₆ in.; D. of lip 2⁵⁄₁₆ in.; Wt. 6 oz., 15 dwt.

MARK: *a* at left of handle.

Globular body with cylindrical neck and tiny everted rim on molded straight baseband. Center point on bottom. Molded domed cover, incised lines on step, with narrow flange for bezel and small turned finial, broad at base. Broad, molded strap handle, made in two unequal parts, affixed halfway on neck and on curve of body; both tips rounded, the lower upcurved. Curved spout not quite at right angles to handle, broad and flattened on body, over small shaped hole.

Engraved ISE over original initials on neck; added later: *1762*, and in light script on bottom: *CWT 1910.*

HISTORY: Early history unknown; Isaac and Elizabeth (Storer) Smith, m. 1746; their son William, m. Hannah Carter, 1787; their son Thomas, m. Frances Barnard, 1831; their daughter Frances, m. Thomas Davis Townsend, 1854; their son Charles Wendell, father of the donor.

NOTES: Listed in Isaac Smith's inventory of plate at 6 oz.

REFERENCES: *Bigelow 1917,* p. 387, fig. 277; *McLanathan 1956,* fig. 18; *Comstock 1958,* p. 87, fig. 14.

EXHIBITIONS: *MFA 1911,* no. 979, pl. 34; *Richmond 1960,* no. 134.

GIFT OF MISS GERTRUDE TOWNSEND 37.568

115

116

116 Porringer, 1725–1730

H. 2 1/16 in.; D. of lip 5 1/8 in.; L. of handle 2 3/16 in.; Wt. 7 oz., 16 1/2 dwt.

MARKS: *b* in center of bowl; *c* on handle.

Narrow everted rim, curved sides, stepped and domed bottom, center point on base. Early keyhole handle with two semicircular cuttings at center (back quite pitted).

Engraved IHM away from bowl.

HISTORY: Unknown.

NOTES: The semicircular cuttings of this handle frequently appear as arches on early so-called keyhole porringers and reflect the center cutting of a geometric handle. The Worcester Art Museum has a Tyler porringer with similar handle and peaked arches. The Cleveland Museum of Art has a porringer with quite high arches on the handle, also engraved away from the bowl. Tyler is known to have fashioned geometric handles also.

REFERENCES: *Hipkiss 1943*, p. 49; *Buhler 1957*, p. 50.

117

117 Gold Mourning Ring, 1729

D. ⅞ in.

MARK: *d* at end of inscription.

Death's-head with modeled wings on slightly curved outer surface; inside flat for inscription.

Engraved *A Brown ob 16 April 1729 AET 9* in semiscript with conjoined block *AE*.

HISTORY: Early history unknown; given to Martha Pickman (Rogers) Codman by her father, J. W. Rogers, in 1850.

JOHN BURT
1692/3–1745/6

The following entry in the goldsmith's hand appears in the family Bible: "John Burt Senr Borne the 6th day of Jany 1692/3 / Abigal [Cheever] my Wife was Borne 20th of May 1690 / And Wee weare maried 3^{tn} of June 1714." A record of their children follows. Burt is thought to have been apprenticed to John Coney, and he carried on Coney's custom of fashioning tutorial plate, the gifts students made to their tutors at Harvard College, whence Burt's firstborn son and namesake was graduated in 1736. He served in minor town offices and trained three sons in his craft: William (1726-1751), Samuel (1724-1754) (see Cat. nos. 237-242), and Benjamin (1729-1805) (see Cat. nos. 297-313). William was the second child given the name, as his twin sister was a second Sarah. The inventory of John's tools was used by R. T. Haines Halsey to describe the craft in the catalogue of the *MFA 1906* exhibition. One of the appraisers of Burt's estate was the goldsmith William Simpkins (q.v.); administration was granted to Burt's widow and their son Samuel.

Burt's first mark showed (*a*) crowned initials with a pellet below in a shield. He later used (*b*) his initial and surname with a colon in a cartouche and (not represented in the MFA) in an oblong. His surname in an oblong (*c*) is rare; his full name in two lines appears in an ellipse (*d*) and (not represented in the MFA) in a shaped ellipse.

a

b

c

d

118 Cann, 1720–1725

H. 5⅟₁₆ in.; D. of base and lip 3⅜ in.; Wt. 8 oz., 17½ dwt.

MARK: *a* at left of handle.
Molded rim, slightly curving sides, molded splayed footband seamed almost at front and very neatly soldered. Center point on bottom. Hollow, cast scroll handle hexagonal in section, the scroll tips flattened at sides (upper with two small vent holes, lower with larger one), molded drop at upper joining, grip over shoulder, disc at lower joining.

Engraved $\substack{W \\ S}$ M C on bottom, the S tangent to oz. 9 = 4 = 0; *MH* almost stoned from front just below rim. The initials on the bottom are the same as those on the William Cowell porringer (see Cat. no. 103).
HISTORY: Unknown.
NOTES: A pair of similar canns by John Burt with mark *b* (see above) was

118

119

given to Nicholas Sever, a Harvard tutor, in 1728.

REFERENCES: *Hipkiss 1943*, p. 47; *Buhler 1957*, p. 50.

THE PHILIP LEFFINGWELL SPALDING COLLECTION. GIVEN IN HIS MEMORY
BY KATHERINE AMES SPALDING AND PHILIP SPALDING, OAKES AMES SPALDING,
HOBART AMES SPALDING 42.253

119 Two-Handled Cup, 1724

H. of body 5⅜ in.; D. of base 2⅛ in.; D. of lip 4¼ in.; Wt. 8 oz., 1 dwt.

MARK: *a* on bottom.

Almost straight sides curve to rounded base on very slightly splayed and
molded footband. Center point on bottom. Molded strap handles, their tips
freestanding, affixed below lip and above curve. Dented at back, one
handle badly bent.

Engraved in semiscript *The Gift of Mr J Floyd to the / Churh of Christ in
Rumney = Mayrsh / 1724.*

HISTORY: See *Notes.*

NOTES: "John Floyd, the donor, was son of Captain John and Sarah (Doo-
little) Floyd, and was born February 20, 1664/5. He died January 7, 1723/4.
He held several public offices at Rumney Marsh, and was one of the founders
of this church. In his will, dated September 27, 1723, and proved February
24, 1723/4, he bequeathed £10 to this church, with which this beaker was
bought" (*Jones 1913*, p. 402). Although Jones gave 1715 as the date of
founding of the Church at Rumney-Marsh (the town's name subsequently
was changed first to Chelsea and then to Revere), Sewall's diary (July 10,
1710) records his going "to Rumney Marsh to the raising of their
meeting house."

REFERENCES: *Jones 1913*, p. 402, pl. CXXII; *McLanathan 1956*, illus. p. 50,
fig. 2.

EXHIBITION: *Cranbrook 1952*, no. 10.

GIFT OF THE FIRST UNITARIAN SOCIETY OF REVERE 51.1524

120 Two-Handled Cup, 1725–1730

H. 5¾ in.; D. of base 3¼ in.; D. of lip 4½ in.; Wt. 8 oz., 15 dwt.

MARK: *b* on bottom.

Similar to Cat. no. 119, flaring at lip, and on splayed footband. Center point on bottom. The handles are narrower but same design.

Engraved in script: *The Gift of De.'n John Tuttle to the / Church of Christ In Rumneymarsh.*

HISTORY: See *Notes* below.

NOTES: E. Alfred Jones records that the donor, Deacon John Tuttle, was the son of John and Mary (Holyoke) Tuttle, and the first signatory to the church covenant. His name, with that of his wife, Martha, appears in the church records immediately after the names of the pastor and his wife, Rev. Thomas and Elizabeth Cheever, followed by those of John Floyd, donor of Cat. 119 and his wife, Rachel. Tuttle's will, dated December 19, 1720, and proved June 13, 1723, is in Rev. Thomas Cheever's handwriting (*Jones 1913*, p. 403). The original records of the Church, given to the MFA library, make no mention of the silver, but the use of Burt's later mark suggests that this cup was not given immediately. See John Dixwell (Cat. no. 96) for a similar cup.

REFERENCES: *Jones 1913*, p. 403, pl. CXXII; *McLanathan 1956*, illus. p. 50, fig. 2.

EXHIBITION: *Towle 1954*.

GIFT OF THE FIRST UNITARIAN SOCIETY OF REVERE 51.1525

120

121

121 Tankard, 1725–1730

H. 8⅛ in. (inc. finial); D. of base 5 in.; D. of lip 4⅛ in.; Wt. 25 oz., 6½ dwt.

MARKS: *b* at left of handle and on bottom.

Straight tapering sides, incised lines below applied molding at lip, applied bead above lower handle joining, molded baseband with thick solder. Stepped domed cover with narrow flange, bezel seamed at side near front, turned bell-form finial. Scroll thumbpiece bent forward (handle dented by it), molded drop from five-part hinge plate. Hollow scroll handle; rounded drop at upper joining, disc at lower, and grimacing mask-tip high on end with vent hole.

Engraved on front in script *F.B.T. 2nd/from/T.C.S. & F.B.S. 1885*. On bottom in script *Wm & Frances Mackay / 1775*. William's name appears on the Liberty Bowl (Cat. no. 356). Scratches, but very slight if any trace of initials on handle.

HISTORY: Original ownership unknown; William and Frances Mackay in 1775; probably Tristram Barnard, executor of Frances Mackay's will; his niece Frances Barnard, m. 1831 Thomas Carter Smith; their daughter Frances Barnard (b. 1832) m. Thomas Davis Townsend (1826-1880); their daughter Frances Barnard Townsend II (b. 1855), aunt of the donors.

NOTES: A tankard with same mask and thumbpiece, but a higher finial, is in the Clearwater Collection of The Metropolitan Museum of Art, New York. In Suffolk Probate, the estate of Wm. Mackay, March 9, 1801, lists "oz. of plate at 1.25" but gives no amounts. Frances Mackay's estate, October 31, 1817 listing no silver, was administered by Tristram Barnard and William Mackay.

The tankard was on annually renewable loan to the Smithsonian Institution from 1963 to 1969.

EXHIBITIONS: *MFA 1911, no. 158; N.Y. 1946; MFA 1956, no. 11; Richmond 1960, no. 9.*

GIFT OF THE MISSES ROSE AND ELIZABETH TOWNSEND 56.673

122

122 Porringer, 1725–1730

H. 1⅝ in.; D. of lip 5⅝ in.; Handle too bent to measure length; W. of handle 2½ in.; Wt. 6 oz., 14 dwt.

MARK: *b* above initials on handle.

Slightly everted rim, curved sides, flat stepped and wide domed bottom (badly battered, edge of dome repaired and bowl at right of handle has line of solder; handle tip badly bent). Center point in bowl and on bottom. Keyhole handle neatly soldered in angle.

Engraved ICS toward bowl on handle.

HISTORY: Original owners unknown; engraved for John and Susannah (Greenleaf) Coburn, m. February 7, 1750; descended in the Langdon family. See biography of John Coburn, p. 302.

GIFT OF THE MISSES CATHARINE LANGDON ROGERS AND CLARA BATES ROGERS 14.898

123

123 Strainer Spoon, c. 1730–1740

L. 5¼ in.; Wt. 6 dwt.

MARK: *c* (corners of punch are somewhat rounded) on back of spoon.

Handle, circular in section and flattened at back near bowl, tapers to a point. Drop and shell on back of almost elliptical bowl pierced with crosses, circles, Y shapes, and scrolls.

Engraved *MS* between bowl and mark on back of handle.

HISTORY: Unknown.

NOTES: The reattribution of this mark, published as Benjamin Burt's, to his father is based on its also being on a porringer (privately owned) definitely datable between 1729 and 1744. It is the only other example of this mark known to us.

REFERENCES: *Buhler 1939,* pp. 114-115, illus. (attributed to Benjamin Burt). GIFT OF ARTHUR D. FOSS *39.14*

124

124 Sugar Bowl, c. 1735

H. 3⅞ in. (covered); D. of base 2¾ in. (uneven); D. of lip 4 in.;
Wt. 6 oz., 5 dwt.

MARK: *d* on bottom over center point.

Deep hemispherical body with paired incised lines below molded rim, on
circular splayed molded foot, incised lines on step. Molded and stepped flat
cover, incised lines on step and flange, edge turned over (or added?). Splayed
molded circular handle on center of cover (smaller, but reverse of foot),
with center point inside.

Engraved ETL on base; in script on side, *EBH* with device.

HISTORY: Ebenezer Turell, m. Lucy Davenport 1735; his sister Christian,
m. Samuel Bass; descended in the family to Elizabeth Bass Hinckley.

NOTES: Ebenezer Turell was born February 5, 1701/2, the youngest child
of Capt. Samuel and Lydia (Stoddard) Turell. He was graduated from
Harvard College in 1721, and studied with Rev. Benjamin Colman; "1724
Nov.ʳ 25 Mr. Ebenezer Turell is ordained Pastor of Meadford Church. Dr.
Mather preach'd the Lecture" (Samuel Sewall's diary.) His first wife, Jane,
died in 1735, and none of their four children lived to maturity. His second
wife, Lucy, was the daughter of Addington Davenport; she died childless on
May 17, 1759. His third wife, Jane (née Pepperell and twice widowed),
was also childless and predeceased her third husband, who died December 5,
1778. His inventory listed "sugar bowl and cover 6½ oz" which passed to
his sister, Christian, who married Samuel Bass, great-great-grandparents
of Mrs. Thomas Hewes Hinckley (1824-1909), in whose name the bowl was
given by her daughter to the Museum.

REFERENCES: *Bigelow 1917*, p. 401, fig. 290; *Wenham 1949*, p. 240, fig. 152.

EXHIBITIONS: *MFA 1911*, no. 125, pl. 6; *ESU 1960*, no. 37.

GIFT OF MISS MARY HEWES HINCKLEY IN MEMORY OF MRS. ELIZABETH
BASS HINCKLEY 13.423

125 Porringer, 1730–1745

H. 1¾ in.; D. of lip 5¼ in.; L. of handle 2¹¹⁄₁₆ in.; Wt. 7 oz., 13 dwt., 12 gr.

MARKS: *d* on handle and in center of bowl.

Slightly everted rim, curved sides, stepped and domed bottom, no center
point but mark in center badly worn. Keyhole handle with many pittings
on back and front.

Engraved IPM, the barred *I* perhaps over an earlier W, toward bowl;
on bottom 8 oz., 3 [*dwt.*]

HISTORY: Unknown.

NOTES: The dating of this porringer is based on the mark.

M. AND M. KAROLIK COLLECTION 39.230

125

126

126 Porringer, 1730–1745

H. 1⅞ in.; D. of lip 5⅛ in.; L. of handle 2¹¹⁄₁₆ in.; Wt. 7 oz., 15 dwt.

MARK: *d* on handle.

Almost straight rim, curved sides, stepped and wide domed bottom. Center point on bottom. Keyhole design of same pattern as Cat. no. 125 but heavier.

Engraved in script on handle *Carroll;* early initials completely erased, probably by stoning when the several oval punch marks were made on the back of the handle.

HISTORY: Unknown.

NOTES: The dating of this porringer is based on the mark. A privately owned porringer (*R.I. 1965*, no. 37) by John Burt is similar, but the dome is smaller.

BEQUEST OF CHARLES HITCHCOCK TYLER 32.382

MOODY RUSSELL
1694–1761

MOODY RUSSELL, son of the Reverend Jonathan Russell and his wife Martha, daughter of Rev. Joshua Moody, was born August 30, 1694. His aunt, Hannah (Moody), was the wife of Edward Winslow, to whom he is believed to have been apprenticed. His uncle, Eleazer Russell, goldsmith of Boston, had died before his birth. His paternal grandfather was Rev. John Russell of Hadley, Massachusetts, who gave shelter to the fleeing regicides, Goffe and Whalley. Although apprenticed in Boston, he worked in Barnstable, where he became deacon of the East Church and died "sick and weak in Body but of Perfect mind" in 1761.

Both marks which he is known to have used are represented in this collection: his initials *(a)* in a shaped shield and *(b)* in a small rectangle.

a   *b*

127

127 Beaker, c. 1715

H. 4⅝ in.; D. of base 3³⁄₁₆ in.; D. of lip 4-4⅛ in. (uneven); Wt. 8 oz., 13 dwt.

MARK: *a* on bottom below center point.

Flaring lip, flat bottom, applied molded baseband. Lumpy solder; one quite large dent near base, other small ones and sharp dent on lip.

Engraved in semiscript on bottom, above mark *This belongs to the Church att Truro.*

HISTORY: See *Notes.*

NOTES: E. Alfred Jones lists five other plain beakers at this church which was founded in 1711; a pair by John Edwards, both inscribed, *This belongs to the Church in Truro/1717* (now privately owned); a pair by Moody Russell, both inscribed, *This belongs to ye Church of Christ in Truro* (one now owned by the Cleveland Museum of Art, one by the Clearwater Collection, The Metropolitan Museum of Art, New York); one by Moody's brother, Joseph Russell inscribed, *This belongs to ye Chh/of Christ in Truro/1730* (Clearwater Collection, The Metropolitan Museum of Art, New York). Moody Russell made beakers without moldings for the churches in East and West Barnstable.

REFERENCES: *Jones 1913,* p. 471. R. McCulloch and A. Beale, "Silversmiths of Barnstable, Massachusetts," *Antiques,* LXXXIV, no. 1 (1963), pp. 72-74, fig. 1.

GIFT OF THE FIRST CONGREGATIONAL CHURCH, TRURO *13.584*

128 Spout Cup, c. 1730

H. of cup 2½ in.; D. of base 2⅛ in.; D. of lip 2¾ in.; Wt. 3 oz., 4 dwt.

MARK: *b* at left of handle.

Everted lip, sides slightly tapering to applied molded baseband (uneven solder). Center point on bottom. Molded strap handle in scroll form, rounded tips, affixed below rim and above baseband. Small tubular spout, incised lines at tip, with flattened body joining and trefoil hole beneath, at thirty-degree angle to handle.

Engraved EAR on bottom; *HH* at right of handle.

HISTORY: Unknown.

NOTES: Two similar spout cups by Edward Winslow (both larger) are in The Currier Gallery of Art, Manchester, New Hampshire and a private collection. Others by Moody Russell are known.

REFERENCES: *Hipkiss 1942,* illus. p. 86; *Hipkiss 1943,* p. 51, illus.; *Buhler 1957,* p. 47.

THE PHILIP LEFFINGWELL SPALDING COLLECTION. GIVEN IN HIS MEMORY BY KATHERINE AMES SPALDING AND PHILIP SPALDING, OAKES AMES SPALDING, HOBART AMES SPALDING *42.237*

128

WILLIAM JONES
1694–1730

WILLIAM JONES, the first recorded goldsmith in Marblehead, Massachusetts, died at the age of thirty-six, probably of smallpox since three
"Nurses in Small pox Each six week Each at 20/-per week" were
recorded in the settlement of his estate. He left three young children
and his widow Sabella, who was instructed to give "a small silver cup
to ye Communion Table" for the town's Congregational Church
founded in 1684. Doubtlessly of his own workmanship, it was unfor-
tunately remade, with another small piece, into a beaker by a vote
in 1772. In the inventory of his estate, wrought silver was valued at
21s and at 18s per ounce, suggesting some at the higher standard
which had been obligatory in England from 1697 to 1720. His "Working Tools, Weights & Scales. Glass Cases & Utensils of the Shop"
were valued at £60.

His two known marks (which may vary only in the striking) show
his initials, the *I* barred, both with *(a)* and without *(b)* a pellet
between them in a cut-cornered rectangle.

a   *b*

129

129 Porringer, 1720–1730

H. 1¾ in.; D. of lip 5 in.; L. of handle 2⅝ in.; Wt. 6 oz., 15 dwt.

MARKS: *b* on body at left of handle and on back of handle.

Slightly everted rim, curved sides, stepped and domed bottom. Center point in bowl. Very neat solder for so-called "urn and crown" cast handle.

Engraved *GN* on handle away from bowl.

HISTORY: Unknown.

NOTES: The porringer was on annually renewable loan to the Smithsonian Institution from 1963 to 1969.

REFERENCE: *Hipkiss, MFA Bulletin*, no. 234, illus. p. 58.

EXHIBITION: *ESU 1960*, no. 82.

GIFT OF MISS AMELIA PEABODY 41.64

130

130 Porringer, 1720–1730

H. 1⅝ in.; D. of lip 5⁵⁄₁₆ in.; L. of handle 2⅝ in.; Wt. 5 oz., 18 dwt.

MARKS: *a* on body at left of handle and on back of handle.

Everted rim, curved sides, flat stepped and domed bottom. Center point in bowl. Handle with shaped piercings below trefoil tip with teardrop holes, lines of engraving on this handle are lacking on the similar preceding one (Cat. no. 129). Very neatly soldered in angle.

Engraved A͞N͞W away from bowl (the W over an A).

HISTORY: Unknown.

REFERENCES: *Hipkiss 1943*, p. 50; *Buhler 1950*, p. 16, illus. p. 15, fig. 6; *Buhler 1957*, p. 50.

THE PHILIP LEFFINGWELL SPALDING COLLECTION. GIVEN IN HIS MEMORY BY KATHERINE AMES SPALDING AND PHILIP SPALDING, OAKES AMES SPALDING, HOBART AMES SPALDING 42.219

GEORGE HANNERS
c. 1696–1740

Robert Hannah and Hannah Matson were married in May, 1695 and their son George is thought to have been born the following year. He advertised in 1720 as "George Hannah goldsmith at his House at the Dock-Head Boston." The marriage of George Hannahs to Rebecca Peirson (or Pearson) was on July 28 of that year. Their son George, who was to follow his father's craft, was born "to George and Rebecca Hanners" in 1721 and, though their surnames continued in varied spellings, his name mark adheres to the spelling under which, in 1740, at Suffolk Probate appears "Inventory of George Hanners Late of Boston Silver-Smith deced Intestate." His tools were itemized and included "1 Belly Pott" anvil, a "Thimble Stamp" and Death head stamp" for mourning rings.

Hanners used a mark of crowned initials with a pellet below *(a)*; his initial and surname mark *(b)* is in italics; he is thought to have had a third mark of his initials in a rectangle.

 a  *b*

131

131 Beaker, 1725–1740

H. 5⅞ in.; D. of base 3½ in.; D. of lip 4¼ in.; Wt. 10 oz., 1 dwt.

MARK: *b* on bottom above center point.
Flaring lip, straight tapering sides, applied simply molded baseband.
HISTORY: See *Notes*.
NOTES: Jones (1913) records a set of five beakers by George Hanners, traditionally given to the church by Mrs. Elizabeth Packer, who died in 1717, age sixty-two. She was the wife of Thomas Packer, physician, colonel, and Judge of Probate at Portsmouth (New Hampshire) who died in 1728. One of the beakers is in the Clearwater Collection, The Metropolitan Museum of Art, New York. Jones' date of 1756 for the founding of this church suggests an earlier church existed.
REFERENCES: *Jones 1913*, pp. 187-188; *Bigelow 1917*, p. 137; *Avery 1920*, pp. 47-48.

EXHIBITIONS: *MFA 1911*, no. 541, pl. 16; *Towle 1954*.
GIFT OF THE CONGREGATIONAL CHURCH
OF GREENLAND, NEW HAMPSHIRE *12.114*

132

132 Bowl, 1725–1740

H. 3⁷⁄₁₆-3½ in. (uneven); D. of base 3½ in.; D. of lip 7¹⁄₁₆-7³⁄₁₆ in.; (uneven);
Wt. 12 oz., 10½ dwt.

MARK: *b* on bottom above center point.

Hemispherical, molded rim, on simply molded splayed footband. Center point
inside and out. Far more hammering visible than in beaker (Cat. no. 131), but
has been banged so that line of footband shows inside as almost cracked.
Repair at rim.

Engraved I*K*E on bowl near rim.

HISTORY: Unknown.

REFERENCES: *Hipkiss 1943*, p. 52; *Buhler 1957*, p. 51; *Wenham 1949*, p. 78-79.

THE PHILIP LEFFINGWELL SPALDING COLLECTION. GIVEN IN HIS MEMORY BY
KATHERINE AMES SPALDING AND PHILIP SPALDING, OAKES AMES SPALDING,
HOBART AMES SPALDING *42.536*

JONATHAN REED
died 1742

Very little is known about Reed. Earlier his mark was attributed to an unknown John Royalston—perhaps confused with John Roulstone, watchmaker (in the Boston Directory of 1789). Two cups bearing this mark were engraved for the New Brick Church in 1723-1724. "An Inventory of the Goods & Effects belonging to the Estate of Jonathan Reed, late of Boston, Goldsmith Deced" was taken on December 28, 1742/3; one of the appraisers was Nathaniel Mors. Reed had "1 spoon test 35 lb £5-5", three spoon punches at twelve shillings, a "large Glass Show Case" at sixty shillings; his detailed shop inventory amounted to £171 18s 6d. in a total of £428 10s. 6d. His widow was Mary Reed.

Reed's mark (a) of capital initials, the top of the shield resembling a crown, is on the New Brick Church cups, and on the MFA spoons is overstamped with a probable second small mark of his initials in a rectangle.

a

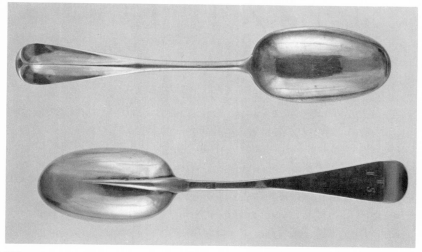

133

133 Pair of Spoons, c. 1720

54.659: L. 7⁵⁄₁₆ in.; Wt. 1 oz., 16 dwt.; *54.660:* L. 7³⁄₈ in.; Wt. 1 oz. 12½ dwt.

MARKS: *a* (double-stamped on 54.659) and each overstamped with *IR* in small rectangle. The outline of the larger mark (with shaped bottom line on 54. 659, straight line on 54.660) has been compared with the first Paul Revere's early shield mark from which it differs.

Rounded handle forward bent with two-thirds midrib and two-thirds rattail on uneven elliptical bowl (their slanting shoulders reversed).

Engraved ITS on back of handle.

HISTORY: John (d. 1737) and Susanna (English) Tousel (Touzel, Towzel) (d. 1739), m. November 7, 1720; descended to the Misses Bailey, from whose heirs the spoons were bought.

NOTES: Captain John Towzel died intestate, and his wife left her wrought silver, amounting only to 12 oz., 5 dwt., 6 gr. to her three children: Susanna, then of age; Mary and John, minors. She specified that her coined silver and gold which in her husband's estate appeared as £ 1669 10s. was to be "put out to such interest as it will fetch." It is interesting to note the great discrepancy between the small amount of wrought silver they owned and the large amount of coin. A pair of spoons owned by The Metropolitan Museum of Art, New York, seems to be part of this set.

EXHIBITION: *MFA 1911,* no. 922 (as "Two Porringer spoons" by John Royalston?).

THE H. E. BOLLES FUND *54.659-660*

JOSEPH KNEELAND
1698/9–1740

JOSEPH KNEELAND, son of John and Mary Kneeland, was born January 29, 1698/9 and is best known for the tankards he fashioned as gifts of the brothers John and William Vassall to Harvard College. There were two at least of his name in the Boston records, and it remains unclear which one is the goldsmith. A Joseph Kneeland and Elizabeth Chamberlain were married November 8, 1722, and children are recorded to them from 1723 through February 1730. A date of February 8, 1728, is given for the marriage of another Joseph Kneeland to Mary Warton. Their first child was born January 3, 1731/2; their last child was Sarah, born April 18, 1740. In September of that year "Joseph Kneeland . . . Goldsmith" died intestate, Nathaniel Green, administrator. In the early books on silver his death was given as 1760 even though there was no silver of the forties and fifties known by him. He died insolvent, and tools and a brass button mold were among the items inventoried by Jabez Hunt, David Cutler, and Joseph Bradford. From a £50 bequest of Jeremiah Atwater in 1735 he fashioned a 13¼-inch baptismal bowl for the First Church of Christ in New Haven, Connecticut.

We know only one mark for Kneeland, his initial and surname with colon between in cartouche *(a)*, although a mark of his initials in a conforming rectangle has also been assigned to him.

a

134

134 Nutmeg Grater, 1720–1740

H. ¾ in.; W. 1⅜ in.; L. 1¾ in.; Wt. 1 oz.

MARKS: *a* in each lid.

Heart-shaped box, deep sides, slight bead applied near each edge to form bezels. Silver grater closes one surface. Two lids with three-part hinges, their tops following heart-shaped contour, the inner hinge-bars spanning indentation of the heart and affixed below bead.

Engraved band of overlapping leaves on each lid, the narrower enclosing a parrot on a leaf. Script *RW* engraved with leaf forms in the point on the lid over the grater.

HISTORY: Unknown.

EXHIBITIONS: *MFA 1956*, no. 105, fig. 43; *ESU 1960*, no. 39, pl. 31.

GIFT OF MRS. LESLIE R. MORE *55.114*

JOHN POTWINE
1698–1792

JOHN POTWINE, of Huguenot descent, was born in England. He was
in Boston in 1700 when he received by the will of his physician-
father "my silver-headed cane, one gold ring and my Chirurgeon's
Chest." His mother married again in 1708, but it is not known to
whom she apprenticed her son. He became a communicant of the
Church in Brattle Square in 1715. He married Mary, daughter of
Thomas and Priscilla (Grafton) Jackson in 1721. The family's removal
to Connecticut may be dated approximately by the birth of Mary
in Boston in 1734 and of Nathaniel in Hartford in 1737. Potwine was
a merchant as well as a goldsmith; his known daybook of 1752-1753
is said to contain no entry of his own plate-making but records
sending "Spanish Dolers" to Daniel Henchman and three charges for
jewelry. His first wife died in Coventry in 1766; five years later he
married Elizabeth (Lyman) Mosely, who was mother-in-law of his
son, the Reverend Thomas, pastor of the North Parish in Windsor,
Connecticut, now the town of East Windsor, where he is buried.
He is said to have assisted his son in pastoral duties until his death
in 1792.

This is Potwine's unquestioned mark *(a)*, his initial and surname with
colon between in cartouche; a mark of *IP* in a rectangle was included
by Miss Potwine in her article in *Antiques* (see *References*, Cat.
no. 135).

a

135

135 Cann, 1723

H. of body 4¾ in.; D. of base 2¾ in. (uneven); D. of lip 3 in.; Wt. 8 oz., 8 dwt.

MARK: *a* at left of handle.

Bulbous body, molded rim, on cast molded splayed footband (dented). Center point on bottom. Hollow scroll cast handle, seams at side and grooved over curve, its short grip flush with edge, turned drop below upper joining, disc at lower joining; ball tip; small vent holes near upper joining and in tip.

Engraved arms used by Ebenezer Storer in asymmetric acanthus scroll and foliate cartouche, crest on torse, on front. *MB* on grip; ESM engraved on bottom; script *MSH* over *1852* below engraved weight *8:13*, also on bottom.

HISTORY: Ebenezer and Mary Storer, m. 1723; interim history unknown; Mary (Ingersoll) Bowditch; Mattie S. Hatch (said to have been a ward of Ingersoll Bowditch); Alfred Bowditch (d. 1912); his daughter, the donor.

NOTES: In the Bowditch genealogy the only Ingersoll was born in 1875, but Nathaniel Bowditch (1773-1838) and his wife Mary (Ingersoll) gave her surname as a middle name to each of five sons, one of whom could have been Mattie Hatch's guardian.

REFERENCES: *Curtis 1913*, illus. opp. p. 49, pl. XVI (with added cover); *Bigelow 1917*, p. 186, fig. 112 (with added cover); E. B. Potwine, "John Potwine," *Antiques*, XXVIII, no. 3 (1935), pp. 106-109, fig. 9.

EXHIBITION: *MFA 1911*, no. 843, pl. 28.

GIFT OF MISS MARY O. BOWDITCH 47.1415

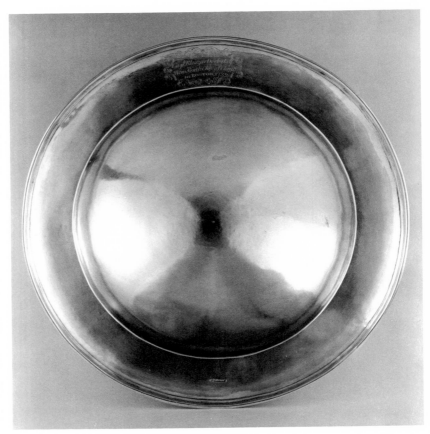

136

136 Baptismal Basin, 1730

H. 3½ in.; D. of rim 13½ in.; Wt. 29 oz., 17½ dwt.

MARK: *a* on rim opposite engraving.

Curved bowl, probably to be used in font or on a stand. Center point in bowl and on back. Slightly upcurved rim with molded edge.

Engraved in frame of foliate scrolls on rim, second and third lines in semiscript: *The Gift of/Cap.ᵗ Eleazer Dorby to yᵉ/New South＝Chh of Christ/in BOSTON 1730.*

HISTORY: See *Notes.*

NOTES: Captain Dorby's inventory, Suffolk Probate in 1736, listed only a "parcell of plate weighing 79¾ at 26/-£ 103-13-6." His gift of this basin to the church thus represented more than a third his own silver. The majority of New England basins had flat or slightly domed bottoms. Paul Revere II, in 1762, fashioned a similarly curved bowl but gave it a splayed foot.

REFERENCES: *Curtis 1913,* illus. opp. p. 49, pl. XVI; *Jones 1913,* p. 73, pl. XXVIII; *Bigelow 1917,* pp. 227-228, fig. 137; E. B. Potwine, "John Potwine," *Antiques,* XXVIII, no. 3 (1935), pp. 106-109, fig. 8.

EXHIBITIONS: *MFA 1906,* no. 215; *MFA 1911,* no. 841, pl. 28.

GIFT OF THE NEW SOUTH CHURCH SOCIETY *12.398*

THOMAS EDWARDS
1701–1755

THOMAS EDWARDS was the first silversmithing son of John and Sybil (Sibella) (Newman) Edwards (q.v.). He married Sarah Burr of Charlestown, Massachusetts on October 19, 1723; their daughter Sarah was born December 11, 1724; another daughter, Elizabeth, was born October 17, 1729. Sarah married her father's apprentice, Zachariah Brigden (q.v.); on May 5, 1749 Elizabeth married William Downes Cheever, sugar baker. In a privately owned manuscript, various real estate transactions of this goldsmith in Cambridge, Plymouth, and Plympton, Massachusetts are recorded in the 1720s and early 30s, yet one of the name is recorded as a Freeman in New York in 1731. From the *Boston Gazette,* October 19/26, 1724: "Some time in September last, when John Winthrop Esq lay Sick at New London some Person broke into his Coach House, and cut out the greatest part of the red Velvet which was the lining of his Coach and likewise took away a great Iron Bolt which fastened the Doors. Whoever shall make discovery of the same, and give notice to the abovesaid Mr. Winthrop, or to Mr. Thomas Edwards, Goldsmith in Boston, shall have Three Pounds Reward & necessary charges paid." In 1746 he advertised the settlement of his father's estate: "NB. The Goldsmith's Business is carried on at the Shop of the deceased, as usual, by his son Thomas Edwards." This sounds as if he might not have had a shop of his own, but he had his own marks. In the next year from Cornhill he advertised stolen silver he had "stop'd." His will, probated September 19, 1755, mentioned "my well beloved wife Eleanor" and "my daughter Sarah" but no second marriage is recorded for him and Sarah, his daughter, was the surviving executrix when the inventory was taken. He left only £10 to his daughter Elizabeth Cheever, perhaps because her husband was a wealthy merchant, the same sum to "cousins," some of whom were actually nephews, and "to my brother Samuel Edwards a handsome Gold Motto Ring." The inventory included wrought silver at 7s. 4d. per ounce, unwrought and household plate at 6s. 8d. His tools were valued at £52 11s. 2d. and "122 books of gold leaf" at £11 1s.

Edwards' first mark resembled his father's late one, crowned initials with pellet between in a shield *(a)*. He also used a mark of his initials in a rectangle *(b)*. A third mark *(c)* includes his surname.

a   *b*   *c*

137 Cup, c. 1723

H. 3½ in. (inc. handle); D. of base 2½ in.; D. of lip 3⅜ in.; Wt. 6 oz., 9 dwt.

MARK: *a* at left of handle.

Heavy gauge, flaring lip, straight sides curving to almost flat bottom (with no center point) on cast molded and splayed footband. Heavy strap handle affixed with rounded tip in curve of lip, tapering to joining above curve at base, broadening to upturned rounded tip.

Engraved coat of arms and crest, used by Ebenezer Storer, in shell and wheat cartouche with acanthus scroll below. On bottom ESM (in another hand) to/MS. Added on side at right of handle, in script, *AWS/to WSE/Jany 1st 1847.*

HISTORY: Ebenezer and Mary (Edwards) Storer m. 1723; their daughter Mary (b. 1725), m. Edward Green, March 23, 1757 and left no issue; her niece Susanna Storer (1782-1853) m. Rev. Asa Eaton, 1813; AWS who made the gift to their grandson, the donor, remains unidentified.

NOTES: Mate bequeathed to MFA by Samuel A. Green (see Cat. no. 138). These arms have been called the "Andrews" (Bolton) and the "Scarming" (Bowditch) arms. However, lists of Ebenezer Storer's plate recently found in the Eaton family papers include frequent references to these as the arms of Ebenezer Storer. It seems clear, therefore, that he had adopted the design for himself.

EXHIBITIONS: *Jamestown 1907*, no. 65; *MFA 1911*, no. 478, pl. 3.

GIFT OF WILLIAM STORER EATON IN THE NAME OF MISS GEORGIANA G. EATON 13.559

137

138

138 Cup, c. 1723

H. 3½ in. (inc. handle); D. of base 2⁹⁄₁₆ in.; D. of lip 3⁷⁄₁₆ in. (uneven); Wt. 5 oz., 18½ dwt.

MARKS: *a* at left of handle; *b* on bottom. Mate to Cat. no. 137.

Engraved arms as on Cat. no. 137; ESM on bottom; added, *to HS*.

HISTORY: Ebenezer and Mary (Edwards) Storer, m. 1723; their daughter Hannah (1739-1811), m. Joshua Green, October 7, 1762; their son Joshua (1764-1847), m. Mary Mosley, 1791, second her sister, Nancy; their son Joshua (1797-1875), m. Eliza Lawrence; their son, the donor.

REFERENCE: *Avery 1930,* illus. opp. p. 255, pl. XLVII.

EXHIBITIONS: *MFA 1911,* no. 477, pl. 3; *Richmond 1960,* no. 60; ESU *1960,* no. 42.

BEQUEST OF SAMUEL A. GREEN *19.1389*

139

139 Pair of Teaspoons, c. 1723

L. 5⅛ in.

MARK: *b,* quite worn, on back of stem.
Rounded tip, forward bent with one-third midrib on long slim stem, rounded drop and shell of eleven lobes on worn elliptical bowl.

Engraved ESM, quite worn, on back of handle.

HISTORY: Same as Cat. no. 138.

EXHIBITION: *MFA 1911,* no. 480.

BEQUEST OF SAMUEL A. GREEN *19.1391-1392*

140

140 Caster, 1730–1740

H. 3½ in.; D. of base 1¹¹⁄₁₆ in.; Wt. 1 oz., 18 dwt.

MARK: *b* in center of base, perhaps obliterating center point.

Rounded bottom on splayed molded foot. Bead molding at joining of slightly curved seamed and tapering neck with everted rim where an applied bead forms a deep bezel, its seam midway between the other two. Low domed lid, molded edge, and applied molded band, piercing in plain holes grouped with slight engraving, faint lines which form bands at rim and over three side groups of holes.

Engraved *AQ* on bottom for Anna Quincy (b. 1719, see Cat. no. 33). Added on side *AQC 1900*.

HISTORY: Descended in the family.

NOTES: Yale has a salver by John Blowers (1710-1748) engraved *AQ* and with Quincy arms but not in the lozenge correct for distaff ownership. Similar casters are known by Jacob Hurd.

EXHIBITION: *R.I. 1965*, no. 79.

GIFT OF ANNA QUINCY CHURCHILL 61.947

141

141 Chafing Dish, c. 1740

H. 3¾ in. (inc. supports); D. of grate 3½ in.; D. of rim 5⅞ in.; Wt. 17 oz., 2 dwt.

MARK: *c* on bottom.

Everted rim, molded on top, straight sides (with piercings in band of symmetrical scroll cuttings and three groups of five upright slots under supports) curve to narrow convex band of simple piercing (three circles, the end two pointed, between shaped rectangles, repeated six times). Slight curve to flat bottom, hole in center for missing screw, cast grate in usual pattern rests well above lower piercings (see Cat. nos. 152, 188, 237). Three scroll supports affixed and forked over rim have molded tips and curve to base with pointed joinings and scroll legs with hoof feet. Grate has tear drop and triangle center and raying slanted slots, alternate ones short with ellipse above, to circle at rim. Support opposite coat of arms flattened for missing handle socket.

Engraved coat of arms used by Ebenezer Storer on front in shell, acanthus scroll, flower, and fruit cartouche; ESM on bottom. *Storer 1723* curved in late script on bottom.

HISTORY: Ebenezer and Mary (Edwards) Storer, m. 1723; their daughter Elizabeth, m. Isaac Smith, 1746; their son William, m. Hannah Carter, 1787; their son Thomas Carter, m. Frances Barnard, 1831; their daughter Frances Barnard, m. Thomas Davis Townsend, 1854; their son, William Smith Townsend, father of the donors.

NOTES: One of the "2 Chaffing dishes 35 oz. 15 dwt" in the estate of Isaac Smith in 1787, the mate still owned in the family. Others in this form: a pair by John Burt (Art Institute of Chicago and a private collection, Milwaukee); several by Jacob Hurd (including Cat. no. 188); one by John Potwine (illus. *Bigelow 1913,* p. 328).

EXHIBITION: *MFA 1956,* no. 70.

GIFT OF THE MISSES ROSE AND ELIZABETH TOWNSEND 56. 670

141

142

142 Child's Porringer, c. 1749

H. 1¼ in.; D. of lip 3¾ in.; L. of handle 2 in.; Wt. 3 oz., 15½ dwt.

MARK: *b* in bowl.

Straight very narrow rim, curved sides, stepped domed bottom. Center point on bottom. Large piercings on keyhole handle, initial area almost triangular. Engraved *ES/to/IS* away from bowl. Weight *3·16·18* engraved on bottom.

HISTORY: Probably Elizabeth (Storer) Smith to her firstborn son Isaac Smith (b. 1749); his niece Elizabeth (1789-1859), m. Edward Cruft, ancestor of donors.

NOTES: Very similar handles occur on pieces by Samuel Edwards, William Breed, and Paul Revere I.

GIFT OF THE ESTATES OF THE MISSES EUNICE McLELLAN AND FRANCES CORDIS CRUFT 42.383

143

143 Spoon, 1755

L. 7¾ in.; Wt. 1 oz., 11½ dwt.

MARK: *c* on back of stem.

Stem broadens to rounded tip with one-half ridge, rounded drop and shell with eleven lobes on back of oval bowl.

Engraved *Mary Storer/Jany 1 1755* over crest used by Ebenezer Storer on back of handle.

HISTORY: See *Notes*.

NOTES: Mary Storer was born in 1725 and married Edward Green in 1757. They died without issue and the spoon doubtless went to her niece Susanna, who married Rev. Asa Eaton (1778-1858), grandparents of the donor.

EXHIBITION: *MFA 1911*, no. 476.

GIFT OF WILLIAM STORER EATON 37.264

BARTHOLOMEW GREEN
born 1701

BARTHOLOMEW GREEN is often confused with Benjamin Greene (1712-1776), brother of Rufus (q.v.). Very little is known about him or his work. His birth date has been consistently given erroneously. His parents, Bartholomew (1666-1732), a printer, and Mary, were married in 1690; their children, Mary (b. October 1692), Samuel, Eliza, and Bartholomew (b. 1697), are all recorded in Volume 9 of the Record Commissioners Reports. In Volume 28, another Bartholomew, who became the goldsmith, was recorded born to them on October 22, 1701, also another Samuel, and a Deborah before Mary died in 1709. In June 1710 the printer married Jane Toppan and a third Samuel (b. 1712) was their only recorded child. The *Boston News-Letter* of December 28-January 4, 1732/3 carried the notice: "In the obituary of Dea. Bartholomew Green, the printer of The Boston News-Letter, who died December 28, 1732, it is stated that his father, Capt. Samuel Green, who arrived in Charlestown in 1630, 'upon their first coming ashore both he and several others were for some time glad to lodge in empty casks to shelter them from the weather, for want of Housing' . . ." Capt. Samuel (1615-1701/2) had come with his parents, Bartholomew and Elizabeth, about 1633. It is not known to whom his grandson was apprenticed, but he married Hannah Hanson of Newtown in 1724, their daughter Mary was the only child recorded to them. His second marriage, by Rev. Timothy Cutler of Christ Church, was to Ann Vaughn, but he is not to be found in the Suffolk Probate Court records.

This mark *(a)* is given to Bartholomew since Benjamin had a terminal *e* on his name (see mark of his brother, Rufus Greene).

a

144

144 Spout Cup, c. 1738

H. 6⅛ in. (inc. finial); D. of base 3⅟₁₆ in.; D. of lip 2¹⁵⁄₁₆ in.; Wt. 12 oz., 3 dwt.

MARK: *a* on bottom near center point.

Bulbous body with molded rim on cast molded splayed foot, thick solder. Center point on bottom. Stepped and domed cover, small turned finial, quite wide molded flange bent under hinge plate. Four-part hinge has plain inner plate over flange of cover, molded and pointed outer one on shoulder of hollow scroll handle with slight body drop at upper joining; slightly angled and pointed tip below lower joining on curve of body. Tubular spout at right angles to handle is broad and flat over elliptical hole with strainer plate (perhaps not silver) set on body, inside spout. Applied to base of spout is shaped plaque decorated with short incised lines.

Engraved IRK on handle.

HISTORY: James (1715-1798) and Katharine (Graves) (1717-1778) Russell of Charlestown, m. April 13, 1738; descended in the family.

NOTES: James Russell survived his wife, two sons, and a daughter, and in his will left to his grandchildren, a son James, and daughters Katherine Henly and Rebecca Lowell, each a mourning ring. His unmarried daughters Sarah and Mary Russell were executors and chief legatees of his estate, for which no inventory is recorded; one granddaughter was Elizabeth Sullivan Russell, to whom the spout cup may have descended.

REFERENCE: *McLanathan 1956*, p. 58, fig. 13.

EXHIBITIONS: *Jamestown 1907*, no. 87; *MFA 1911*, no. 532 (as by Benjamin Greene); *MFA 1956*, no. 73.

GIFT OF MISS SARAH SULLIVAN PERKINS AND MRS. ELIZABETH PERKINS CABOT
20.1844

PAUL REVERE I 1702–1754

Apollos Rivoire, son of Isaac and Serenne (Lambert) Rivoire of Riaucaud, France, was born November 30, 1702, and on November 21, 1715, he set out for Guernsey, whence his uncle had fled the religious persecutions. From there he came to Boston and was apprenticed to John Coney. The latter's inventory in 1722 notes: "Paul Rivoire's Time abt Three Year & half as pr indenture £30-0-0." Miss Esther Forbes records that he bought his freedom from his master's estate (*Paul Revere and the World He Lived In*, Boston, 1942). In 1730 the *Weekly News Letter* carried the notice "Paul Revere Goldsmith is removed from Capt. Pitts at the Town Dock, to North End over against Col. Hutchinson." Francis Hill Bigelow included in his collection a piece he had attributed to an otherwise currently unlisted "John Pitts, Boston, c. 1730"—one cannot but wonder if he had provided the money to pay the Huguenot apprentice's unexpired time.

Although John Coney had been one of the subscribers to King's Chapel in 1689, Revere (he shortly anglicized his surname as well as his given name) and his son are recorded as members of the New North Church (founded in 1714 and disbanded in 1872) and its seceding New Brick Church (founded in 1721). In 1729 Revere had married Deborah Hitchbourn (Hichborn), their firstborn a daughter, their second a son, each named for the appropriate parent. Rivoire's only recorded church silver is the pair of strainer spoons in the Second Church, Boston; his silver is rare and is not known to include any tutorial plate—that activity of his master falling first on John Burt. His creampot in this collection shows the careful craftsmanship worthy of his training; and the teapot, regrettably altered, discloses his ability in decorative engraving. Probably the greatest evidence which has survived of his training is in that which he gave his son, the patroit.

The mark of his initials in a rectangle *(a)* on the Second Church in Boston spoons is on the miniature caudle cup; his more decorative, and larger, mark *(b)* shows a line across and below the top of a shield-shaped punch. He also had a mark of initial and surname in a rectangle *(c)* and in a rectangle with a wavy upper line *(d)*. He also used capital letters with a period in a cartouche, or scalloped rectangle *(e)*, and with a pellet in a plain rectangle *(f)*. The last mark was continued in use by his son.

a   *b*   *c*   *d*   *e*   *f*

145

145

145 Miniature Caudle Cup, c. 1720

H. 1⅝₆ in. (inc. handles); D. of base 1⅛₆ in.; D. of lip 1¹¹⁄₁₆ in. (uneven); Wt. 9½ dwt.

MARKS: *a* on bottom twice.

Somewhat straight sides tapering to a curve, stepped flat bottom. Lower part of body chased, in imitation of cup attributed to John Coney (Cat. no. 37), with edges of leaves formed by short separate strokes. Leaf on base has dots in angles, long strokes for outlines of triangle, which is seemingly punched with an oval tool of crosshatching or gridwork almost obliterating the center point.

HISTORY: Unknown; see Cat. no. 37.

REFERENCE: *Revere 1956*, no. 9.

EXHIBITION: *MFA 1956*, no. 117, figs. 42 and 42b.

BEQUEST OF MRS. F. GORDON PATTERSON *56.116*

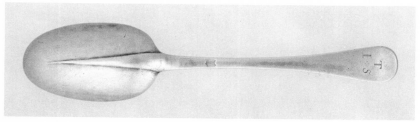

146

146 Spoon, c. 1725

L. 7½ in.; Wt. 2 oz.

MARK: *b* on back of stem.

Heavy stem, rounded tip bent forward with one-half ridge, long heavy rattail on elliptical bowl.

Engraved ITS for John and Susanna Touzel.

HISTORY: See Cat. no. 133.

THE H. E. BOLLES FUND 54.661

147

147 Cann, c. 1730

H. 5½ in. (inc. handle); D. of base 3³⁄₁₆ in.; D. of lip 3⅛ in.; Wt. 11 oz., 12 dwt.

MARKS: *d* at left of handle and a broken stamp of the same mark on bottom.
Bulbous body with deeply incised paired lines below everted rim, cast molded splayed foot. Center point on bottom. Cast hollow scroll handle with molded body drop at upper joining, slight grip, vent (?) hole below; disc at lower joining and upcurved scroll tip with vent hole below. Bottom battered.
Engraved *C/WM/AG*. The *C*, *W*, and *A* each spans the seam of the handle. Engraved on bottom: *12¼ oz.* at center point.
HISTORY: Unknown.
REFERENCE: *Revere 1956*, no. 5.
EXHIBITIONS: *Worcester 1916; Washington 1925*, no. 80.
PAULINE REVERE THAYER COLLECTION *35.1757*

148

148 Spoon, 1725–1740

L. 8¹⁄₁₆ in.; Wt. 1 oz., 19½ dwt.

MARK: *f* on back of stem.
Rounded handle bent forward with ridge halfway; rounded drop and shell on back of (worn) elliptical bowl.
Engraved in semiscript with italic capitals *Sarah Dole* across back of tip.
HISTORY: Sarah Dole (b. 1720), m. James Knight, May 2, 1740.
NOTES: A matching spoon lent to an exhibition at the Towle Manufacturing Company (1953), had the date 1739 added and was owned by a descendant of Sarah Dole.
EXHIBITION: *Washington 1925*, no. 115.
PAULINE REVERE THAYER COLLECTION *35.1818*

149

149 Teapot, c. 1740

H. 5⅝ in. (inc. finial); D. of base 3⅛ in.; Wt. 18 oz., 19 dwt.

MARK: *c* just above center point on bottom.

Almost globular and raised upside down. The bottom, with center point, shows neat solder inside and for the cast molded splayed footband. Flat cover cut with a jog for five-part hinge with molded wedge, molded band around inside of cover does not seem to be applied, strap under rim of body for its support. A turned and flame finial, as for the patriot's tankards, has been pegged through the cover, incised circles near its base perhaps mark original finial width, and the vent hole is just beyond them at the back. The upper handle socket, molded at its joining high on the body, has a leaf grip, incised line near edge, and horizontal pin for the wooden scroll handle with scroll grip. The lower socket is cylindrical with an everted edge and horizontal pin. The spout, over original strainer holes in an ellipse unusually high on the body, is straight and tapering and was changed within the memory of the donor. Quite large dent at right of spout.

Engraved on pourer's side, Foster arms in shaped shield on imbricated ground within leaf and scroll cartouche high at sides to surround crest. *S. L. Robbins/ 1813* added on bottom in a curve. The cover has a scroll and bellflower border of engraving, as has the shoulder with wider area at front and back.

HISTORY: Descended in the family (see *Notes*).

NOTES: Since the Winslow mug from the same source bears the name of Edward Hutchinson (1678-1752), this perhaps descended from his wife, Lydia Foster (1686-1748), whom he married in 1705; although Thomas Hutchinson (1674/5-1739), father of the royal governor, had a daughter Lydia, who married in 1736 George Rogers. The quillwork sconce given to the Museum by Miss Howe is worked with Foster arms, signed LH, and dated 1737, which suggests the work of the younger Lydia, whose maiden coat of arms seems more appropriate to her time and that of the teapot. Each of the brothers was survived by children.

EXHIBITION: *MFA 1911*, no. 849.

BEQUEST OF MISS LOIS LILLEY HOWE 64.2048

150

150 Covered Milk Pot, 1730–1750

H. 4⅝ in. (inc. finial); D. of base 2⅛ in.; D. of lip 1¹³⁄₁₆ in.; Wt. 5 oz., 7 dwt.

MARKS: *b* at left of handle and over center point on bottom.

Bulbous body on cast molded splayed foot (holes in thick solder), applied molded rim and small triangular spout with turned body drop below V cut of body. Molded domed cover with turned bell form finial pegged through it, tiny three-part hinge. V from inner part of hinge over the flange, molded shaped outer plate extends to slight grip on shoulder. Scroll handle has long drop at upper joining flush with rim, lower joining on curve of body, upturned scroll and forked tip.

HISTORY: Unknown.

NOTES: Jeweler's incised numerals under foot. Similar pieces: one by John Edwards (*MFA 1956*, no. 61) and one by Jacob Hurd in the Cleveland Museum of Art (Hollis French Collection), both without covers; Bigelow

(1913, fig. 299) shows one by Tobias Stoutenburgh of New York with a hinge on the handle to prove a lost cover, but it is tripod.

REFERENCES: *Buhler 1950*, pp. 43-44, fig. 35; *Revere 1956*, no. 4.

EXHIBITIONS: *Chicago 1949*, no. 195, illus. 119; *Detroit 1951*, no. 355; *Richmond 1960*, no. 102.

BEQUEST OF FREDERICK W. BRADLEE 28.45

151 Caster, 1740–1750

H. 5¼ in.; D. of base 1¾ in.; Wt. 3 oz., 12 dwt.

MARK: *b* on bottom.

Hemispherical bowl on cast splayed molded foot with added vertical rim; rather sharply curved seamed section joined with molding has applied bezel and molded rim, its seam slightly to right of body seam. Seamed domed cover engraved in rectangular panels of diaper work with plain holes, molded edge on disc below turned bell-form finial, pegged through disc.

Engraved *DT* under foot.

HISTORY: Unknown.

REFERENCE: *Revere 1956*, no. 6.

BEQUEST OF CHARLES HITCHCOCK TYLER 32.403

151

152

152 Chafing Dish, 1740–1750

H. 3¾ in. (inc. supports); D. of grate 3½ in.; D. of lip 6⅝ in.; L. 12⁹⁄₁₆ in. (inc. handle); Wt. 22 oz., 18 dwt.

MARKS: *e* twice, both stamps in same direction on bottom.

Everted rather wide molded rim, piercing on upper curve, lower curve quite thick and cut for wide concave band pierced in reverse heart motifs, applied at edge of body and inside flat plate with upcurved edge. Upper piercing consists of four areas of crosses in diamond form with horizontal scroll designs and slight engraving flanking small area of cresent and dot designs. Support to which turned handle socket is affixed is over one area of crosses. Pierced cast grate overlapping center has scribed molded edge and inner circle, rayed piercings of uneven length, the short ones topped by cut ellipses, the center six ovals forming triangular holes, the outer edge scalloped. Screw with rounded head affixed through plate is threaded only at tip and has square nut with shaped corners. Three cast supports have scroll tips, affixed at rim, and C curve, with small inner scroll below a band of molding, affixed by a strap above concave band of piercing and ends in a scroll foot. Handle socket with moldings almost covers the band of molding of one support. Turned wooden handle pinned into socket.

Engraved WWR on bottom over partially erased engraving TIGM.

HISTORY: See *Notes*.

NOTES: The engraving perhaps stands for William and Rebecca White of Haverhill, Massachusetts; he died childless in 1773 and the estate was divided among his brothers and sisters. Goss (1891) gave the piece as the property of D. F. Appleton, and Jamestown (1907) recorded the initials as of Revere II's second wife, an attribution unfamiliar to their descendant, Mrs. Thayer. The unusual double initials for the man fit Thomas James Grouchy, who was married to Mary Dumaresq in Trinity Church on October 11, 1741, but no one of the surname can be found in later records. The same initials are on a caster by John Burt, carefully concealed by crosshatching, and on a sugar bowl by the patriot (Yale University Art Gallery, Garvan Collection). Similar chafing dishes are by John Burt (The Metropolitan Museum of Art, Clearwater Collection), and Samuel Burt (Cat. no. 237); and similar inner plates by Jacob Hurd (Cat. no. 188).

REFERENCES: *Goss 1891*, p. 412, illus.; *Buck 1903*, p. 141, illus.; *Hipkiss 1931*, illus. p. 88; *Buhler 1936*, illus. p. 43, fig. 9; *Revere 1956*, no. 2.

EXHIBITIONS: *MFA 1906*, no. 226, pl. 21, 13; *Jamestown 1907*, no. 129; *Washington 1925*, no. 82; *Hartford 1946*.

PAULINE REVERE THAYER COLLECTION *35.1756*

152

153

153 Saucepan, 1740–1750

H. of bowl 2⅞ in.; D. of base 2¾ in.; D. of lip 2½ in.; L. of handle 6⅛ in.;
Wt. 5 oz., 19 dwt. (inc. handle).

MARK: *f* above center point on bottom.

Everted lip with incised line below, hammered on side left of handle to form
small pouring lip; body rounded to flat base. Conical socket affixed with
heart-shaped disc below rim for turned wooden handle pinned below tiny
everted rim. Dented.

Engraved *5¼ oz.* above mark in lettering comparable to that on Cat. no. 147.

HISTORY: Early history unknown; owned by 1907 by Mrs. Thomas Bailey
Aldrich, mother of the donor.

REFERENCE: *Revere 1956*, no. 3.

EXHIBITIONS: *Jamestown 1907*, no. 124; *MFA 1911*, no. 847.

GIFT OF TALBOT ALDRICH *53.2081*

154 Cann, 1740–1750

H. of body 5 in.; D. of base 3⁵/₁₆ in.; D. of lip 3⅛ in.; Wt. 10 oz.

MARK: *f*, slightly broken stamp, above center point on bottom.

Very slightly everted thickened lip with single incised line on it, paired incised lines below. Bulbous body on cast molded splayed foot. Double scroll handle, the scroll tips flattened at sides, plain grip, vent under convex upper body joining, applied disc at lower joining, handle affixed with hole in solder. Has been burnished.

Scratched on bottom in script *Edes* and *10 oz., 16 dwt.*

HISTORY: Owned by Thomas Edes (1737-1792), m. Mary (1739/40-1818) daughter of Daniel Wood; descended to their great-grandson, H. H. Edes (1849-1922).

REFERENCE: *Goss 1891*, p. 14.

EXHIBITION: *MFA 1906*, no. 228.

GIFT OF MR. AND MRS. HENRY HERBERT EDES 36.47

154

KNIGHT LEVERETT
1702/3–1753

KNIGHT LEVERETT, son of Thomas Hudson and Rebecca Leverett, was born January 1, 1702/3. He was a great-grandson of Governor John Leverett, whose order of knighthood conferred by Charles II is thought to have been the source of the boy's name. His uncle, John Leverett, was president of Harvard College. He is said to have been apprenticed to Andrew Tyler; he served the town of Boston as hog reeve, scavenger, and clerk of the market, but paid to avoid being a constable. The settlement of the estate of Sarah Dennie in 1752 records: "To Cash p^d Knight Leverett his Bill for rings for fun^a £136-11/Jacob Hurd for a ring for funeral [£] 5-16." He died in 1753, intestate and insolvent; one of the appraisers of his estate, which included fishing equipment, was Jacob Hurd; its total value was but £27 1s.

Leverett's initial and surname mark is shown with a pellet (a) in a cartouche. He used a mark of his initials in a rectangle (too blurred on the MFA spoon [see *Appendix*] to reproduce) and his name mark has been drawn in a rectangle.

a

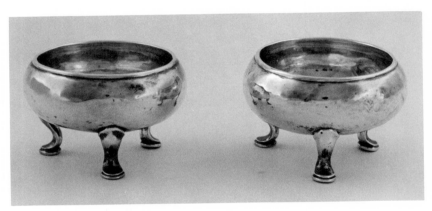

241

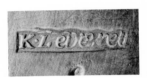

a

185

186

Clapp arms on a teapot (*French 1939*, no. 266).
REFERENCE: *French 1939*, p. 35, no. 76 (as Barrett arms).
BEQUEST OF CHARLES HITCHCOCK TYLER 32.375

187

187 Grace Cup, 1740–1745

H. 13½ in. (inc. finial); D. of base 5¹¹⁄₁₆ in.; D. of lip 6¾ in.; W. 12 in. (inc. handles); Wt. 76 oz., 2 dwt.

MARKS: *a* below center point on bottom; *e* on bezel of cover.

Two-handled cup with slightly flaring rim, sides taper to curve above wrought splayed and stepped foot with added band at edge; applied molded midband. Molded stepped cover flattened at top (dented) for turned and molded finial with vent hole in cover. Hollow cast scroll handles, inner surface slightly faceted, outer curved; molding at upper joining below flare, scroll grip on shoulder, extension for lower joining, a scroll above scroll tip with flattened sides and forked tip (very small vent hole).

Engraved with Rowe arms without tinctures and crest, all enveloped in an elaborate scroll and acanthus cartouche, with shell in base tangent to midband. Scratched on bottom *oz* over *76-6-0* .

HISTORY: John Rowe (b. Exeter, England, November 27, 1715; emigrated 1735; d. 1787) m. Hannah Speakman (1725-1805) 1743; his nephew, John Rowe; his granddaughter, Mrs. Caleb Loring Cunningham (née Anne Rowe), from whom it was purchased.

NOTES: Similar cartouches by Hurd on a salver with the Colman arms (Cat. no. 184) and a salver with the Clarke arms (Yale University Art Gallery, Garvan Collection). Similar cups by Hurd: Tyng cup, dated 1744, wt. 100 oz. (Yale University Art Gallery, Garvan Collection); Comet-Bomb cup presented to Richard Spry, dated 1744 (privately owned); monogrammed cup, The Metropolitan Museum of Art, New York. William Swan made a similar cup presented in 1749 by the Commonwealth to Benjamin Pickman (on deposit at the Essex Institute, Salem, Massachusetts).

REFERENCES: *Jones 1928*, p. 43; K. C. Buhler, "John Rowe's Cup," *MFA Bulletin*, XXXIV, no. 206 (1936), pp. 103-105, illus.; *French 1939*, p. 39, no. 129, pl. XIX; Buhler, *Antiques*, no. 6 (1945), pp. 348-349, fig. 3; *Ensko 1948*, illus. p. 13; *Phillips 1949*, pp. 74-75; *Wenham 1949*, illus. opp. p. 61, pl. XVI; *Buhler 1950*, pp. 31-32, fig. 25; *McLanathan 1956*, illus. p. 61, fig. 19; *Comstock 1958*, p. 82, fig. 8.

EXHIBITIONS: *MFA 1911*, no. 603, pls. 21, 33; *ESU 1960*, no. 47, pl. 10.

HELEN AND ALICE COLBURN FUND 36.415

188

188

188

188 Chafing Dish, 1745

H. 4 in. (inc. supports); D. of grate 3¾ in.; D. of rim 6⅛ in.; L. 12³⁄₁₆ in. (inc. handle); Wt. 19 oz. 10 dwt.

MARK: *d* on bottom.

Everted rim with paired incised lines near edge; sides curve to narrow concave band with piercing around flat bottom with hole for screw. Band of piercing below rim has five vertical slots under each support, two rows of shaped scrolls between. Dish supports extend over rim and end in molded scroll, a freestanding curve from these is affixed under the dish, attached curved leg with slight scroll ends in hoof foot. To one curve is affixed turned socket for turned wooden handle. Cast grate slightly domed is similar to that of Cat. no. 189 but with incised lines in place of outer piercings. The screw of the grate has a ball tip on turned base, its shaped nut has an arched guard.

Engraved with Phillips coat of arms in rocaille cartouche and crest on front between piercings; on bottom, mostly in script: *The Gift / of M͞r W͞m Blair Townsend Merc͏t / to / Cap͏t John Phillips i / in Boston 1745.* On bottom: *oz gr* over *18-15-00.*

HISTORY: William Blair Townsend (1723-1782), only son of wine cooper James and Elizabeth (Phillips) Townsend, nephew of John Phillips (d. 1747) and one of the administrators of his estate. Subsequent history unknown.

NOTES: The inventory of Phillips' estate, taken June 20, 1747, included "1 pr Chaffin dishes."

REFERENCE: K. C. Buhler, "American Silver on View in London," *Antiques,* LXXVIII, no. 3 (1960), illus. p. 230.

EXHIBITIONS: *ESU 1960,* no. 49, pl. 10; *R.I. 1965,* no. 102.

GIFT OF MRS. JOHN WELLS FARLEY *60.1467*

189

189 Chafing Dish, 1740–1750

H. 4¼ in. (inc. supports, one bent); D. of grate 4 in.; D. of rim 6%₁₆ in.; L. 13 in. (inc. handle); Wt. 23 oz., 1½ dwt.

MARK: *e* on bottom.

Everted molded rim, sides curve to cut out center (3 in. across). Concave band of piercing, larger than center hole, is affixed to bowl and flat bottom with hole in center. Cast grate, pierced with center design and raying straps to trefoils, circles, and scrolls near rim with incised line, is held by bud finial on turning for long screw (replaced nut). Upper half of dish pierced with grouped X's under supports, scrolls flanking quatrefoils between. Cast dish supports are everted scroll forms above rim, C scrolls from rim to midbody, forks with scroll to high curve of scroll foot, an angled support to base of body. Turned socket for wood handle attached to one C scroll with dish support attached to it.

Engraved weight *oz* over *22-5-0* on bottom; scratched weight *22-3-0* .

HISTORY: Unknown; owned by the donor by 1928.

NOTES: *French 1939* recorded ten chafing dishes, mostly in this form, of which one, listed as a pair (nos. 51-52) was really a single dish. Three other chafing dishes have appeared since the book was published to make an even dozen known today.

REFERENCES: *French 1939*, p. 34, no. 57; *Hipkiss 1942*, illus. p. 86; *Hipkiss 1943*, p. 57, illus.; *Buhler 1957*, fig. 7.

THE PHILIP LEFFINGWELL SPALDING COLLECTION. GIVEN IN HIS MEMORY BY KATHERINE AMES SPALDING AND PHILIP SPALDING, OAKES AMES SPALDING, HOBART AMES SPALDING 42.239

189

190

190 Cann, 1740–1750

H. 5⅜ in. (inc. handle); D. of base 3¼ in.; D. of lip 3¼ in.; Wt. 12 oz.

MARK: *d* poorly stamped at left of handle.

Bulbous body, incised lines below molded lip, on cast molded splayed foot (resoldered above). Double scroll cast handle in two parts, slight grip, scroll at upper joining with extension, flattened and incised at sides, disc at lower joining (repaired), scroll on handle tip with applied curl beneath. Vent hole in upper scroll, center point on bottom.

Engraved in shell and foliate cartouche with Lynde coat of arms.

HISTORY: Benjamin Lynde, Chief Justice (b. October 5, 1700, eldest son of Chief Justice Benjamin [Harvard 1686] and Mary Browne Lynde), m. Mary (Bowles), widow of Walter Goodridge, November 1, 1731; to one of two daughters: Mary, m. Andrew Oliver (Harvard 1749); Lydia, m. Rev. William Walters (Harvard 1756); descended in family to the donor.

NOTES: The same coat of arms, also attributed to Lynde, is on a tankard by Pygan Adams (Yale University Art Gallery).

REFERENCE: *French 1939*, p. 36, no. 84.

BEQUEST OF EDITH, LADY PLAYFAIR *Res. 32.36*

191

191 Ladle, 1740–1750

D. of bowl 2¹³⁄₁₆ in.; L. of silver 3⅞ in.; L. of wood 8½ in.

MARK: *e* in center of bowl.

Circular bowl, curved sides, everted rim, center point on almost flat bottom. Conical socket, clumsily resoldered to broken bowl, for turned wooden handle pinned in (which precludes weighing).

Engraved *HE* above center point on back of bowl.

HISTORY: Edes family.

REFERENCE: *French 1939,* p. 39, no. 135.

GIFT OF MR. AND MRS. HENRY HERBERT EDES 36.40

192

192 Spoon, c. 1746

MARKS: *f* twice on back of stem.

Rounded handle forward bent, slight ridge, rounded drop and shell (?) with cross-hatched triangles at sides, on back of elliptical bowl.

Engraved IHS on back of handle at tip.

HISTORY: John and Susanna Hathorne, m. 1746, descended to the Misses Bailey, from whose heirs it was bought.

EXHIBITIONS: *MFA 1911,* no. 686 (not attributed).

THE H. E. BOLLES FUND 54.662

193

193 Salver, 1740–1756

H. 1¾ in.; W. of dish 13⅜-13½ in. (uneven); Wt. 32 oz., 9 dwt, 12 gr.

MARK: *e* tangent to one bellflower.

Octagonal with curves at angles, applied (?) curved rim with molded edge, on four legs with pad joinings and paw feet.

Engraved and chased border inside rim with acanthus scrolls, shells suspending bellflowers between shaped panels of diaper groundwork, and pendent bellflowers at angles. Added script *AM / to / SM* in center (center point in *t*).

HISTORY: Although the initials are not Hurd's engraving, the salver could have belonged to Abigail May, who gave it to her daughter Sophia (1784-1870) who married Edward Tuckerman III as his second wife; descended in the family to Mrs. Orton Loring Clark (Margaret Tuckerman), from whom it was bought.

NOTES: The only published salver made by Hurd in this hexagonal form and size. He made two smaller ones: one with Quincy-Sturgis arms, no border (*French 1939*, no. 295) and one with what is probably Hubbard coat of arms, no border, small bellflowers at angles (*French 1939*, no. 292).

REFERENCES: French 1939, p. 49, no. 288; *McLanathan 1956,* illus. p. 66, fig. 28.

EXHIBITIONS: *MFA 1956*, no. 97; *Richmond 1960*, no. 81.

GIFT OF GUY WARREN WALKER, JR. 53.2849

194

194

194 Teapot, c. 1750

H. 6⅜ in. (inc. finial); D. of base 3¼ in.; Wt. 20 oz., 14 dwt.

MARK: *e* on bottom.

Spherical body, the bottom set in, on cast molded splayed foot, very thick solder and a lump of it inside. Three-part hinge from wedge with neatly incised lines across on cover thicker than those of other teapots in this collection. Turned wood finial has lower turned silver part soldered and pineapple tip, vent hole at tip of leaf decoration. Thirteen-panel spout, scalloped at body with turned drop, has sharp collar at midpoint; the tip has double scroll on top and a long underlip. Upper handle socket molded, lower socket plain for wooden scroll handle (a replacement?), pinned horizontally in both (vertical pin in upper socket missing). Wide scroll and flower embossing with dotted outer line on shoulder, four very narrow bands of decoration on rim; edge of cover has engraved border of overlapping leaves, rayed leaves chased around base of finial; at upper handle socket, body has dotted and chased design.

Engraved with Fleet coat of arms in shell, scroll, and foliate cartouche on pourer's side, crest on torse above (the base of the cartouche has what *French 1939* noted as a waterfall). Scratched on bottom: *18-6-1* and in cover: *B Oliver* over *1861*.

HISTORY: (conjectured) Elizabeth Vergoose, m. 1715 Thomas Fleet, printer (1685/6-1758); their son, Thomas (d. 1797), m. Elizabeth (not in Boston records), her will written 1821, proved 1827 (the inventory included a teapot); their daughter Mary, m. Ephraim Eliot (Harvard 1780, d. 1827), druggist, grandparents of donor.

NOTES: A pineapple finial is noted on four teapots in *French 1939*. Workmanship of embossing is similar to that on creampots by Hurd at Yale University Art Gallery, Garvan Collection, and to that on a teapot by Thomas Edwards (see *Addenda*).

REFERENCE: *French 1939*, p. 48, no. 275.

BEQUEST OF MISS MARY LINCOLN ELIOT 27.192

195

195 Gold Mourning Ring, 1752

Attributed to JACOB HURD

D. 1³⁄₁₆ in.

MARKS: None.

Painted (?) skull beneath rectangular faceted crystal in rayed bezel; four conjoined lettered scrolls with black enamel (some chipped).

Engraved *HON: MRS .K / DUMMER / OB: 13 JAN / 1752 AE 62.*

HISTORY: Katherine (daughter of Gov. Joseph Dudley), m. William Dummer, April 26, 1714; gift to a mourner; descended to donor.

NOTES: The attribution to Hurd is based on the fact that of the goldsmiths known to have been patronized by William Dummer, Jacob Hurd was the only survivor in 1752. The curved inner surface precludes a mark. A marked mourning ring by Hurd, a plain engraved band, is in the Essex Institute, Salem, Massachusetts (*French 1939*, no. 173).

EXHIBITION: *Presentation Silver 1955*, p. 14.

GIFT OF MISS ELIZABETH G. NORTON 52.980

WILLIAM SIMPKINS
1704–1780

Nicholas Simkins, great-grandfather of the goldsmith, was a tailor in Boston and was referred to as Captain as early as 1634. He had a son, Pilgrim, whose son, Thomas, born in 1671, became a mariner and married Margery Barton. Thomas and Margery had a son Thomas, born January 27, 1702, who became a brazier, and a son William, who became the goldsmith. The latter's birth is not in the published records, but it is given as March 20, 1704. He married Elizabeth Simms on May 16, 1726 (his name given as "Simkins" in the marriage records, and in the intentions hers was "Sines"). He advertised as William Simpkins, goldsmith, near the Draw Bridge, Boston, when selling the library of the late Rev. Robert Stanton of Salem.

Although he is thought to have ceased his goldsmithing about 1750, his inventory had a large assortment of tools; Josiah Waters, Benjamin Burt, and John Stanton were the appraisers. His total estate was valued at £ 32,117 - 3 - 4. Thomas Barton Simpkins, goldsmith (1728-1804), was his son.

Several marks are given for Simpkins: his initial and surname, with pellet between, in an ellipse (a) may also be in a rectangle (not represented in the MFA), or in a cartouche. His surname alone (not represented in the MFA) is given in a cartouche and in a rectangle. His initials marks are recorded both with (b) and without a pellet in a rectangle.

a   *b*

196

196 Bowl, 1736 or 1744

H. 3⅞ in.; D. of base 4⅞ in.; D. of lip 8½-8¹¹⁄₁₆ in. (uneven); Wt. 33 oz., 5 dwt.

MARKS: *a* twice near rim.

Very heavy gauge, hemispherical bowl with very slightly flaring rim, on cast molded and splayed foot.

Engraved sₕₑ around center point on bottom. In a curve, in script (probably not by Simpkins judging by his lettering on tankards owned by the First Parishes of Brookline and West Roxbury): *The Gift of Rebecca Sanders to her Daughter E Hall 1744;* added horizontally in upper half: *and of / John Gray / Great Grandson of the original / donor, to Dr. Thomas Gray, Jr. / his Nephew. May 15ᵗʰ 1845.*

HISTORY: Stephen and Elizabeth (Sanders) Hall, m. April 27, 1736; their grandson, John Gray; his nephew, Dr. Thomas Gray, Jr., 1845; descended in the family to the donor.

GIFT OF MISS RUTH K. RICHARDSON IN MEMORY OF T. FALES GRAY AND MRS. GEDNEY K. RICHARDSON 63.2767

197 Porringer, c. 1740–1750

H. 2⅛ in.; D. of lip 5³⁄₁₆ in. (uneven); L. of handle 2¾ in.; Wt. 7 oz., 13½ dwt.

MARK: *a* in center of bowl.

Slightly everted rim, curved sides, stepped and domed bottom. Battered. Center point on bottom. Keyhole handle, tip worn, uneven solder in angle underneath.

Engraved ELS on handle toward bowl. Scratched on bottom *7 - 16;* on back of handle *8 - 2.*

HISTORY: Edward Langdon (1698-1766), tallow chandler, m. Susanna Wadsworth December 2, 1718; his son Edward (d. 1755), m. Mary Parkman, 1752; descended in the family to the donors.

NOTES: The younger Edward predeceased his father, leaving in 1755 his wife and a daughter Mary. Edward, Jr.'s inventory included "1 can 3 porringers 4 large spoons 6 Tea spoons." His father's, a decade later, included two groups of silver: his own and some that was "the property of Edward Langdon jun. dec'd." He had four porringers of which this was surely one; his son's "large spoons" as well as his own were recorded as "Table spoons."

GIFT OF MISSES CATHARINE LANGDON ROGERS AND CLARA BATES ROGERS *14.897*

197

198

198 Cann, 1740–1750

H. of body 5 in.; D. of base 3⅜6 in.; D. of lip 3⅝6 in.; Wt. 10 oz., 5 dwt.

MARK: *b* at left of handle.

Bulbous body, applied molded rim, on cast splayed molded foot, center point on bottom. Scroll handle, rather long drop at upper joining, disc at lower; slight grip of short, flat piece with notched edge; tapering surface of handle broadening below lower joining has slightly angled and pointed tip, flush with underpart which has a large semicircular vent hole.

Engraved *HL,* separated by an ornamental device, on handle.

HISTORY: Initials said to be for Sarah Hersey and Thomas Loring. (This cannot be proved and would be unusual.)

NOTES: Simpkin's inventory included a high-priced "Stake for Can: £30."

GIFT OF THOMAS L. SPRAGUE *18.323*

SAMUEL EDWARDS
1705–1762

"Samuell Son of John Edwards and Sibell his Wife Born 21 June 1705" appears in the Boston records. His father and his brother Thomas were both goldsmiths. Marriage intentions of Samuel Edwards of Boston and Sarah Smith of Charlestown were filed August 23, 1733—seven years before her widowed mother Abigail married his father. They were childless and evidently particularly attentive to Abigail, who, widowed again, in 1760 left much of her estate to them in gratitude.

Samuel served in various town offices, published the usual notices of stopping stolen goods, and was recorded in the *Boston Gazette* of April 19, 1762: "Last Wednesday Night (Apr 14) died here after a few Days Illness of a Violent Fever, in the 57th Year of his Age, Mr. Samuel Edwards, goldsmith: who, for several Years had been one of the Assessors of the Town; and esteemed as a Man of Integrity; exact and faithful in all his Transactions; His Death is lamented as a publick Loss".

He bequeathed to his nephew, Joseph, "a swage for tea and large spoons," yet three years later Joseph was advertising from his uncle's estate "Table and tea spoons large and small," and *tablespoon* has been the usual designation since. He specified the division of his estate after his wife's death. Joseph Edwards, doubtless his brother, the stationer, and his brother-in-law Isaac Smith were executors; his inventory was taken by William Simpkins, Joseph Bradford, and John Coburn.

Samuel Edwards had four distinct punches of his crowned initials mark: *a, b, c,* and *d.* He also used simple marks of his initials in a rectangle *(e)*, in an ellipse *(f)* and in an ellipse with a colon between the initials (not represented in the MFA).

a   b   c

d   e   f

199

199 Plate, c. 1730

D. 5¹⁵⁄₁₆ in.; Wt. 4 oz., 4 dwt.

MARK: *b* almost in center of bottom.

Broad flange very slightly curved, shallow curve to flat bottom, center point in plate.

Engraved on rim with Jackson arms in sheaf and scroll cartouche; crest on opposite rim, both facing center. In semiscript in curve on bottom: *E. Jackson*.

HISTORY: Edward Jackson (1707/8-1757), m. Dorothy Quincy, 1738; their son Jonathan; his daughter Hannah (Mrs. Francis Cabot Lowell), great-grandmother of Guy Lowell.

NOTES: The inventory of Edward Jackson's estate taken in 1757 included "a pr butter plates." The second is still owned in the family. The rarity of small plates need hardly be pointed out (see Dummer, Cat. no. 19).

REFERENCE: *Buhler 1951*, pp. 290-291, fig. 8.

EXHIBITION: *Richmond 1960*, no. 58.

GIFT OF MRS. GUY LOWELL 50.745

200

200 Communion Cup, c. 1740

H. 8 in.; D. of base, 4 in.; D. of lip 4⅛ in.; Wt. 13 oz., 15½ dwt.

MARK: *b* on bowl.

Straight-sided bowl with everted rim; sharp curve to rounded bottom with applied disc below for attachment of cast baluster stem on wrought, slightly domed, splayed, and molded foot with applied strap for strengthening edge. No visible center point. A domed cover (not shown), probably made by Lewis Carey (1798-1834), is scratched with the numerals *IIII*. Scratched on bottom: *IIII*.

Engraved in semiscript in cartouche matching the original one on Cat. no. 88:

Belongs / To the Church / in Lynde Street / Boston.

HISTORY: See *Notes.*

NOTES: An old account book, now lost, of West Church is said to have had the following record: "1739 Nov. 2 To cash paid Mr. Samuel Edwards for 2 silver cups £49.0.7 / To Engraving H. Hall Esqʳ Coat of Arms £1.1.0." The second of the two cups which Edwards fashioned is in the Clearwater Collection, The Metropolitan Museum of Art, New York; the cup on which Edwards engraved the Hall arms is that fashioned in 1737 by his father (Cat. no. 88). A second church record, also now lost, implies a confusion in the dates of this commission: "At a meeting of the Brethren of the Church in New Boston Sept. 22, 1741 appointed for the disposing of some money belonging to the Church, Voted—That with the Money in Church stock two silver cups be purchased for the Communion Table and that the Deacons take the trouble to do this." It is unlikely that the church would have ordered two cups in 1739 and an additional two in 1741. One or the other of these records is seemingly in error. For further comment on these church records, see Cat. no. 159.

REFERENCES: *Buck 1903,* illus. opp. p. 225; *Jones 1913,* p. 87, pl. XXXIII; *Avery 1920,* p. 82; *Ensko 1948,* illus. p. 14; *McLanathan 1956,* illus. p. 49, fig. 1.

EXHIBITIONS: *MFA 1906* (as by Stephen Emery), no. 119, pl. IV; *MFA 1911,* no. 446, pl. 13.

GIFT OF THE WEST BOSTON SOCIETY 92.2847

201

201 Punch Strainer, 1743–1749

H. 1¼ in.; D. of bowl 4¼ in.; L. 10¹³⁄₁₆ in.; Wt. 3 oz., 10½ dwt.

MARK: *c* on bottom of bowl.

Molded everted rim on circular bowl pierced with crosses within a border of scrolls and dots with four shell (?) or fan (?) forms equally spaced. Two cast flat handles, scroll outline, loop and simple tip at end, affixed with ellipse below scroll under rim (one repaired).

Engraved PTH under handle; added under other handle, *J.J.* above *M.L.;* at sides, script *ECW* and *1867.*

HISTORY: Patrick Tracy (b. 1711, Ireland), m. first 1742/3 Hannah Carter (1723/4-1746), second 1749 Hannah Gookin (1723/4-1756), third Mary (1713-1791), widow of Michael Dalton; Hannah (daughter of Patrick and Hannah Gookin Tracy), m. Jonathan Jackson, 1772; their daughter Mary,

m. Henry Lee, June 21, 1809; to Elizabeth Cabot Ware and the donor.
EXHIBITION: *Richmond 1960*, no. 59.
GIFT OF ROBERT TRACY JACKSON 44.775

202

202 Punch Strainer, c. 1746

H. 1⅝₁₆ in.; D. of bowl 4³⁄₁₆ in.; L. 11½₂ in.; Wt. 4 oz., ½ dwt.

MARK: *b* in bowl.
Like Cat. no. 201 with the addition of pierced dots between the crosses.
Engraved ISE under one handle on bowl (not centered) and added, in plane of given initials under handle joining, *1746*.

HISTORY: Isaac and Elizabeth (Storer) Smith, m. 1746; their son William, m. Hannah Carter; their son Thomas, m. Frances Barnard; their daughter Frances Barnard Smith, m. Thomas Davis Townsend; their son William, father of the donors.

NOTES: This appears as a "punch Strainer 4 oz" in Isaac's inventory of 1787. Strainers similar to this and the preceding piece were made by Paul Revere I (Yale University Art Gallery, Garvan Collection); Jacob Hurd (Minneapolis Institute of Arts); Thomas and Samuel Edwards (private collection); James Ridgway (private collection); John Coburn (Clearwater Collection, The Metropolitan Museum of Art, New York); Ebenezer Austin (see *Curtis, 1913*, unnumbered plate following p. 115).

REFERENCE: *Bigelow 1917*, pp. 363-364, fig. 261.

EXHIBITIONS: *MFA 1911*, no. 461; *MFA 1956*, no. 68; *ESU 1960*, no. 53 (illus. pl. 23 was erroneously of the Jackson strainer, Cat. no. 201).

GIFT OF THE MISSES ROSE AND ELIZABETH TOWNSEND 56.671

203 Spoon, c. 1748

L. 8½₂ in.; Wt. 1 oz., 13½ dwt.

MARK: *d* on stem.
Rounded handle forward bent with halfway midrib, long rattail not quite straight on worn elliptical bowl.
Engraved in semiscript on back *The Gift of / H. Storer / to / H. Storer.*
HISTORY: Perhaps Hannah (Hill) Storer (d. 1748) to her granddaughter

203

Hannah (b. 1734), m. 1762 Joshua Green; descended in the family to the donor.

EXHIBITION: *MFA 1911*, no. 468.

BEQUEST OF DR. SAMUEL A. GREEN *19.1387*

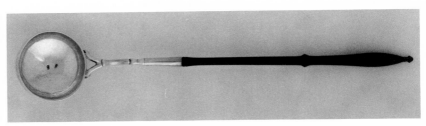

204

204 Ladle, c. 1750

H. of bowl 1⅛ in.; D. of bowl 2⅜ in.; L. 13³⁄₁₆ in. (overall).

MARK: *e* in bowl.

Circular bowl with slight curve below rim, center point on bottom. Handle socket with an open scroll, faceted on top, between forked joinings with turned tips and conical section, molded at scroll, for long turned wooden handle.

Engraved Storer crest on back of bowl toward handle and above center point.

HISTORY: See *Notes* and Cat. no. 137.

NOTES: On a list of plate owned by Ebenezer Storer, Jr., taken January 1, 1775, this appears: "a Ladle S E 1 oz 14 The Crest of Storer on the bottom."

EXHIBITIONS: *Jamestown 1907*, no. 64 (as by S. Emery); *MFA 1911*, no. 486.

GIFT OF WILLIAM STORER EATON *37.265*

205

205 Gold Mourning Ring, 1754

D. ¾ in.-1³⁄₁₆ in. (uneven).

MARK: *e* after engraving before seam (opposite skull).
Raised death's-head one-eighth-inch wide on band.
Engraved on flat inside surface *I. Quincy Ob. 16 May. 1754. AE 18.* commemorating an unknown youth in the family of Anna Quincy
(see Cat. no. 33).
HISTORY: See description above.
GIFT OF THE HEIRS OF ANNA QUINCY THAXTER CUSHING THROUGH
DR. ANNA QUINCY CHURCHILL *24.275*

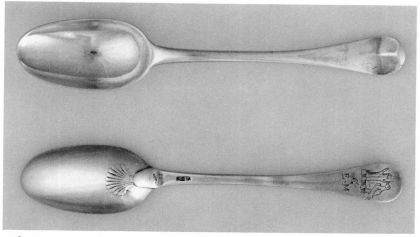

206

206 Pair of Teaspoons, c. 1757

L. 4⁹⁄₁₆ in.; Wt. of *37.266:* 7 dwt.; of *37.267:* 7½ dwt.

MARKS: *e* on one, *f,* on the other.
Rounded tip forward bent, slight ridge, drop and a clearly delineated shell
on back of almost elliptical bowl.
Engraved EGM with Green crest above, on back of handle.
HISTORY: Edward and Mary (Storer) Green, m. April 14, 1757 in Brattle
Street Church, died without issue; her niece Susanna, m. Rev. Asa Eaton;
their granddaughter Georgiana G. Eaton; her brother, the donor.
NOTES: The inventory of the silver belonging to Edward Green (1733-1790)
included only buckles and six teaspoons.
EXHIBITION: *MFA 1911,* no. 485 (as by S. Emery).
GIFT OF WILLIAM STORER EATON *37.266-267*

207

207 Mug, 1758

H. 3¾ in. (inc. handle); D. of base 3³⁄₁₆ in.; D. of lip 2⁷⁄₁₆ in.; Wt. 6 oz., 1½ dwt.

MARK: *a* on bottom.

Straight tapering sides, molded rim and applied baseband (very neat soldering). No center point. Sturdy molded strap handle with slight grip affixed with rounded tip at and below rim and above baseband, rounded lower tip curved.

Engraved with Storer arms and crest on front in cartouche (see Cat. nos. 137 and 168); on bottom *The Gift of Mary Storer. / to / Mary Smith. / 1758.*

HISTORY: Mary (Edwards) Storer, sister of the silversmith; her grandchild Mary (b. March 28, 1757), daughter of Elizabeth (Storer) and Isaac Smith; her niece, Elizabeth, m. Edward Cruft; descended in the family to the donors.

NOTES: A matching cup by the same maker (still owned in the family) is inscribed: *The gift of Mary Storer / to / Mary Storer Junʳ. / 1758* for the daughter of Ebenezer and Elizabeth (Green) Storer, who was born March 11, 1758.

REFERENCE: *Buhler 1951,* p. 291, fig. 10.

EXHIBITION: *Richmond 1960,* no. 57.

GIFT OF THE ESTATES OF THE MISSES EUNICE MCLELLAN AND FRANCES CORDIS CRUFT 42.384

208

208 Gold Mourning Ring, 1760

Attributed to SAMUEL EDWARDS

D. ¾ in.

MARKS: None.

Square faceted crystal over skull in rayed mount; four black enameled lettered scrolls—legend beginning at right of mounting.

Legend reads: · *MRS.AB' / EDWARDS / OB.9.JAN / 1760. AE.81.*

HISTORY: For a mourner at the funeral of Abigail (Fowle) (Smith) Edwards, wife of John Edwards and mother-in-law of Samuel; descended in the family to the donor.

GIFT OF MISS GERTRUDE TOWNSEND *41.853*

209

209 Porringer, c. 1762

H. 1⅞ in.; D. of lip 4⅞ in.; L. of handle 2⅝ in.; Wt. 6 oz., 17 dwt.

MARKS: *c* in bowl below center point, on rim at left of handle, and on back of handle.

Narrow everted rim, curved sides, stepped and domed bottom. Keyhole handle neatly soldered in angle. Center point in bowl, very sharp small one on bottom.

Engraved with Green crest on handle; IGH on back of handle, both toward bowl.

HISTORY: Joshua and Hannah (Storer) Green, m. October 7, 1762 in Brattle Street Church; descended in the family to the donor (see Cat. no. 138).

NOTES: The maker had died suddenly in April. The engraving is attributed to Joseph Edwards.

EXHIBITION: *MFA 1911,* no. 449.

BEQUEST OF DR. SAMUEL A. GREEN *19.1388*

JOSEPH GOLDTHWAITE
1706–1780

JOSEPH GOLDTHWAITE, son of John and Sarah (Hopkins) Goldthwaite, was born November 11, 1706, and married Martha Lewis in 1727/8. Seven children were born to the couple. In the *Boston News-Letter* of April 15/22, 1731 appeared: "Joseph Goldthwait, goldsmith, is removed from Mr. Burrill's shop to the House adjoining to the Sign of the Red Lyon, where any Gentleman or Woman may be supplied with any sort of Pocket Instrument Cases at a very Reasonable Rate." This had led to a belief that he was an apprentice of Samuel Burrill, but a book on the family, published by Charlotte Goldthwaite in 1899, discloses that Mr. Burrill was Joseph's wife's grandfather, and a sailmaker. Goldthwaite's silver for the New Brick Church in Boston was assigned in 1911 and by E. Alfred Jones to Joseph Glidden who has since been found to have been a shipwright. Joseph was mentioned as a gentleman in 1744 and is thought perhaps to have gone into innkeeping. He held town offices and was Captain in the Seige of Louisburg. He died in Weston, Massachusetts; sales of his estate were recorded in 1782 and 1783.

Only one mark *(a)* is credited to Goldthwaite: his initials, crowned, with a pellet between, a cross below, in a shield.

a

210

210 Tankard, c. 1760

H. 8⅝ in. (inc. finial); D. of base 5¼ in.; D. of lip 4⁄₁₆ in.; Wt. 26 oz., 16½ dwt.

MARK: *a* at left of handle.

Tapering sides with incised lines below molded rim, applied midband and rather deep molded baseband seamed at back. Stepped and domed molded lid (cracked) with turned finial and flange turned down (cut at back for handle and at front for spout) with bezel inside. Scroll thumbpiece, repaired and reversed; plain hinge plate extends to five-part hinge with molded and shaped plate on shoulder of hollow scroll handle; slight body drop at upper joining of handle; disc at lower joining, the handle tip a disc placed high on the tip with a vent slot beneath. Large spout added at front has been removed; strainer holes were cut but the rim is intact. Center point on bottom.

Engraved + *c* + over + *N* + *H* on handle. Scratched on bottom: *28-10*.

HISTORY: Unknown.

BEQUEST OF CHARLES HITCHCOCK TYLER *32.373*

JEFFREY LANG
1707–1758

H. W. Belknap in *Artists and Craftsmen of Essex County* writes that
Jeffrey Lang was born on January 16, 1707 in Salem, Massachusetts;
married Hannah Symmes on August 24, 1732; and probably died in
1758. Elsewhere this date of his death is given as definite. Jeffrey
had three sons, all of whom followed his craft: Richard (1733-1820),
Nathaniel (1736-1826), and Edward (1742-1826). Of Edward, the
Reverend William Bentley wrote: "June 1793 . . . We then passed to
the East School, which had been under Mr. Lang ever since it was
opened. It was formerly the fullest school, & has had several assistants
. . . . Mr. Lang, the Master, is a most worthy man. He was a Silversmith by profession, but reduced in his circumstances, he accepted this
School, in which he does not succeed to the public wishes. . . ."

Lang had a large mark *(a)* with his initial and surname with a pellet
between; his initials mark *(b)* by its position on a very narrow strainer
spoon handle is here incomplete. He has been credited with a surname
mark also.

a   *b*

211

211 Salver, c. 1730

H. 2³⁄₁₆ in.; D. of base 3³⁄₈ in.; D. of dish 8¹⁵⁄₁₆ in.; Wt. 9 oz., 18 dwt.

MARK: *a* near rim (strange punch, some letters raised, others scraped).
Circular, edge curved and everted with very thin molding applied. Center

point in dish with very lightly engraved daisy pattern within three circles. Trumpet foot with narrow flange for fastening, splayed quarter-round molding with narrow edge.

Engraved under the dish: *MB* and in script: *MTP*.

HISTORY: Mary Barton, m. June 27, 1734, Bezaleel Toppan (Harvard 1722); their daughter, Mary Toppan (1744-1817), m. Benjamin Pickman; see Cat. no. 39.

REFERENCES: *Avery 1930*, p. 70; *Clark [Buhler] 1931*, p. 50, illus. p. 48; *Ellis 1961*, p. 27.

GIFT OF MR. AND MRS. DUDLEY LEAVITT PICKMAN 31.234

212

212 Salver, c. 1730

Attributed to JEFFREY LANG

H. 1¹³⁄₁₆ in.; D. of base 2¹³⁄₁₆ in.; D. of dish 5¼ in. (uneven); Wt. 4 oz., 12 dwt.

MARKS: None.

Circular with very slight rim, perhaps added molding; foot not as on the Jeffrey Lang salver (Cat. no. 211) but relatively heavier and in one sweep to edge, small flange for fastening. Daisy pattern, lightly engraved and in-complete, in a single circle around center point.

HISTORY: Descended in the family of the donors.

NOTES: The attribution is based on Lang's work for the family (see Cat. nos. 211-215). This salver is not in Benjamin Pickman's 1819 inventory, but could have been given to a child before he died.

REFERENCES: *Clark [Buhler] 1931*, p. 50, illus. p. 48; *Ellis 1961*, p. 27.

GIFT OF MR. AND MRS. DUDLEY LEAVITT PICKMAN 31.233

213 Spoon, c. 1730

L. 8¹⁄₁₆ in.; Wt. 1 oz., 18 dwt.

MARK: *a* on back of handle near the bowl.

Thick stem with upturned rounded tip ridged; double drop and thin rattail on almost elliptical bowl.

Engraved T͟B͟M on back of handle.

HISTORY: Thomas and Mary (Willoughby) Barton, m. 1710; descended in the family to the donors (see Cat. no. 39).

213

NOTES: When given this was one of a set of six; Benjamin Pickman's inventory listed "10 large spoons, 29 small do," and "37 large spoons, 20 teaspoons."

REFERENCES: *Bigelow 1917*, p. 268, fig. 168; *Clark [Buhler] 1931*, p. 50, illus. p. 48; *Ellis 1961*, pp. 25, 27.

GIFT OF MR. AND MRS. DUDLEY LEAVITT PICKMAN 31.235

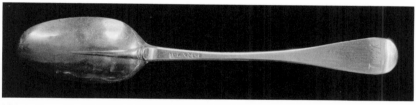

214

214 Porringer Spoon, c. 1735

L. 5⅞ in.; Wt. 13 dwt.

MARK: *a* on back of handle near bowl.

Stem chamfered, ridged on front; double drop and long rattail on back of almost elliptical bowl.

Engraved *WT* on back of handle.

HISTORY: Willoughby Toppan, firstborn child of Bezaleel and Mary (Barton) Toppan (baptized November 9, 1735; buried May 10, 1760); descended in the family to the donors (see Cat. no. 39).

REFERENCES: *Clark [Buhler] 1931*, p. 50 (described as teaspoon); *Ellis 1961*, p. 27.

GIFT OF MR. AND MRS. DUDLEY LEAVITT PICKMAN 31.236

215

215 Strainer Spoon, 1735–1750

L. 5¾ in.; Wt. 4½ dwt.

MARK: *b* (incomplete) on back of handle near bowl.

Circular stem, slight lines near pointed tip, flattens near bowl; rounded drop on oval bowl, its outer edge engraved in a band of stylized leaf pattern, row of shaped holes with lined engraving inside; shaped holes in center with simpler engraving.

HISTORY: Descended in the family to the donors (see Cat. no. 39).

NOTES: Marked strainer spoons are rare, doubtless due to the narrowness of their stems.

REFERENCES: *Bigelow 1917*, p. 278, fig. 180; *Clark [Buhler] 1931*, pp. 49-50, (illus. described as mote spoon); *Ellis 1961*, p. 27.

GIFT OF MR. AND MRS. DUDLEY LEAVITT PICKMAN 31.237

RUFUS GREENE
1707–1777

Born May 30, 1707, Rufus Greene was the second son of Nathaniel
and Anne (Gold) Greene, who were married in 1703. His brother
Benjamin (1712-1776) also was a goldsmith. The diary of his son
William indicates that Rufus was apprenticed to William Cowell, who
was one of the witnesses to his grandmother Gold's will in 1711.
In 1728 the estate of the Hon. John Menzies paid Rufus £ 27-18
for mourning rings. In the same year, he married Katharine Stanbridge, and in 1733 an advertisement of stolen spoons mentions "the
Maker's name, R. Greene, at length" indicating perhaps the newness
of a surname mark. His wife died in 1768 and was survived by seven
children, two of whom, including Katherine, who had married John
Amory, predeceased their father, whose will was written in 1772 and
probated in January, 1778. The inventory of his estate mentioned a
house occupied by the goldsmith Benjamin Pierpont; his silver was
itemized but not valued: "1 tankard 3 Porringers 2 Cans 1 Caster / 1
Cup 6 table & 15 tea Spoons 1 Sugar Tongs / 1 Creampot 2 knives
& 1 fork." The tankard was that by David Jesse (Cat. no. 74); one
of his porringers is still owned by descendants and was exhibited
in London in 1960 (ESU 1960, no. 17).

Greene's two marks, (a) his initial and surname, with pellet between,
in a cartouche, as mentioned above; and (b) his initials in a cartouche, are together on the small pepper box (Cat. no. 216). A small
mark (c) is of similar initials in a rectangle.

a   b   c

216

216 Pepper Box, c. 1728

H. 3⅞ in. (inc. finial); W. of base 2¹⁄₁₆ in.; Wt. 3 oz.

MARKS: *a* on bottom and *b* at left of handle.

Octagonal, seamed under handle, flaring at base with applied bottom forming tiny molding. Applied molded bands above each handle joining, upper band forming bezel. Domed cover flattened under turned finial broad at base, pierced in stars with line of shaped holes above and below, molded edge and applied vertical molding. Scroll handle, both tips small cylinders, broad at upper joining, applied grip on shoulder with long rattail over curve, slight scroll above lower joining.

Engraved R$\overset{G}{\underset{*}{}}$K on bottom, the upright strokes crosshatched.

HISTORY: Rufus and Katharine (Stanbridge) Greene, m. December 10, 1728; descended in the family to Martha (Codman) Karolik (see Cat. no. 74).

NOTES: Despite the fact that Rufus Greene's inventory called this a caster, the term pepper box was more frequently used for a piece of this form (see Cat. no. 61, by Coney, and Cat. no. 221, by Samuel Gray).

REFERENCES: Hipkiss, *MFA Bulletin,* no. 235 (1941), illus. p. 86; *Hipkiss 1941,* p. 228, no. 155; Norman-Wilcox, *Antiques,* Part 2 (1944), p. 82, no. 20.

M. AND M. KAROLIK COLLECTION 39.195

217 Pair of Casters, c. 1730

31.414: H. 4⅜ in. (inc. finial); D. of base 1⅝ in.; Wt. 2 oz., 10½ dwt.
31.415: H. 4½ in. (inc. finial); D. of base 1½ in.; Wt. 2 oz., 12½ dwt.

MARKS: *31.414: b* on bottom, *31.415:* crosshatched bottom, lacks mark and earliest initials.

Slightly curving seamed sides, rounded base on circular splayed molded foot with strengthening band (badly bent on 31.414); no center point; applied molding at joining and rim. Straight sides of seamed cover engraved with six panels of diamond design, small darts between, and a hole pierced in almost every diamond; applied molding forms bezel. Slightly domed top has turned finial, engraved rayed design from its base, and row of circular piercings.

Engraved sᴛʀ below joint molding; sᴛʀ below rim at right of seam; ᴍʜʙ over *1878* opposite. On 31.415 the *B* is over the seam, the sᴛʀ opposite but the original initials are lacking. Could this crosshatched lower bowl be a replacement?

HISTORY: Samuel and Ruth (Chapin) Jackson, m. August 27, 1722; their daughter Ruth, m. Simon Tufts, June 1, 1747; their daughter Lucy, m. Benjamin Hall, Jr. (1754-1807); see Cat. no. 75.

NOTES: Benjamin Hall, Jr. left "1 sett of Casters $3" and "1 Do [silver] creampot."

REFERENCES: *Bigelow 1917*, pp. 322-323; fig. 227; *Buhler 1947*, pp. 38-39, fig. 12.

EXHIBITION: *MFA 1911*, no. 535.

BEQUEST OF HENRY W. CUNNINGHAM 31.414-415

217

218

218 Box with Ivory Lid, c. 1750

H. ⅜ in.; W. 1¾ in.; L. 2¼ in.

MARK: *b* on bottom.

Elliptical straight sides seamed at end fit within the quite thick flat bottom. Edge molded. The cover is very yellowed ivory flat-carved with the "Flight into Egypt" set within a molded rim and broken at seam. Box contains colored cardboard discs of uncertain age and usage.

Engraved below maker's mark: *II;* added across top: *Jany 1st 1816;* in slightly curving script below: *by her grandmother* with *J.A. to J.E.C.* beneath in block letters; in script: *5th generation it has pass'd,* both in straight lines (Jane Austin to Jane Eliza Chapman).

HISTORY: James Ivers, m. Hannah Trecothick, 1753; their daughter Jane, m. Benjamin Austin; their granddaughter Jane Eliza Coolidge, m. Dummer Rogers Chapman; descended in the family to the donor.

NOTES: Various subjects were used for boxes. The *Boston Gazette* in 1752 carried a notice: "Lost . . . an oval silver snuff box, the cover Gilt inside and out, and the Rivell of the heathen gods in raised work on the cover."

GIFT OF MISS EMILY D. CHAPMAN *Res. 25.23*

DAVID NORTHEY
c. 1710–1778

In 1732 David Northey was married in Lynn to Miriam Bassett. Their eldest son William followed his father's craft; six children and his wife survived him. He styled himself a goldsmith but his inventory shows general merchandise, "watchmakers Tools," and a large quantity of pewter, "Pewter Tools," and "1 pair of Goldsmiths Bellows." His initials mark *(a)* consists of his initials in a rectangle; his mark of *D. NORTHEE* is on a porringer in the Clearwater Collection, The Metropolitan Museum of Art, New York, but his will was written and probated as Northey.

a

219

219 Gold Mourning Ring, 1748

D. ⅝ in. (inside); outside ¾ in.

MARK: *a* between seam and beginning of inscription.
Plain band with very slightly curved surface.
Engraved inside: *E · H · Ob · Aug^t · 19 · 1748 AE · 34* (AE conjoined).
HISTORY: Unknown.
REFERENCE: *Hipkiss 1943*, p. 66.

THE PHILIP LEFFINGWELL SPALDING COLLECTION. GIVEN IN HIS MEMORY BY KATHERINE AMES SPALDING AND PHILIP SPALDING, OAKES AMES SPALDING, HOBART AMES SPALDING 42.250

SAMUEL GRAY
working 1732–1750

SAMUEL GRAY is said to have been a nephew of the goldsmiths Samuel (1684-1713) and John Gray (1692-1720) who were born in Boston and worked in New London, but the early deaths of his uncles preclude any influence on their nephew. He was probably born to Joseph and Rebecca Gray of Boston on January 19, 1710/11. The Thwing Catalogue at the Massachusetts Historical Society lists him for a deed in 1732/3; Ensko records that he bought land for a shop in Boston in 1732, the deed witnessed by William Simpkins and Basil Dixwell. Very little of his work has been published. The Samuel Gray recorded in Suffolk Probate Court was a baker and was of an earlier date.

A small mark of his surname in a rectangle (a) is on the MFA pieces; a mark of his initial and surname has also been recorded.

a

220

220 Porringer, c. 1742

H. 1⅞ in.; D. of lip 5⅜ in.; L. of handle 2¹¹⁄₁₆ in.; Wt. 7 oz., 12½ dwt.

MARK: *a* in bowl near center point.

Slightly everted rim, curved sides, stepped and domed bottom, keyhole handle. Engraved SAM on handle toward bowl.

HISTORY: Silas Atkins, mariner, m. Mary Gyles, March 30, 1742; their son Silas, m. Martha Howland, 1770 (granddaughter of John Burt, goldsmith); descended in the family to the donor.

NOTES: The younger Silas was also a mariner but was called a merchant in 1781. He was administrator for the estate of his father, Captain Silas Atkins, probated in 1779. This was one of three porringers listed among his plate, which was valued at £160-10 in a total estate of £3321-12-6.

REFERENCE: Hipkiss, *MFA Bulletin,* No. 234 (1941), p. 61, illus. p. 59.

GIFT OF MISS AMELIA PEABODY 41.63

221 Pepper Box, c. 1742

H. 3¾ in. (inc. finial); W. of base 1⁵⁄₁₆ in.; Wt. 2 oz., 9 dwt.

MARK: *a* on bottom.

Octagonal with straight sides seamed under handle; applied band near rim to form bezel; flaring and slightly molded base with flat bottom extending to form edge (base repaired). Domed cover (dented) with shaped piercings and turned finial soldered through, has molded edge and vertical band seamed at back to repeat contour at base. Scroll handle with slight grip affixed below upper bead with longer scroll tip above lower joining.

Engraved SAM on bottom. Stars on front panel of body and cover to indicate proper closure.

HISTORY: Captain Silas Atkins' inventory, 1779, listed one pepper box (see Cat. no. 220).

REFERENCES: Hipkiss, *MFA Bulletin,* no. 234 (1941), p. 61, illus. p. 59; Norman-Wilcox, *Antiques,* Part 2 (1944), p. 82, no. 19.

EXHIBITIONS: *Richmond 1960,* no. 62.

GIFT OF MISS AMELIA PEABODY 41.65

221

222

222 Creampot, c. 1750

H. 3⅝ in. (inc. handle); Wt. 3 oz., 9 dwt.

MARK: *a* on bottom toward center point.

Bulbous body, short narrow neck, scalloped rim, small drawn spout. Pad joinings for three triple-toed angled feet. Triple scroll handle affixed over rim, grip on shoulder, forked tip with small upper scroll.

Engraved in double-lined circle on front, in script with faint guidelines; *The Gift of / The Honb̧e / J:Hancock, Esq̧ŗ / to Lydia Bowes;* engraved on bottom *LB.*

HISTORY: Early history unknown; Lydia Bowes (b. 1749), daughter of Rev. Nicholas and Lucy (Hancock) Bowes, m. Rev. Phineas Whitney (Harvard 1759), April 19, 1770; their second son, Rev. Nicholas Bowes Whitney; descended in the family to Lucretia Fall Whitney (1839-1922).

NOTES: John Hancock was Lydia's considerably older first cousin.

GIFT OF GEORGE P. NASON IN MEMORY OF LUCRETIA FALL WHITNEY 61.114

JOHN BLOWERS
1710–1748

Born in 1710, John Blowers was the son of Rev. Thomas Blowers (Harvard 1695) and Emma (Eliot), widow of Andrew Woodbury. His father was the second pastor of the First Church in Beverly; his brother Pyam (Harvard 1721) was a merchant who married Jerusha Fayerweather in 1732. Blowers married Sarah Salter in 1735; their son Sampson Salter Blowers was junior counsel in 1770 in defense with Adams and Quincy of the British soldiers concerned with the Boston Massacre. He later became Chief Justice of Nova Scotia. His only daughter married William Blowers Bliss, the son of the Chief Justice of New Brunswick (see Cat. no. 328). A porringer and cann (*MFA 1911*, nos. 48 and 49), a salver (Yale University Art Gallery, Garvan Collection), a strainer and pepper box (private collection) and a now lost cann of his workmanship are known to us.

Two advertisements quoted by George Francis Dow from the *Boston Gazette* mention lost or stolen silver with a maker's mark of *I.Blowers;* his few published pieces, however, bear simply the mark *(a)* of his surname in semiscript in a long oval.

a

223

223 Tankard, c. 1740

H. 8³⁄₁₆ in. (inc. finial); D. of base 5¼ in. (uneven); D. of lip 4-4³⁄₁₆ in.; Wt. 23 oz., 7 dwt.

MARK: *a* at left of handle.

Straight tapering sides, incised lines below thickened rim, applied midband and molded baseband (bent). Stepped molded cover, flattened on top with turned bell-form finial, incised lines on flange turned over rim (cut for handle and dented at left front), bezel missing. Modeled scroll thumbpiece; plain inner plate for five-part hinge; molded shaped drop on shoulder of scroll handle; rounded drop at upper joining, disc at lower; disc tip with vent slot below. Center points on bottom and in lid.

Engraved *EF* on handle.

HISTORY: See *Notes*. Descended in the Storer family to the donor.

NOTES: In Ebenezer Storer, Jr.'s list of plate, taken in 1785 when he had received silver from Seth and Mary Storer, this piece is included without explanation of its initials. It seems significant, however, that one of the witnesses of Seth Storer's will was Edmund Fowle.

EXHIBITIONS: *Jamestown 1907*, no. 109; *MFA 1911*, no. 50.

GIFT OF FRANCIS S. EATON 47.1487

THOMAS SKINNER
1712/13–1761

H. W. Belknap records that Thomas Skinner was born on March 8, 1712/13 in Boston and that he married first Sarah Caswell of Charlestown, and second the widow Hannah (Kemball) Felton of Marblehead on December 21, 1758. He died in Marblehead in 1761. The published Boston records, in marriage intentions, give: "Thomas Skinner of Boston & Sarah Casswell of Charlestown, Aug. 1, 1734," which would indicate working years in Boston.

The initials mark is listed both in a rectangle *(a)* and in an ellipse; his surname in capitals and in capitals and lowercase are also cited.

a

224

224 Gold Mourning Ring, 1750

D. ⅞ in.

MARK: *a* at end of inscription.
Very worn death's-head with trace of wings on slightly curved surface; flat inside.
Engraved in semiscript: *I • Leg = ob^t 9^t = Feby 1750 -AE^t 25 -*
HISTORY: Unknown.
BEQUEST OF MAXIM KAROLIK 64.856

JOHN JAGGER
1713–1764

Born on December 28, 1713, John Jagger was the son of John and Mary (Tyhurst) Jagger, who were married by Dr. Cotton Mather on May 10, 1711. Jagger married Sibella, widow of William Jones, goldsmith, of Marblehead in 1735 and is said to have moved to Boston in 1739. He died prior to her death on December 24, 1764.

This piece is the only one known by him, its mark *(a)*, of his initial and surname in slanting capitals in a rectangle, is clear.

a

225 Tankard, c. 1738

H. 7⅞ in. (inc. finial); D. of base 5¼-5⅜ in.; D. of lip 4¹⁄₁₆ in.;
Wt. 22 oz., 11 dwt.

MARKS: *a* at each side of handle and on bottom.

Straight tapering sides, incised lines below molded rim, applied bead midband, and molded splayed baseband. Flattened dome on stepped and molded cover, flange turned down and cut for a handle and a shorter width at front than the removed spout required. Turned finial; scroll thumbpiece with grooved support; five-part hinge, forward plate repaired. Turned drop below hinge plate on scroll handle (resoldered around rounded drop and disc at lower joining), mask tip. Center points on bottom and in lid. Handle badly broken under mask, where there is a wide if not enlarged vent hole.

Engraved below drop on handle SBM with device between initials on applied square plaque with incised lines at edge and wiggle-work framework; *oz* over *22-15* engraved in very small figures on bottom.

HISTORY: Simon and Mary (Strahan Hills) Bradstreet, m. 1738 in Marblehead; descended in the family to Frederick Silsbee Whitwell, who sold it to the donor.

NOTES: The spout, added in a deep triangle below molding of rim, was removed by Joseph Sharrock in 1953.

GIFT IN MEMORY OF T. JEFFERSON NEWBOLD 53.382

225

WILLIAM SWAN
1715/16–1774

On January 5, 1743, William Swan was married in King's Chapel to Levinah Keyes, and the births of three children to them in 1745, 1749, and 1751 are in the Boston records. Their fourth child was born in 1754 in Worcester, where William was to dwell for another twenty years. In 1749 the silversmith had been commissioned to make the large two-handled covered cup presented by the Province of Massachusetts to Colonel Benjamin Pickman for his services with the Louisburg expedition, and this cup remains his most impressive piece. In Worcester, Swan sang in the Old South Church (see Louisa Dresser, *Worcester Art Museum Annual*, Vol. 1 [1935-1936], pp. 49-57), suffered the usual advertised robbery, and served in various town offices. The *Boston News-Letter* carried the notice of his death, April 18, 1774, "a Man of a very respectable Character."

The lettering of his surname in a cartouche *(a)* is also known in a rectangle; a third mark shows his initial and surname in the cartouche of this one, and a fourth mark is given of his surname in capitals in a rectangle.

a

226 Set of Three Porringers,
1750–1755

H. 1⅞ in.; D. of lip 5⅜ in.; L. of handles 2¹¹⁄₁₆ in.; Wt. of *39.190*, 7 oz., 18 dwt.; of *39.191*, 8 oz., 4 dwt.; of *39.192*, 8 oz., 8 dwt.

MARK: *a* on back of handle of each.

Narrow everted rims, curved sides, stepped and domed bottoms, center points in bowls and on bottoms (except in *39.192*). Cast keyhole handles. Engraved *K ∴ C* away from bowl on each.

HISTORY: Katharine Chandler (1735-1791), m. c. 1755 Levi Willard (1727-1775); their daughter Katharine (1761-1831), m. John Amory, Jr. (1759-1832), January 15, 1792; their daughter Catherine Willard Amory (b. March 24, 1796), m. Henry Codman (1789-1853), grandfather of Martha Codman Karolik, to whom the pieces descended.

NOTES: Porringers in greater number than a pair are very rare (Revere II's daybooks record none). Tradition erred in assigning the several pieces by Swan to the Codman ancestors of the donor, née Martha Catharine Codman.

226

The mistake is readily explained by the unusual change in the spelling of Katharine (Chandler) Willard's name. In the Chandler genealogy, where she appears as the youngest surviving child of the fourth John Chandler of Worcester, and in her husband's will, written in 1771 and probated in 1775, she was Katharine; but on her funeral ring (Cat. no. 278) sixteen years later, Catherine. The three porringers are listed in Levi Willard's inventory.

REFERENCE: *Hipkiss 1941*, p. 239, no. 166.

M. AND M. KAROLIK COLLECTION *39.190-192*

227 Creampot, c. 1755

H. 3⅜ in.; Wt. 3 oz., 1½ dwt.

MARK: *a* above center point (double) on bottom.

Bulbous body, everted scalloped rim, and short drawn lip. Three triangular pad joinings (one beneath handle) above rounded knees and notched pad feet. Double scroll cast handle with slight grip, affixed under (broken) rim and crudely soldered above forked scroll tip.

Engraved *KC* on front; *J.W* on bottom below center point.

HISTORY: Katharine Chandler Willard; her second son, John (b. 1758), who died unmarried; presumably thence to his sister or niece.

NOTES: Levi Willard's inventory includes this "1 cream pott." See similar creampot by Swan (now in the Harrington Collection, Dartmouth College: *Bigelow 1917*, fig. 301) for longer lip and slightly higher handle in the form which this one probably was originally. It has its owner's initials on the bottom.

M. AND M. KAROLIK COLLECTION *39.188*

227

228 Cup, c. 1755

Attributed to WILLIAM SWAN

H. 3½ in. (inc. handles); D. of base 2 in. (uneven); D. of lip 2½ in.;
Wt. 3 oz., 2½ dwt.

MARKS: None.
Cylindrical body, no center point, slightly flaring rim; sides tapering to
applied molded baseband (crude solder). Molded strap handle with curved
tips repaired at both joinings and bent out of original contour.

Engraved *KC* on bottom. The device between the initials is different
from that on other pieces.

HISTORY: See Cat. no. 226.

NOTES: The attribution to Swan is based on the characteristic simplicity of
the piece and on the fact that he made the other known pieces for Katharine
Chandler. This cup is probably the one in Levi Willard's inventory.

REFERENCE: *Hipkiss 1941*, p. 242, no. 169 (as unknown maker and as for
Katherine Codman).

M. AND M. KAROLIK COLLECTION *39.189*

228

229

229 Cann, 1755–1760

H. of body 5½ in.; D. of base 3⁷⁄₁₆-3½ in. (uneven); D. of lip 3⁷⁄₁₆ in.;
Wt. 13 oz., 13 dwt.

MARK: *a* above center point on bottom.

Bulbous body, incised line below slightly flaring rim, on cast molded splayed
foot. Double scroll cast handle, slight grip, vent in upper scroll, extension
for upper joining, disc at lower, where solder is poor; flattened sides on scroll
tips, lower one forked.

Engraved *KC* below grip on handle. Scratched on bottom *27-18-0*.

HISTORY: See Cat. no. 226.

NOTES: Levi Willard's inventory included "2 p*ᵗ* Kans." The weight on the
bottom of this one must have been for the pair.

REFERENCE: *Hipkiss 1941*, p. 238, no. 165.

M. AND M. KAROLIK COLLECTION *39.187*

WILLIAM HOMES
1716/17–1783

The son of Captain Robert and Mary (Franklin) Homes, William
Homes was a nephew of Benjamin Franklin. His marriage to Rebecca
Dawes on April 24, 1740 was recorded under the spelling of Holmes,
but his maker's mark indicates his preference. Four children were
recorded to them, including the namesake who was to follow his
father's craft (see *Appendix*). He was a member of the Artillery Company in 1747 and rose to be Captain. He was a member of the Old
South Church, of which his wife's family were among the founders, and
in 1757 served on a committee there to obtain subscriptions toward
printing Rev. Thomas Prince's revised New England version of the
Psalms. Homes died in 1783, but his will is not recorded in Suffolk
Probate Court.

His surname mark *(a)* on Cat. no. 231, italic capitals in a rectangle,
substantiates the attribution of the mark *(b)* of his initials, a pellet
between, in a rectangle, which appears on the same piece. The initials
mark *c* in the lettering of *b* with upper serifs joined has long been given
to him; there were other goldsmiths with these initials, including his
son who may have used his punches.

    a   *b*   *c*

230

230 Child's Porringer, c. 1750

H. 1⁷⁄₁₆ in.; D. of lip 4⁹⁄₁₆ in.; L. of handle 2½ in.; Wt. 5 oz.

MARK: *c* on back of handle.

Sharply everted narrow rim, curved sides (battered), stepped and domed bottom, center point inside and outside.Keyhole handle with shield cutting in center at rim, very neatly soldered.

Engraved *MC / to / DS* in decorated script around shield opening.

HISTORY: Unknown.

NOTES: The shield-shaped hole in the area commonly reserved for initials is unusual. The first so-called keyhole handles had paired arches near the bowl (see Cat. no. 116).

BEQUEST OF CHARLES HITCHCOCK TYLER 32.384

231 Punch Bowl, 1763

H. 4⁷⁄₈ in.; D. of base 5¼ in.; D. of lip 9⁷⁄₈ in.; Wt. 32 oz., 17½ dwt.

MARKS: *a* below center point over *b*.

Plain bowl, very slightly flaring rim, sides curve to almost flat bottom on cast circular molded splayed foot. Center point on bottom.

Engraved with Dawes arms in scroll and foliate cartouche with drapery below on one side. Inscription in several letterings on other side, within engraved and bright-cut medallion with instruments of war and British flags: *The Gift / of the Field Officers and / Captains of the Regiment / of the Town of BOSTON. to / THOMAS DAWES Esqʳ / for his past Services as Ad- / jutant to said Re- / giment Sept. 13 / 1763.*

231

231

HISTORY: Thomas Dawes (d. 1808); his grandson Thomas Dawes; descended in the family to the donor.

NOTES: Dawes served as Senator, Moderator, and a member of the Governor's Council. He was a builder and worked with the renowned architect Charles Bulfinch. His will, probated on January 2, 1809, left "to my Grandson Thomas Dawes Tertius after the decease of his Grandmother Dawes my Gold Watch and Silver Bowl, which was presented to me by the Officers of the Boston Regiment." Thomas Dawes was a cousin of the goldsmith's wife.

REFERENCES: *Paull 1913*, pp. 22-23, illus.; *Bigelow 1917*, pp. 421-422, fig. 311; *Jones 1928*, pp. 29-30; *Avery 1930*, pp. 152, 339; Buhler, *Antiques*, no. 6 (1945), p. 349, inscription fig. 6; *Ensko 1948*, illus. p. 51; *Phillips 1949*, p. 96; *Wenham 1949*, p. 77, illus. pp. 224-225; *McLanathan 1956*, pp. 52-53, fig. 4; *Comstock 1958*, p. 90, fig. 18.

EXHIBITIONS: *MFA 1911*, no. 566, pl. 18; *Chicago 1949*, no. 178, illus. no. 120; *London 1954*; *Presentation Silver 1955*, illus. p. 6; *Minneapolis 1956*, no. 233, fig. 31; *Richmond 1960*, no. 69; *ESU 1960*, no. 56, pl. 14; *R.I. 1965*, no. 97, fig. 55.

GIFT OF MRS. AMBROSE DAWES IN MEMORY OF HER HUSBAND 13.381

JOSIAH AUSTIN
1719–1780

Baptized in Charlestown on January 24, 1719, Josiah Austin married
Mary Phillips on August 25, 1743. Records show that he was a
landowner in Charlestown, Massachusetts until 1765. Initials (IA)
marks attributed to him are on pieces which seem too early to be his
(see biography of John Allen and Cat. nos. 75 and 76; also *MFA 1956*,
no. 1).

An initials mark with a pellet was used during his brief partnership
with Samuel Minott. His script mark in a rectangle *(a)* has an initial *I*;
another uses all capitals with *J* and a pellet.

a

232

232 Papboat, c. 1750

H. of body 1⅜ in.; L. 6 in. (inc. handle); Wt. 2 oz., 8½ dwt.

MARK: *a* in bowl at center point.

Sides curve to almost flat bottom, lip drawn but not quite centered. Loop handle, flat beneath, affixed with curved tips at back. Three legs with molded pad joinings and feet. One leg is under handle, as in Parker sauceboats (see Cat. no. 294).

Engraved in late script on side *S. R. 1750. / I.D.R. 1836;* scratched on bottom *SR 1750.*

HISTORY: Early history unknown; Mrs. Henry R. Dalton by 1907.

NOTES: Other published papboats include one without handles or feet by Paul Revere (private collection); two without handles or feet by Thomas Edwards (Amherst College Collection and The R. W. Norton Art Gallery, Shreveport, Louisiana); two with handles by John Ewan of Charleston, South Carolina.

EXHIBITIONS *Jamestown 1907,* no. 123; *MFA 1911,* no. 24, pl. 3 (as "small sauceboat").

GIFT OF MISS ELIZABETH L. DALTON IN MEMORY OF HER BROTHER, HENRY R. DALTON 47.1344

JOSEPH CLARK
working 1737–1770 (?)

JOSEPH CLARK appears as a maker of mourning rings for the estate of Seth Parker in the Suffolk Probate Court in 1750. This gives a first name to the long-listed I Clark who fashioned silver for churches in Lynn and Saugus, Massachusetts, presumably at the time of Theophilus Burrill's bequest in 1737. His own estate is not recorded in Suffolk Probate Court.

He used his initial and surname in capitals, with pellet between, in a rectangle *(a)*. His surname in a cartouche is found with *a* on a teapot in the Rhode Island School of Design. A possible third mark *(b)* is on Cat. no. 234.

a

b

233

233 Teaspoon, c. 1740

L. 4⅝ in.; Wt. 6 dwt.

MARK: *a* (worn) on back of stem.
Rounded handle forward bent, rounded drop and shell on back of bowl.
Engraved *WE* with serifs on back of tip.
HISTORY: Traditionally, engraved for Mary Wood and Thomas Edes, but this would be an unusual use of surnames.
GIFT OF MR. AND MRS. HENRY HERBERT EDES 36.58

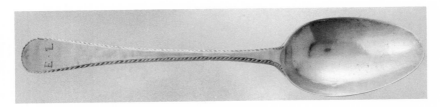

234

234 Tablespoon, c. 1770

Attributed to JOSEPH CLARK

L. 8½ in.; Wt. 1 oz., 18 dwt.

MARK: *CLARK* preceded by a pellet in a cartouche, the initial preceding the pellet partially obliterated.

Rounded handle backward bent; feathered or bright-cut edge; rounded drop and carefully delineated shell on oval bowl.

Engraved *EL* on front of handle.

HISTORY: Unknown.

NOTES: The shape of the cartouche and the position of the remaining letters in it lead us to attribute this piece to Joseph Clark.

GIFT OF MR. AND MRS. WILLIAM BELTRAN DE LAS CASAS *30.741*

ANDREW OLIVER
1724–1776

ANDREW OLIVER, jeweler (André), was born on September 20, 1724, son of Anthoine and Mary (Johonnot ?) Olivier, in Annapolis Royal, Nova Scotia. His older brothers and sisters had been born in Boston. He was in Ipswich, but the only record of him in that town's publications seems to be in 1750 when "formerly admitted to the First Church here in full communion" he was dismissed to the South Church in Boston. In the records of the baptism of his son in the Old South Church, his wife was given as Susan Boyer, daughter of the jeweler James and sister of Daniel Boyer (q.v.). There is a confusion of Andrew Olivers in Boston Records at this period, but the anglicization of his name removes him from the well-known family. In 1753 Andrew Oliver jeweler was so specified as one of the Clerks of the Market for the ensuing year. In 1776, Ezekiel Price's diary records "Feb. 17 Heard at Watertown of the death of Mr. Andrew Oliver jeweller." This is not amplified in the published records of that town. His gold ring inscribed "A Friend's gift," is in the Yale University Art Gallery.

His mark of his initials in a rectangle *(a)* appears on Cat. no. 235. *Worcester 1913* recorded a mark of initial and surname, in capitals and lowercase, on spoons engraved for a couple married in 1778.

a

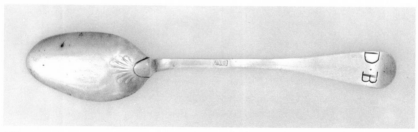

235

235 Teaspoon, c. 1750

L. 4½ in.; Wt. 4½ dwt.

MARK: *a* on back of stem.
Rounded handle forward bent, one third midrib, slim stem, drop and shell on back of worn oval bowl.
Engraved *D·B* in crude letters on back of handle.
HISTORY: Unknown.
GIFT OF MRS. EUGENE C. HULTMAN 48.235

JOHN BRIDGE
born 1723

JOHN BRIDGE, the goldsmith, is believed to be the son born to Ebenezer and Mary Bridge on July 21, 1723. Bigelow called him a blacksmith *(Bigelow 1917)*, but the two flagons of his fashioning in 1751 and 1753 firmly belie that occupation, as does his strainer (Cat. no. 236). With no mention of his profession, the Boston records (vol. 14) note that in 1752 John Bridge was sworn constable, was excused, but was sworn constable again in 1753 and in 1754 "for the ensuing year". We do not find his death recorded in Boston.

His New North Church (now King's Chapel) flagon bears two different marks in capital letters: his surname in a cartouche, and with initial *I* and a pellet in a scalloped rectangle. The mark *(a)* on the strainer is a third variation, consisting of his initial and surname in roman capitals and semiscript lowercase letters in a rectangle.

a

236

236 Punch Strainer, c. 1750

H. 1 in.; D. of bowl 3¾ in.; L. 8½ in.; Wt. 4 oz., 15 dwt.

MARKS: *a* on back of each handle.
Shallow circular curved bowl with everted molded rim; eight short pierced rays surround the center hole, eight rows of somewhat random piercings circle the bowl. Rather short strap handles, looped with tip at ends, have angled bars for joining under the rim.
Engraved with an old English *H* under rim of bowl between handle joinings.
HISTORY: Unknown.
GIFT OF THE PAUL REVERE LIFE INSURANCE COMPANY 66.497

SAMUEL BURT
1724–1754

The eldest of John's silversmithing sons, Samuel Burt was born on September 4, 1724. His craft was undoubtedly learned under his father's instruction. He was married to Elizabeth White in 1747. In 1748 he fashioned the two fine armorially engraved flagons for the First Congregational Church in Marblehead, Massachusetts. In 1749 he was married to Elizabeth Kent of Newbury, whose maternal grandmother's second husband was the silversmith John Edwards. Samuel's death is recorded in the family Bible "Sept. 23 1754 in the 31 year of his age." In 1752 and in 1754 he had been excused from serving as constable. His will, dated September 19, named his widow as sole executor; no inventory of his estate was filed.

His more frequently found mark is of his full name in capital letters on two lines in a cartouche *(a);* but that of his initial and surname in capital letters separated by a colon and contained in a rectangle *(b)* is also known.

a   b

237 Chafing Dish, 1740–1750

H. 3⅝ in. (inc. supports); D. of grate 3⅝ in.; D. of rim 6⅛ in.; L. 12¼ in. (inc. handle); Wt. 19 oz., 8 dwt.

MARKS: *a* on bottom at each side of nut, both toward handle.

Bowl with curved sides, cut-out bottom, everted rim molded on surface to a line above piercing in three panels of scrolls and hearts, divided by spaced areas of cut scrolls flanking squares of crescent and plain holes. Three lines of engraving connect panels to flanking scroll designs. A slightly curved band of open guilloche centering alternately reversed hearts is affixed between bowl and upcurved rim of flat base. Three cast scrolls, their sides flattened, are affixed equidistant at the rim for scroll supports and to the body below a square of piercing. A scroll from below is affixed to angled knee of leg ending in a wide scroll foot. Attached to one support (at end above its band of molding) is a turned and banded socket for the turned wooden handle (the scroll of the support is affixed to the band). A cast grate with curved rayed open-work design and molded edge has a fixed peg rectangular in section with disc top above plate and screw tip through bottom for modeled square nut.

HISTORY: Unknown.

NOTES: Other chafing dishes with the heart in guilloche band: one by Paul Revere I (Cat. no. 152); one by Thomas Dane (Harrington Collection, Dartmouth College); one by John Burt (Clearwater Collection, The Metropolitan Museum of Art, New York); one by Philip Syng, its bowl without pierced sides (Philadelphia Museum).

GIFT OF LEVERETT SALTONSTALL, MURIEL SALTONSTALL LEWIS, AND RICHARD SALTONSTALL 62.809

237

238

238 Sauceboat, 1745–1750

H. 4½ in. (inc. handle); L. 7⁷⁄₁₆ in.; Wt. 14 oz., 10 dwt.

MARK: *a* on bottom, above initials.

The mate to Cat. no. 239. Broad elliptical body, curved sides incurved below everted scalloped rim, long lip apparently drawn. Three cabriole legs, molded body joinings, separately cast hollow shell feet. Cast double scroll open handle, bent out of shape, with acanthus grip; pointed tip affixed on rim; disc at body joining; both scroll tips flat at side, applied tip below lower one. No center point.

Engraved on the bottom NᶜM (the *N* is over an unfinished *M*); below: *14=11=12;* beneath the weight is scratched: *1764.*

HISTORY: Nathaniel Carter, m. Mary Beck, Newburyport, 1742; their daughter Hannah (1764-1836), m. William Smith; their daughter Elizabeth Storer Smith (1789-1859), m. Edward Cruft; descended in the family to the donors.

NOTES: A creampot by Samuel Burt with the same initials is owned by the Minneapolis Institute of Arts.

EXHIBITIONS: *MFA 1956,* no. 16 (with its mate); *ESU 1960,* no. 58.

GIFT OF THE ESTATES OF THE MISSES EUNICE MCLELLAN AND FRANCES CORDIS CRUFT 42.379

239

239 Sauceboat, 1745–1750

H. 4⅝ in. (inc. handle); L. 7⁷⁄₁₆ in.; Wt. 14 oz., 7 dwt.

MARK: *a,* both ends worn, above initials.

The mate and identical to Cat. no. 238, but handle not bent.

Engraved on bottom NMC within guidelines and *14=9=12.*

HISTORY: Nathaniel Carter, m. Mary Beck, Newburyport, 1742; their daughter Hannah (1764-1836), m. William Smith; their son, Thomas Carter Smith, m. Frances Barnard; their great-granddaughters, the donors.

REFERENCE: *Jones 1928,* p. 42.

EXHIBITIONS: *MFA 1911,* no. 176; *MFA 1956,* no. 17 (with its mate).

GIFT OF THE MISSES ROSE AND ELIZABETH TOWNSEND *56.674*

240 Caster, c. 1750

H. 5⅜ in.; D. of base 1¹³⁄₁₆ in.; Wt. 3 oz., 5 dwt.

MARK: *b* near rim.

Vase-shaped with hemispherical body on (cast?) rather high foot, splayed and molded. Seamed sides sharply curved at joining with molded band, almost straight to applied rim. Seamed domed cover with molded disc below turned bell-form finial, paired chased lines form six panels, in alternate ones plain holes in diaper design, in others larger and fewer holes with chased lines which form scroll patterns. Center point on bottom.

Engraved *LA* on body.

HISTORY: Unknown.

REFERENCE: *Buhler 1939*, pp. 114-115, illus. (as unrecorded mark).

EXHIBITION: *Richmond 1960*, no. 14.

GIFT OF ARTHUR D. FOSS 39.5

240

241 Pair of Salts, c. 1750

H. 1¾ in.; D. of base 2¾ in.; Wt. of *65.885:* 2 oz., 4½ dwt; of *65.886:* 2 oz., 4 dwt.

MARK: *a* on bottom below center point.

Circular, incurved to narrow rim; three scroll legs, triangular joinings, line on pad feed. Center points. Battered.

Engraved DWR on bottom.

HISTORY: David Wood (1710-1797), m. 1733 Ruth Hopkins (d. 1792); their daughter Mary (1740-1818), m. Thomas Edes, 1761, and second John Stanton; Thomas Edes, Jr. (1762-1818), m. Mary Ball (1764-1839), 1788; their son Robert Ball Edes (1789-1862), m. Sarah Barker, 1818; their daughter Mary (1818-1880), m. James Sullivan Noyes, ancestor of the donor. R. B. Edes' son Henry Augustus Edes was father of Henry Herbert Edes, cousin of the donor's father. See also Cat. no. 242.

EXHIBITION: *MFA 1906*, nos. 48, 49, pl. IX.

GIFT OF MISS PENELOPE B. NOYES 65.885-886

241

242

242 Cann, c. 1750

H. 6³⁄₁₆ in. (inc. handle); D. of base 3³⁄₁₆ in.; D. of lip 3½-3⁹⁄₁₆ in. (uneven); Wt. 13 oz., 18½ dwt.

MARKS: *a* each side of handle.

Flaring lip with incised lines, bulbous body, on molded footband seamed near front. Center point on bottom. High scroll handle, slight grip has scalloped edge; flat surface tapers to (bent) tip; vent hole patched over.

Engraved DWR / *1733* on handle; added in script on side: *This Can / Descended from / David & Ruth Wood / 1733, / To their daughter / Mary (Wood) (Edes) Stanton / 1797, / To her grandson / Robert Ball Edes / 1818. / To his grandson / Henry Herbert Edes / 1870.* (See Cat. no. 241.)

HISTORY: See description of engraving.

EXHIBITION: *MFA 1906,* no. 51, pls. IX, XV.

GIFT OF MISS PENELOPE B. NOYES 65.884

JOHN BALL advertised 1763–1767

JOHN BALL "goldsmith of Concord" advertised land and buildings for sale in the Boston newspapers of 1763 and 1767. He is not mentioned by Lemuel Shattuck in *The History of the Town of Concord* published in 1835. He made beakers engraved for the churches in Lincoln and Westborough in 1761 and 1762, but his work is rare.

The goldsmith is said to have married Sarah Brooks of Concord in 1746, and if this is true, he was born 1723/4, one of five of the name in the fifth generation from the first New England John Ball, a freeman in Concord in 1650 from Wiltshire in England. Sarah and John Ball had seven children from 1747 to 1762, but neither his death date nor his occupation is given in the family genealogy.

The New England origin of pieces with this mark of his surname in capital letters in a rectangle *(a)* precludes its belonging to the Pennsylvania or Maryland goldsmiths of the name. John Ball's full name in two lines in italic capitals and *J BALL* with a pellet in a rectangle are also recorded.

a

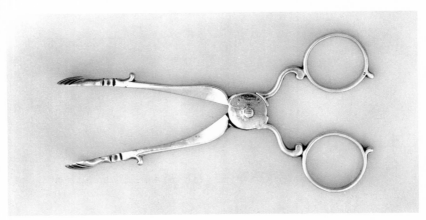

243

243 Sugar Scissors, 1750–1760

L. 4¾ in.; Wt. 1 oz., 5 dwt.

MARKS: *a* inside each tip.
Circular finger holes with short scrolls, scroll to circular pivot hinge, shaped shanks (not matching or meeting), scroll and molding just above neatly finished hollow shell tips.
HISTORY: Unknown.
REFERENCE: *Bigelow 1917*, p. 406, fig. 295.
GIFT OF THE MISSES CATHARINE LANGDON ROGERS AND CLARA BATES ROGERS 14.896

WILLIAM BREED
active c. 1740

No birth for one of this name is to be found in the Boston Town Records, though children are recorded to Timothy and Sarah, Nathaniel and Sarah, and Amos and Elizabeth Breed in the early 1700s. William Breed and Susanna Barrington were married on October 20, 1743.

Other known pieces by William Breed are a porringer with the same marks in the same position as on Cat. no. 244 (The Henry Francis du Pont Winterthur Museum, Delaware); a porringer with the same name mark, the handle tip broken, also engraved away from bowl (present location unknown); a pepper box (private collection); a pair of salts (Yale University Art Gallery, Garvan Collection); a child's coral and bells (privately owned, on loan to the MFA); a punch strainer (Massachusetts Historical Society, on loan to the MFA) and a teapot (Phillips Academy, Addison Gallery of American Art, Andover, Mass.).

Breed's name mark *(a)* initial and surname in semiscript with capitals conjoined in a rectangle, appears on Cat. no. 244 with an initials one *(b)*, top serifs joined, in a rectangle, making attribution of the latter concise and simple.

a *b*

244

244 Porringer, c. 1750

H. 1¾ in.; D. of lip 5³⁄₁₆ in.; L. of handle 2¹³⁄₁₆ in.; Wt. 8 oz., 4½ dwt.

MARKS: *a* on handle; *b* on handle tip.

Almost straight rim, curved sides, stepped and domed bottom, center point inside. Small splash of solder (?) has been spilled inside. Spotty solder under keyhole handle.

Engraved A!E away from bowl.

HISTORY: Unknown.

NOTES: As on the William Homes punch bowl (Cat. no. 231), it is reassuring to have the maker's initials mark with his surname mark.

REFERENCE: *Buhler 1950*, p. 36.

EXHIBITION: *MFA 1911*, no. 63.

BEQUEST OF WILLIAM BELTRAN DE LAS CASAS 30.732

245

245 Set of Gold Sleeve Buttons,
c. 1750

UNKNOWN MAKER

W. ½ in.

MARKS: None.

Four octagonal buttons with rim rolled under, small loop on back of each for elliptical joining link to form pairs.

Engraved with rather stylized rosette within framework of lines.

HISTORY: Rev. Jacob Cushing of Waltham, Massachusetts (Harvard 1748); descended in family to donor.

GIFT OF MISS ELEANOR E. BARRY *62.959 a-b*

246

246 Cream Pail, c. 1750

UNKNOWN MAKER

H. 3⅛ in. (inc. handle); D. of lip 1¹³⁄₁₆ in.; Wt. 2 oz., 3 dwt.

MARKS: None.

Engraved *H∴D* on bottom; added in script on side *William Dawes Sr. / to Hannah Lucas / 3ᵈ Nov. 1765.*

Straight sides, seamed under one handle joining, taper to inset bottom. Rim elaborately scalloped; five very thin bands of three reeds each are applied, the lowest extending slightly below the bottom. Circular hinge for twisted bail handle has turned body drop over top band at each side.

HISTORY: Hannah, daughter of William and Lydia (Boone) Dawes (b. September 18, 1743), m. John Lucas, November 3, 1765; descended to her niece, grandmother of the donor.

NOTES: Other pails are known: by Thomas Dane (Yale University Art Gallery, Garvan Collection); by William Simpkins (private collection); with flat straps (or bands) by Nathaniel Hurd (Worcester Art Museum, reproduced *R.I. 1965*).

GIFT OF MISS E. E. P. HOLLAND *11.1347*

247

247 Pin Ball and Chain, c. 1750

UNKNOWN MAKER

D. of ball 2 in. (approx.); L. of chain 11 in.

MARKS: None.

Scalloped strap of silver, with raised midmolding and punched dots below incised notches, encircles linen-covered pin cushion (outer cover missing). A molded ring for figure-eight fastener of link chain with ring and S loop at end.

HISTORY: Unknown.

NOTES: References to pin balls and chains indicate that a pair of scissors was usually suspended from the chain (see advertisement, *N.Y. Journal,* August 31, 1741: "Stolen . . . a silver Scissors Chain . . . a Silver Watch Chain and Pincushion Chain . . ."; or Paul Revere's account book November 18, 1780: "a Chain for Scissors and Pin-ball, 1 oz. 18". Sewing implements of silver and gold such as hooks and eyes, buttons, needle cases, bodkins, thimbles and their cases, and scissors and their cases, are known mainly from inventories.

EXHIBITION: *ESU 1960,* no. 81.

GIFT OF MRS. JASON WESTERFIELD *60.981* (Withdrawn)

248

248 Cup, 1750–1760

UNKNOWN MAKER

H. of body 1⅞ to 1¹⁵⁄₁₆ in. (uneven); D. of base 1⅝₁₆ in.; D. of lip 2⅝ in.; Wt. 2 oz., 17 dwt.

MARKS: None.

Raised with flaring sides, three plain bands soldered slightly below rim, at midbody, and at flat bottom extending very slightly below it. Cast scroll handle affixed with curves at rim and at midband and, with sharp angle, at baseband, its forked tip bent sharply upward; slight downward grip on shoulder. Center point on bottom.

Engraved with guidelines on bottom in semiscript: *The gift of Sarah Thwing / to Mrs Mary Austin.* An extra pair of guidelines is at the center point.

HISTORY: See *Notes.*

NOTES: The fact that several Sarah Thwings are recorded makes the original ownership of this piece difficult to ascertain. The following possibilities exist: Sarah, daughter of Nathaniel and Joanna Thwing, was born May 4, 1737 and died September 3, 1753. The marriage of another Sarah Thwing to Jonathan Williams took place on February 4, 1762, and a third Sarah Thwing was married in 1775.

248

Mary Smith (1710-1800), whose sister Sarah was the wife of Samuel Edwards, goldsmith, married in 1732 Ebenezer Austin (d. 1742) of Charlestown. Their sons were Ebenezer (b. 1733), goldsmith, and Nathaniel (b. 1741), pewterer. A pail by Nathaniel Hurd (Worcester Art Museum) has similar wide bands (*R.I. 1965*, fig. 47).
GIFT OF FRANK L. HARRINGTON 65.472

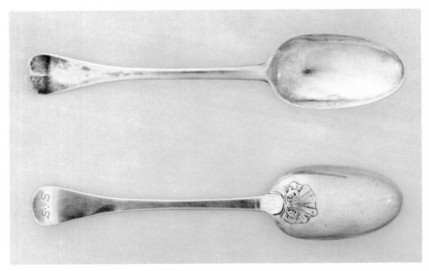

249

249 Pair of Spoons, 1750–1760

UNKNOWN MAKER

L. 7¾ in.; Wt. of *61.1090*, 1 oz., 18 dwt.; of *61.1091*, 1 oz., 17 dwt.

MARKS: None.
Rounded tip forward bent with slight ridge; broad drop on oval bowl with ornate shell and scroll stamping.
Engraved *SS* on back of tip.
HISTORY: Made for Samuel Scarborough (d. 1789); descended in the family of his first wife to the donor.
NOTES: This pair of unmarked spoons emphasizes the importance of the possession of silver inasmuch as the inventory of the original owner's comfortable estate listed in plate only "Two tablespoons and 6 tea spoons."
He left a mahogany dining table to put them on and, of interest for its terminology, a "Snap tea table". He married twice and his household furniture

was divided between his first wife's brother's children and "Elizabeth my beloved wife." Two well-known goldsmiths of Huguenot descent have used this unusually decorative device for the bowls of spoons in the MFA collection, neither in quite the proportion of these. Revere II's similar spoon (Cat. no. 342) bears the crest of his Huguenot patrons, the Johonnots, on its forward bent handle. Daniel Boyer's large spoons (see *Appendix*) with the later backward bending are very worn; his forward bent teaspoon shows the same design. Benjamin Hurd had slightly shorter rays on his similar swage (see Cat. no. 428), and John Gibbs of Providence had another comparable with this (see *Appendix*). It would be unwise, in the light of their condition, to assign a definite maker to this pair.

GIFT OF JOSEPH LORING RICHARDS IN MEMORY OF HIS FATHER JOSEPH DUDLEY RICHARDS *61.1090-1091*

250

250 Gold Mourning Ring, 1756

UNKNOWN MAKER

D. ¹³⁄₁₆ in.

MARKS: None.

Six conjoined lettered curves enameled in black, the first two longer, and in alternating directions.

Inscribed *MADM D. / DUDLEY / OB:24 / OCTO / 1756 / .AE. 72.* .

Small triangular devices flank the date and follow the month.

HISTORY: Descended in the family of the donor.

NOTES: Despite the erroneous initial, this undoubtedly commemorates Mrs. Paul Dudley (née Lucy Wainwright) whose death date this was. Her will, dated October and probated November 19, 1756, specified rings to her brother-in-law Mr. Dummer (Lieutenant Governor William Dummer); sisters-in-law Sewall, Miller, and Atkins; niece Mrs. Turell; nephews Henry Sewall, John Still Winthrop; and kinswoman Mrs. Hatch.

GIFT OF MISS HELEN P. DEMARAS *20.848*

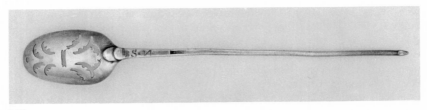

251

251 Strainer Spoon, c. 1760

L. 5⅝ in.

MARK: Indecipherable letters in a rectangle on back of stem.
Circular stem tapering to small pointed spade tip, flattened above double drop on back of elliptical bowl pierced with bar in center and shaped scrolls raying from it.
Engraved *S = N* (the *N* reversed) on back of stem.
HISTORY: Unknown.
BEQUEST OF CHARLES HITCHCOCK TYLER 32.400

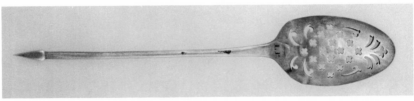

252

252 Strainer Spoon, c. 1760

L. 5 in.

MARKS: None.
Handle, elliptical in section, tapers to spade tip with sharp point. Rounded drop on oval bowl pierced with scrolls at both ends, crosses in center.
Engraved *LP* on drop.
HISTORY: Unknown.
GIFT OF MR. AND MRS. HENRY HERBERT EDES 36.38

253

253 Gold Mourning Rings, 1761 and 1762

<small>UNKNOWN MAKER</small>

D. of *54.1477:* ¹³⁄₁₆ in.; of *54.1479:* ¹¹⁄₁₆ in.

<small>MARKS:</small> None.

Rectangular faceted glass over a small paper skull is in a rayed mount held by the forked scroll tips of the band with a center line holding a small square crystal, three scroll panels of cut lettering filled with black enamel.

Engraved 54.1477: *J.WENDELL / OB• 7.SEPT / 1761• AE 71;*
54.1479: *MS• WENDELL / OB 22 JUL / 1762• AE 66.*

<small>HISTORY:</small> Descended in the family to Edward Jackson Holmes (see Cat. no. 34).

<small>NOTES:</small> Similar rings commemorate Jacob Wendell (1691-1761) and Sarah (1696-1762), his wife, although the stones of hers were smaller and the panels were in a single curve.

<small>GIFT OF MRS. EDWARD JACKSON HOLMES</small> *54.1477* and *54.1479*

254

254 Gold Mourning Ring, 1762

UNKNOWN MAKER

D. ⅞ in.

MARKS: None.

Four reverse curve panels joined at their scroll tips are lettered and enameled in black.

Enameled lettering: *MRS. DORO / JACKSON / OB • 27 • JULY / 1762: AE: 54.*

HISTORY: See *Notes.*

NOTES: Born Dorothy Quincy, she was the widow of Edward Jackson. Oliver Wendell was executor of her estate. No mention is made in its settlement of the maker of her commemorative rings. On September 9, 1762 their daughter Mary married Oliver Wendell; their daughter Sarah married Rev. Abiel Holmes in 1801; descended to their great-grandson.

GIFT OF MRS. EDWARD JACKSON HOLMES *54.1478*

255

255 Gold Mourning Ring, 1768

Unknown Maker

D. ¹⁵⁄₁₆ in.

Marks: None.

Four ornamented conjoined scrolls, lettered and enameled in white (chipped). Inscribed *E.QUINCY / TERTS OB • / 24 MARCH: / 1768.AE. 35 /*.

History: Edmund Quincy, son of Col. Josiah and Hannah (Sturgis) Quincy, (b. October 1, 1733; Harvard College 1752); died at sea, unmarried. Descended in the family of his aunt, Dorothy (Quincy) Jackson, to the donor.

Notes: Quincy's estate is recorded at Suffolk Probate Court, but no maker is given for his funeral rings. The use of white enamel for an adult is very rare.

Exhibition: *Presentation Silver 1955*, p. 15.

Gift of Mrs. Edward Jackson Holmes *54.1480*

256

256 Gold Mourning Ring, 1770

Unknown Maker

D. ¹¹⁄₁₆ in.

Marks: None.

A simple ring of gold wire with tightly woven hair held under glass in a narrow ellipse of gold.

Engraved in very worn script on back of ellipse *S Jackson / ob 22 / June / 1770 . . . 29*.

History: See *Notes*.

Notes: This ring for a third generation of Jacksons (see also Cat. nos. 158 and 254) is dated surprisingly early for its form. This one commemorates Sarah (Barnard) Jackson, the first wife of Jonathan (1743-1810), son of Edward and Dorothy (Quincy) Jackson. Jonathan's son by his second wife, Hannah Tracy (1755-1797), was Charles (1775-1855), father of Amelia Lee Jackson (1818-1888), who married the first Oliver Wendell Holmes, grandfather of Edward Jackson Holmes.

Gift of Mrs. Edward Jackson Holmes *54.1481*

JOHN COBURN
1725–1803

JOHN COBURN is said to have been born in 1725 and probably served
his apprenticeship with the Edwards family. He advertised in 1750
as "goldsmith at the head of the Town Dock" and in that year married
Susanna Greenleaf, who died in 1783. He served in various town
offices, left town during the British siege but advertised in 1776 that
he had "removed into Boston again and carries on the goldsmith's
business in King Street. . . . He likewise continues to take ladies and
gentlemen to board as usual". Eighteen months after his wife's death
he married Catharine Vans. He appears in the first Boston Directory in
1789 not as a silversmith but with "gentlemen boarders"; in 1796 he
appeared as a "gentleman." His will was probated in 1803. He had no
children, and after his wife's death, her sisters Mary (Mrs. Jonathan
Mason) and Sarah (Mrs. Timothy Langdon) were to share what
remained of his estate.

Coburn's initials mark (a) on pieces descended through his heirs is in
the lettering of his name mark (b).

a   b

257

257 Sugar Bowl, c. 1746

H. 4³⁄₁₆ in. (inc. cover); D. of base 2¾ in.; D. of lip 4⁵⁄₁₆ in.; Wt. 12 oz.,
19½ dwt.

MARKS: *b* in reel handle and on base.

Hemispherical, its everted molded rim has applied upright bezel; its almost
straight sides curve to rounded base on rather high cast molded and splayed
foot. Cover has a molded rim fitting over the bezel, and a reel-shaped molded
handle, slightly bent and cracked. The cover center point is both inside
and out.

Engraved ISE on bottom around decorated center point. Scratched on bottom
13 oz. Cover has band of rayed foliate engraving in a circle on its curve with
incised lines below.

HISTORY: Isaac Smith, m. Elizabeth Storer, 1746; their son William, m.
Hannah Carter; their daughter Elizabeth Storer Smith, m. Edward Cruft;
descended in the family to the donors.

REFERENCES: *Bigelow 1917*, pp. 400-401, fig. 289.

EXHIBITIONS *MFA 1956*, no. 21, fig. 61.

GIFT OF THE ESTATES OF THE MISSES EUNICE McLELLAN AND FRANCES
CORDIS CRUFT 42.380

258

258 Salver, c. 1750

H. 1 in. (uneven); W. of dish 5¾ in.; Wt. 6 oz., 2½ dwt.

MARK: *b* on face, near rim, above arms.

Octagonal, in the form of Jacob Hurd's large salver (Cat. no. 184) and his known smaller ones; four legs at deepest curves have triangular fastenings; slight drops and scroll feet.

Engraved with Storer arms in shell, scroll, and foliate cartouche in the center. Scratched weight 6-6½ on bottom.

HISTORY: Ebenezer Storer (d. 1761), m. Mary Edwards; their daughter Elizabeth, m. Isaac Smith; for subsequent history, see Cat. no. 257.

NOTES: The similarity of this to salvers made by Jacob Hurd is one of many reasons for believing that Coburn trained with the Edwards family.

REFERENCE: *Comstock 1958*, pl. 47a.

EXHIBITION: *MFA 1956*, no. 22.

GIFT OF THE ESTATES OF THE MISSES EUNICE MCLELLAN AND FRANCES CORDIS CRUFT 42.381

259 Pair of Teaspoons, c. 1750

L. 4¹³⁄₁₆ in.; Wt. of *37.268:* 9½ dwt.; of *37.269:* 10 dwt.

MARKS: *b* on back of stem of each.

Each has rounded handle forward bent with slight ridge, long drop with molded tip on back of oval bowl.

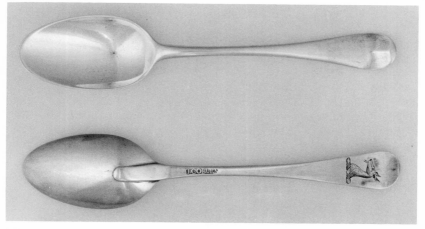

259

Engraved with Storer crest on back of handle.

HISTORY: Ebenezer Storer, m. Mary Edwards; their granddaughter
Susannah, m. Rev. Asa Eaton (1778-1858), minister of Christ Church,
Boston, 1803-1829; grandparents of the donor.

EXHIBITION: *MFA 1911*, no. 222.

GIFT OF WILLIAM STORER EATON 37.268-269

260

260 Caster, c. 1750

H. 5 ins.; D. of base 1⅝ ins.; Wt. 2 oz., 16 dwt.

MARK: *a* almost indistinguishable near rim.

Hemispherical bowl on molded splayed foot with applied edge; molding at joining of seamed curving neck with heavier applied molding below rim (inside built up with two extra bezels). High domed cover, the flattened disc on top pierced around base of turned and pointed finial. Triple engraved lines form six panels of diaper design with three vertical rows of holes. Molded edge has row of diamond and scroll piercing, backed by silver, and applied band below, which no longer closes properly. Very poorly repaired.

HISTORY: The donors were presumably descendants of one of Coburn's chief heirs, his sister-in-law, Sarah Langdon.

GIFT OF THE MISSES CATHARINE LANGDON ROGERS AND CLARA BATES ROGERS 14.893

261

261 Nutmeg Grater, c. 1750

H. 3⅛ in.; D. 1⅛ in.; Wt. 1 oz., 10½ dwt.

MARKS: *b* on bottom and inside cover.

Seamed cylinder with base forming slight molding; applied bezel, its seam opposite that of cylinder's; detachable cover, very slightly domed with incised line on narrow seamed sides.

Engraved with Greenleaf crest on side and *SG* on bottom; bands of engraving near each end; a band of overlapping leaf engraving around edge of cover with circular floral design in center.

HISTORY: Susanna Greenleaf (1722-1783), m. John Coburn, February 7, 1750; descended in family to the donors.

REFERENCE: *Bigelow 1917*, p. 396, fig. 284.

EXHIBITIONS: *Richmond 1960*, no. 20; *ESU 1960*, no. 60, pl. 31; *R.I. 1965*, no. 43.

GIFT OF THE MISSES CATHARINE LANGDON ROGERS AND CLARA BATES ROGERS *14.894*

262

262 Teapot, c. 1750

H. 5¼ in. (inc. finial); D. of base 3 in.; Wt. 15 oz., 16 dwt.

MARK: *b* on bottom.

Curved shoulder, almost globular body tapers to flat inset bottom, on cast splayed molded foot. Domed cover with vent hole extends at back for center of hinge with heavy applique beneath, flanking it to meet applied bezel. Pine cone finial on turned base riveted into lid. Spout, scalloped at body with shell on lower curve and slightly molded tip, is over simple strainer holes, rather high on body. Upper handle socket with scroll and slight shaping on shoulder, lower straight socket for pinned wooden handle with grip.

Engraved with Gardner arms in shell, wheat, and scroll cartouche with pendent device on pourer's side; *S*G* on bottom. Engraving of overlapping points raying from finial and band of overlapping leaf forms at its rim; shoulder has panels of diaper work between scroll and shell forms at sides, lozenges centered front and back, acanthus scroll for lower line.

HISTORY: Samuel Gardner (d. April 7, 1769); subsequent history unknown.

NOTES: The inventory of Samuel Gardner, of Salem, Massachusetts, included "1 large Tea Pott 17 - 17 / 1 small Do 15 oz. 8 dwt." The large teapot is owned by the Heritage Foundation, Deerfield, Massachusetts.

REFERENCE: *Buhler 1934*, p. 48, illus.

BEQUEST OF CHARLES HITCHCOCK TYLER *32.402*

263

263 Coffee Pot, 1750–1760

H. 11⅛ in. (inc. finial); D. of base 5 in.; Wt. 42 oz., 5 dwt.

MARK: *b* at left of handle.

Molded rim with incised lines below on almost straight sides to broad curve at rounded bottom with center point, on cast molded splayed foot. Flat incised flange with heavy bezel on stepped domed cover, turned finial soldered to disc and through cover, which has vent hole. Right-angle open hinge to upper scroll handle socket affixed to shell plaque on body; lower upright socket, scrolled and grooved, has extension to double disc on body. Double-scroll wooden handle with grip. Curved spout, acanthus on shaped tip and boldly fluted and scalloped lower half, affixed to body over small oval hole.

Engraved with Symmes arms on pourer's side (see Guillim's *Display of Heraldry,* p. 90) in somewhat asymmetrical cartouche of flowers, fruit, and foliage with garlands and pendent flowers; added script O on other side said to be for Oxnard.

HISTORY: Unknown.

NOTES: The Symmes arms appear on six canns by Daniel Boyer which were gifts of Edward Kitchen to the Tabernacle Church in Salem, Massachusetts, described in his bequest as "six Silver Pint Cans with the three half Moons and the Sun engraven thereon." Kitchen's description suggests his lack of knowledge of the Symmes arms, which appear again, impaled with Wolcott, on a teapot by Jacob Hurd (*French 1938*, no. 383, pl. XX). An almost identical Coburn coffee pot with the Barrett arms is owned by the Sterling and Francine Clark Museum, Williamstown, Massachusetts.

REFERENCE: *Winchester 1956*, p. 74, illus.

EXHIBITIONS: *London 1954*; *Minneapolis 1956*, no. 188; *Richmond 1960*, no. 17; *ESU 1960*, no. 59, pl. 16.

HELEN AND ALICE COLBURN FUND 50.3595

264 Cann, c. 1755

H. 5⅞ in. (inc. handle grip); D. of base 3¹⁵⁄₃₂ in.; D. of lip 3⅜ in.; Wt. 10 oz., 5½ dwt.

MARK: *b* at left of handle.

Bulbous body, rather thin neck, incised paired lines below molded slightly flaring lip, on simply molded cast splayed foot. Hollow scroll handle, rather long upper drop, disc at lower joining and disc tip with vent slit below. A strap of silver with shaped edge forms grip. Rim nicked at front. Center point on bottom.

Engraved *ES* on bottom with rayed lines from center point to form device between initials. Scratched on bottom *1755* and *10 oz. 13*.

HISTORY: Elizabeth Storer (1726-1786), m. Isaac Smith (1719-1787), 1746; for subsequent history see Cat. no. 257.

NOTES: Isaac Smith's inventory had "1 pair pint canns 20 oz. 10."

GIFT OF THE ESTATES OF THE MISSES EUNICE MCLELLAN AND FRANCES CORDIS CRUFT 42.382

264

265 Cann, c. 1760

H. 5½ in. (inc. handle grip); D. of base 3⅜ in.; D. of lip 3½ in.;
Wt. 13 oz., 14 dwt.

MARKS: *b* at left of handle and on bottom at center point.

Bulbous body, molded lip, on cast molded splayed foot. Double scroll cast handle, extension at upper joining, disc at lower joining, slight grip, scroll tips flattened at sides, lower forked. Vent holes in upper scroll and in tip. Foot has been banged into body.

Engraved on front with Gardner arms in leaf, scroll, and shell cartouche.

HISTORY: Samuel Gardner (1712-1769) m. first Esther Orne, 1738, second, Elizabeth (Clarke) Winslow, 1758; see Cat. nos. 48 and 262. Subsequent history unknown.

NOTES: Samuel Gardner's inventory included a pair of canns weighing 27 oz., 2 dwt.

REFERENCE: *Buhler 1934*, pp. 49-50, illus.

BEQUEST OF CHARLES HITCHCOCK TYLER 32.380

265

266

266 Porringer, 1750–1770

H. 2 in.; D. of lip 5½ in.; L. of handle 2¾ in.; Wt. 9 oz., 12½ dwt.

MARK: *b* on back of handle.

Everted rim, curved sides, stepped and domed bottom, center point inside; keyhole handle.

Engraved *C*W* toward bowl.

HISTORY: See *Notes*.

NOTES: Originally one of a pair (the mate privately owned), it was engraved presumably for Catherine Willard, widow, when she had so unaccountably changed the spelling of her given name (see Cat. no. 226).

REFERENCE: *Hipkiss 1941*, pp. 226-227, no. 153, illus.

M. AND M. KAROLIK COLLECTION 39.193

267

267 Teapot, c. 1762

H. 6¼ in. (inc. finial); D. of base 3⁷⁄₁₆ in.; Wt. 23 oz., 2 dwt.

MARKS: *b* four times on bottom.

Elongated globular body, the bottom set in above joining of cast splayed molded foot; reinforcing strip inside at lip from sides of three-part hinge for domed lid; tall turned and chased finial soldered through cover. Simple strainer holes under curved spout, cast with large shell and molded body drop at base; shaped molded long underlip and engraved acanthus leaf on top. Upper socket scrolled and molded, lower straight, for wooden scroll handle with grip. Repairs at hinge.

Engraved with the Pickman arms in leaf and scroll cartouche on pourer's side; on other side, script initials *SPL* have been added; on bottom, original engraving *LP* to *MP*.

HISTORY: Love Pickman to her daughter-in-law Mary Toppan, m. Benjamin Pickman, 1762; their son Thomas; his granddaughter, Sally Pickman Loring Dwight, cousin of the donor.

NOTES: Benjamin Pickman's inventory, taken with scales unaligned with ours, in 1819 listed "1 teapot 22 oz. at 1.20 $26.40."

REFERENCES: *Bigelow 1917*, pp. 341-342, fig. 243; *Clark [Buhler] 1931*, p. 50, illus. p. 49; Buhler, *Antiques,* no. 6 (1945), p. 349, fig. 4; Phillips, *Antiques,* no. 1 (1949), p. 41; *Buhler 1950*, p. 56; *McLanathan 1956*, illus. p. 60, fig. 16; *Ellis 1961*, p. 27, fig. 9

EXHIBITIONS: *Chicago 1949*, no. 145, p. 118; *Baltimore 1959*, no. 438.

GIFT OF MR. AND MRS. DUDLEY LEAVITT PICKMAN 31.239

268

268 Pair of Salts, c. 1762

H. 1½ in.; D. of lip 2⅝ in.; Wt. of *31.240:* 3 oz., 5 dwt.; of *31.241:* 3 oz., 4½ dwt.

MARKS: *b* below center point on bottom of each.

Circular, paired incised lines at contracted rims with applied cast gadrooned and scalloped everted borders; sides curve to flat bottoms. Three cabriole legs with molded body joinings and pad feet on each salt.

Engraved BPM with tiny chased rays from center point which form device between the initials.

HISTORY: Benjamin Pickman, m. Mary Toppan 1762; descended in the family to the donors.

NOTES: Benjamin Pickman's inventory in 1819 listed "4 pr salt cellars & spoons 13 oz. 15 at 1.30 17.87". The matching pair is in a private collection.

REFERENCES: *Clark [Buhler] 1931,* p. 48, illus.; *Ellis 1961,* p. 27.

GIFT OF MR. AND MRS. DUDLEY LEAVITT PICKMAN *31.240-241*

268, 269

269

269

269 Pair of Casters, c. 1762

31.242: H. 5⅜₆ in.; D. of base 1⅞ in.; Wt. 4 oz., 3½ dwt.; *31.243:* H. 5⅜ in.; D. of base 1⅞ in.; Wt. 4 oz., 7 dwt.

MARKS: *b* below center point on bottom of each.

Each has raised pear-shaped body, on cast molded splayed foot with added strengthening edge, incurved for seamed cylindrical section with molded edge at joining and applied molded rim. High domed cover, turned disc below turned and bell-form finial. On *31.243* the cover holes are punched, not pierced, and the seam is darkened.

Engraved *MT* under foot near edge on both; on covers, paired double lines engraved vertically to form six panels and, crossing obliquely, diaper design pierced in plain holes.

HISTORY: Mary Toppan, m. Benjamin Pickman 1762; descended in the family to the donors.

NOTES: Benjamin Pickman's inventory in 1819 listed "1 set of Castors 35 oz. 15 / 2 pepper boxes 7 - 15". The latter probably refers to the present pieces even though one of ours is unpierced and therefore is for mustard rather than for pepper.

REFERENCES: *Clark [Buhler] 1931,* p. 48; *Ellis 1961,* p. 27.

GIFT OF MR. AND MRS. DUDLEY LEAVITT PICKMAN *31.242-243*

270

270 Pair of Salt Spoons, c. 1762

Attributed to JOHN COBURN

L. 4 in. (each); Wt. of *31.244:* 3½ dwt.; of *31.245:* 3 dwt.

MARKS: None.

Each has rounded handle tip, no ridge on back, shovel-shaped bowl or scoop with slanting sides, almost straight front edge.

Engraved *B*P* on tip of each; feathered edges.

HISTORY: Benjamin Pickman, m. Mary Toppan 1762; descended in the family to the donors.

NOTES: The attribution to Coburn is based on the number of pieces he fashioned for this couple. Jacob Hurd also made a pair of salt spoons in this form. Paul Revere II in 1790 charged Benjamin Pickman for "4 silver salt spoons / To engrav*g* 5 cyphers". Since styles were then quite different, this is probably irrelevant. Pickman's inventory of 1819 included "4 pr salt cellars & spoons 13 oz 15" and "2 pr salt spoons" weighed with other pieces.

REFERENCES: *Clark [Buhler] 1931,* p. 49, illus.; *Ellis 1961,* p. 27.

GIFT OF MR. AND MRS. DUDLEY LEAVITT PICKMAN 31.244-245

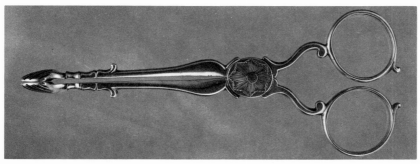

271

271 Pair of Sugar Scissors, c. 1762

Attributed to JOHN COBURN

L. 4¹³⁄₁₆ in.; Wt. 1 oz., 2 dwt.

MARKS: None.

Circular finger holes with slight scrolls to center pivot; shaped shanks molded and terminating in shell tips, insides of shells roughly cut. Decorated with rayed star-shaped design on each side of pivot.

HISTORY: Benjamin Pickman's inventory included "1 pr sugar tongs."

NOTES: The attribution is based on the fact that Coburn made many pieces for the Pickman family, and the workmanship is sufficiently fine to be his.

REFERENCES: *Clark [Buhler] 1931,* p. 49, illus.; *Ellis 1961,* p. 27.

GIFT OF MR. AND MRS. DUDLEY LEAVITT PICKMAN 31.246

272

272 Communion Dish, 1764

D. 13¾₆ in.; Wt. 25 oz., 5 dwt.

MARKS: *b* on bottom at center point and upside down on rim in left wing framing cherub.

Large plain dish with shallow depression, slightly domed in center; flat rim with incised line to simulate slight molding on under side. Center point on bottom.

Engraved with Hancock arms and crest in scroll and floral cartouche, torse of crest forming upper frame; winged cherub's head in frame of spread wings and curled fronds opposite. In semiscript and block letters around rim *The Gift of the Honble THOMAS HANCOCK ESQR / to the CHURCH in Brattle Street Boston 1764.* Scratched on bottom No. 2 *wt 26oz.*

HISTORY: See *Notes.*

NOTES: One of three dishes made by John Coburn for this church; of the other two, one is privately owned and one is in the Smithsonian Institution (bequest of Arthur Michael, formerly collection of E. Alfred Jones). Hancock's will had specified £100 for "two silver Flaggons for the Communion Table," but six dishes were made (see Cat. no. 321). These dishes, often wrongly called alms dishes, are suggested to be for communion by the inscription on the pair owned by the First Parish in Brookline: "Do this in remembrance of me".

REFERENCES: *Jones 1913,* pp. 68-69, illus.; *Paull 1913,* pp. 23-24, illus.; *Buhler, Antiques,* no. 6 (1945), pp. 350-351, fig. 8; *Ensko 1948,* p. 132, illus.; *Phillips, Antiques,* no. 4 (1949), p. 285; *McLanathan 1956,* p. 56, fig. 9.

EXHIBITIONS: *MFA 1906,* no. 57; *MFA 1911,* no. 215 or 217; *Cranbrook 1952,* no. 114; *Minneapolis 1956,* no. 189, fig. 48; *Richmond 1960,* no. 18; *Buffalo 1965,* no. 98.

GIFT OF THE BENEVOLENT FRATERNITY OF CHURCHES *13.394*

273 Sugar Bowl, 1760–1770

H. 5 in. (inc. cover); D. of base 2¾ in.; D. of lid 4¾ in.; Wt. 13 oz., 17 dwt.

MARKS: *b* inside foot and inside reel of cover.

Pear-shaped on molded splayed foot, two incised lines on applied upright rim. Cover has bezel, incised lines on flange, and step to flattened dome on which flaring reel handle is affixed. Center point on bottom and in handle of cover.

Engraved with Orne arms in shell and flower cartouche, crest on torse on opposite side. *RO* under edge of foot.

HISTORY: (Conjectured.) Rebecca (1748-1818), daughter of Timothy and Rebecca Orne, m. 1768 Capt. Joseph Cabot (1745/6-1774), son of Joseph (1720-1767) and Elizabeth (Higginson) Cabot (d. 1781); their daughter Rebecca Orne Cabot (b. 1769); in 1860 probably bequeathed to her nephew, Joseph Sebastien Cabot (1796-1874), m. Susan Burley, childless; subsequent history unknown.

NOTES: The initials are unusual and appear identically on the Revere II creampot, Cat. no. 338.

EXHIBITION: *R.I. 1965*, no. 45, fig. 50.

MARION E. DAVIS FUND *64.55*

273

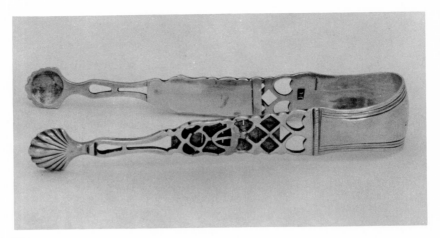

274

274 Sugar Tongs, 1760–1770

L. 5 1/16 in.; Wt. 1 oz., 6 dwt.

MARKS: *a* just above piercing in each end of bow.

Bow form, the shaped and curved arch with molded edges has band of very fine reeding above scallop-edged openwork arms tapering to shell tips. Both arms have been broken and repaired with comforming-edged silver plates inside, one in four sections.

Engraved *LCS* in script of about 1790 on top of bow.

HISTORY: Unknown.

GIFT OF THE MISSES CATHARINE LANGDON ROGERS AND
CLARA BATES ROGERS *14.895*

275

275 Tankard, 1760–1770

H. 8½ in. (inc. finial); D. of base 5 in.; D. of lip 3¾ in.; Wt. 27 oz., 7½ dwt.

MARKS: *b* at base of finial and at left of handle.

Straight tapering sides, molded rim, applied narrow bead midband and molded baseband. Five-part hinge with molded drop on handle for molded domed cover, bell-form finial. Scroll thumbpiece. Wide flange with double paired incised lines has turned-over edge cut for hollow scroll handle with disc at lower joining, both crudely joined and perhaps resoldered, and disc tip; wide vent hole. Narrow bezel with crude soldering that is even cruder for baseband. Center point on bottom.

Engraved EGS on handle; scratched on front between slight curving wheat sheaves, *BG* with devices above, between, and below initials.

HISTORY: Unknown.

EXHIBITIONS: *MFA 1906*, no. 56, pls. XIV, XXVI; *MFA 1911*, no. 220.

BEQUEST OF MR. AND MRS. GEORGE W. HAMMOND 08.312

276

276 Gold Mourning Ring, 1751

Attributed to JOHN COBURN

D. ⅞ in.

MARKS: None.

Elliptical beveled glass over a painted skull in rayed mount held in forked scroll ends of band with center bar on which a smaller glass chip is mounted (missing at one end). Hoop of three scrolled panels.

Lettered and enameled in black in scrolled panels T:BARTON: / ESQ.OB ·APR / 28:1751·AE 71.

HISTORY: Thomas Barton (d. 1751); descended in the family to Martha Codman Karolik.

NOTES: Barton's daughter, Mrs. Benjamin Pickman, was to employ John Coburn for silver, and he may have been the fashioner of the ring. Thomas Barton had bequeathed "unto my dearly beloved Wife . . . All her Maiden Plate as a Tanckard Spoons etc. and as much more as she may want to be useful for her and all my Gold Rings had at funerals saving what may be made use of for my own funeral". This would not have been a used one.

BEQUEST OF MAXIM KAROLIK 64.862

277

277 Gold Mourning Ring, 1773

Attributed to JOHN COBURN

D. ¹¹⁄₁₆ in.

MARKS: None.

A distinctly coffin-shaped glass covers a full painted skeleton (outlined in hair?) in a rayed mount with four notched scroll panels.

Lettered and enameled in black in the panels *HON.B / PICKMAN / OB.20 AUG / 1773 · AE 66.*

HISTORY: Benjamin Pickman (d. 1773); descended in the family to Martha Codman Karolik.

NOTES: This Benjamin is the father of the Benjamin who in 1819 died possessing twelve gold rings, of which this may well have been one, which descended to his several times great-granddaughter née Martha Codman.

BEQUEST OF MAXIM KAROLIK 64.866

278

278 Gold Mourning Ring, probably 1791

UNKNOWN MAKER

D. ¾ in.

MARKS: None.

Two colors of hair are loosely plaited as a background for the monogram, set under glass in an elliptical curved frame on a band which tapers to a straight back.

Engraved monogram *LCW* in gold; at each end flanking the frame in script *Levi Willard, died July 11. 1775. aged 48.* Inside in four lines on the broad part in script *Catherine / Willard, / died Jany 10, 1791. / aged 56.*

HISTORY: Descended in the family to Martha Codman Karolik.

NOTES: The initials are those of Levi and Catherine Willard, and the style of the ring suggests the date of her death. Winthrop Chandler's portraits of the Willards are in the M. and M. Karolik Collection of Eighteenth Century American Arts, and their daughter Katharine married John Amory.

BEQUEST OF MAXIM KAROLIK 64.870

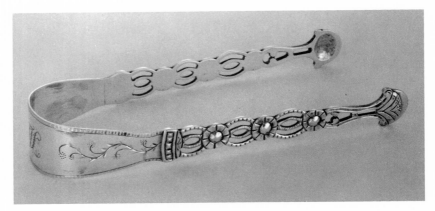

279

279 Sugar Tongs, c. 1780

UNKNOWN MAKER

L. 6 in.; Wt. 1 oz., 17½ dwt.

MARKS: None.

Bow form; the flat bow tapering to juncture of thicker arms of three successive areas of vertical curved straps divided by carved rosettes. Outer straps have effect of gadrooning, inner ones more closely incised, molded long scrolls to shell grips with plain tips. Band of framed nail-head design across top of arm from which rises an incised floral tendril almost to monogram.

Engraved script *TJL* on bow.

HISTORY: Thomas and Joanna (Quincy) Loring (1757-1836), m. 1780; descended collaterally in the family to the donor.

GIFT OF THOMAS L. SPRAGUE *18.333*

280

280 Nutmeg Grater, c. 1810

UNKNOWN MAKER

H. 3⁹⁄₁₆ in.; W. 2 in.; Wt. 2 oz. 17½ dwt.

MARKS: None.
Flattened urn form in two parts, the hinged slightly domed cover with chased ball finial closes to hold the two halves which are hinged at the rectangular base. The shoulder is embossed with the design chased on the edge of the cover; the stems of the urn are cast and, fastened to the back, fitting into the front, is a steel grater with riveted silver edge.
Engraved on front with shield enclosing *H,* leafy sprigs and bird at top.
HISTORY: "a family piece."
NOTES: A box on the same principle is in the Essex Institute, Salem, made by Joseph Hiller (1748-1814). Two of similar construction, also unmarked, are in the Clearwater Collection, The Metropolitan Museum of Art, catalogued under date of 1770-1810 (*Avery 1920,* page 158).
GIFT OF MISS CAROLINE HOOPER FABENS 47.1488

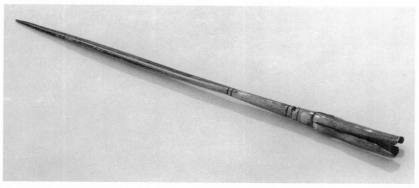

281

281 Larding Pin, c. 1790

UNKNOWN MAKER

L. 5½ in.; Wt. 7 oz.

MARKS: None.
Four thin rectangular strips in calyx form on a partly hollow tapering stem with three incised lines near the tip and paired ones above an also tapering but solid pin, rectangular in section to its point.
HISTORY: Benjamin Pickman (d. 1819); descended in the family to Martha Codman Karolik.
NOTES: Benjamin Pickman's inventory of 1819 included "1 larding pin" in a group of silver articles weighing 98 ounces. Silver larding pins were luxury items and this is the only one known to the author. However, Paul Revere II recorded a larding pin in his account book in 1797; its weight was not given but the cost was twelve shillings.
REFERENCE: *Hipkiss 1941,* p. 241, no. 168 (as belonging to the Amory family).
M. AND M. KAROLIK COLLECTION 41.622

282

282 Chatelaine Hook, c. 1790

UNKNOWN MAKER

L. 1⅝ in. (front); 1⅜ in. (back strap).

MARKS: None.
From its tip, with a hole in each of two scallops, a strap narrows and is looped almost at midpoint.
Engraved script *HG* near tip.
HISTORY: Hannah (Storer) Green (1739-1811), wife of Joshua Green (1731-1806); descended in the family to the donor.
EXHIBITION: *Towle 1956-1957*, no. 24
BEQUEST OF SAMUEL A. GREEN *19.1405*

283

Massachusetts: UNKNOWN

283 Caster, 1790–1800

UNKNOWN MAKER

H. 5⅞ in.; W. of base 1⅞ in.; Wt. 3 oz., 12½ dwt.

MARKS: None.

Deep ovoid body with concave shoulder joined with narrow band of molding, incised line at rim, on splayed molded foot and square plinth with applied vertical edge. Domed lid, curved sides with plain piercing, molding above bezel and pointed finial from disc on top.

Engraved script *A* on body.

HISTORY: Amory family; descended to Martha Codman Karolik.

NOTES: Other known casters in this form include a pair by Paul Revere II (Fogg Art Museum, Cambridge, Massachusetts); a single one by Paul Revere II (Phillips Academy, Addison Gallery of American Art, Andover, Massachusetts); and an unmarked one which has engraving in the patriot's style (private collection).

BEQUEST OF MAXIM KAROLIK *64.926*

284

284 Twenty-three Buttons, 1790–1800

UNKNOWN MAKER

D. ¾ in. (each).

MARKS: None.

Each is a flat round disc with narrow strap looped and soldered at or near the middle of the back.

Engraved script monogram *JL*.

HISTORY: John Lowell (1769-1840), great-great-grandfather of the donor.

GIFT OF RALPH LOWELL *53.33*

285

285

285 Tinder Box, 1790–1800

J R, Unidentified

H. ¾ in.; W. 1⅝ in.; L. 2¹³⁄₁₆ in.; Wt. 4 oz., 3 dwt. (inc. steel).

MARKS: *JR* with pellet between in rectangle with cut corners in lid.

A rectangular box, its straight sides seamed at midback, the flat base extending slightly beyond sides. The front has a centered latch and equidistant from it are notches for a shaped steel striking bar hinged into inside posts at front. Adjacent to and inside one is a partition with shaped top, one end angled and soldered to back of box with molded strip for hinge. Tiny bezel on slightly overhanging flat cover is broader at back with molded strip for two extensions of five-part hinge.

Engraved in the center of the lid is a bird with one twig in its beak and one across its back, standing on a book between letters *A* and *M*. Scratched on bottom *E+H*. Around the base of the box is an engraved band of overlapping leaves right and left from center, repeated at the top of the sides and front. A different leafy band is near the edges of the cover, with a flower-shaped form in each corner.

HISTORY: Unknown.

NOTES: At one time attributed to Joseph Richardson, but the mark is not known to be his.

GIFT OF MRS. GEORGE L. BATCHELDER, JR., BY EXCHANGE *63.1080*

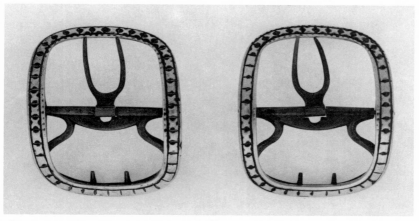

286

286 Pair of Shoe Buckles, 1790–1800

UNKNOWN MAKER

H. 2½ in.; W. 3 in.

MARKS: None.

Oblong, curved, thickened at back for bar of steel chape and tongue. Simple nail-head decoration, very worn except at tongue side of each.

HISTORY: See *Notes*.

NOTES: Said to have been owned by Ensign Ebenezer Craft (1679-1722) of Roxbury, but these buckles were surely made too late for this to have been so.

GIFT OF G. ALEXANDER ROBERTSON *65.428a-b*

287

287 Pair of Shoe Buckles, 1790–1800

UNKNOWN MAKER

H. 1⅝ in.; W. 3⅛ in.

MARKS: None.

Rectangular, curved, thickened at back for bar of steel chape and tongue. Frame is molded with gadrooned edge, enclosing curved feathered lines from inner corners with rosettes between frame and curve at bar.

HISTORY: Unknown.

NOTES: Published *(see Reference)* as "New York 1775-1800," but the present author feels that there is insufficient evidence for this localization.

REFERENCE: *Hipkiss 1943*, p. 78, illus.

GIFT OF PHILIP LEFFINGWELL SPALDING 30.36-37

288

288 Ladle, c. 1790

UNKNOWN MAKER

L. 13¾ in.; Wt. 5 oz., 15 dwt.

MARKS: None.

Stem, almost square in section, slightly chamfered on top, flattens to wide pointed backward-bent tip; oval drop soldered to hemispherical bowl.

Engraved *S H* with serifs on top.

HISTORY: Said to be for Sarah Henry (1719-1798); descended in the family to the donor.

GIFT OF THOMAS L. SPRAGUE 18.657

289

289 Porringer, 1790–1800

UNKNOWN MAKER

H. 1½ in.; D. of lip 4⅝ in.; L. of handle 2³⁄₁₆ in.; Wt. 4 oz., 14 dwt.

MARKS: None.

Narrow everted rim, curved sides, stepped and domed bottom. Center point on bottom, small one inside. Keyhole handle with triangular center, soldered on both sides.

Engraved script on front of bowl *Bradley*.

HISTORY: See *Notes*.

NOTES: Said to have belonged to John Bradley of Concord, New Hampshire (b. 1819, drowned 1825). The style of the porringer and the quality of the silver, which lacks the proportion of zinc characteristic in the nineteenth century, suggests that Bradley was not the original owner.

GIFT OF MRS. GEORGE P. SANGER *17.1431*

DANIEL BOYER
1725–1779

Although the final numeral is missing from the records, Daniel Boyer almost surely was born on June 14, 1725. He was the son of James Boyer, Huguenot emigrant jeweler, who married in Boston in 1724 Mary Ann, daughter of Daniel and Susan (Sigourney) Johonnot. Daniel, the goldsmith, married Elizabeth Bulfinch in 1749; they had two daughters who married, successively in 1771 and 1788, Joseph Coolidge, who was trained in the goldsmith's craft, an importer of jewelry, and listed in 1789 as a merchant. In 1767 Boyer advertised "at his shop opposite the Governor's," as an importer of jewelry and tools as well as "most sorts of Jewellers and Goldsmiths Work, cheap for cash." Four years later he was "opposite the Province House," with the same type of wares and services. His brother Peter and his son-in-law Coolidge were executors of his estate in 1779.

Boyer used two surname marks, *(a)* in capitals in a rectangle, and another with capital and lowercase letters in a cartouche. His initials mark, a device between, in conjoined circles *(b)* has also been drawn without the device.

a *b*

290

290 Serving Spoon or Punch Ladle, c. 1760

L. 14⅛ in.; Wt. 7 oz., 11 dwt.

MARKS: *a* twice, in opposite directions, or back of stem.

Long rounded handle bent forward with one-third ridge, rounded drop and shell on back of almost elliptical bowl.

Engraved on back of handle a scallop shell (crest) and below, in script: *AM / -to- / CM.*

HISTORY: Early history unknown; owned by Miss Mary Ella Bryant in 1906; by Arthur Currier in 1929.

EXHIBITIONS: *MFA 1906*, no. 7; *Detroit 1951*, no. 364.

GIFT OF ST. PAUL'S ROYAL ARCH CHAPTER MASONIC TEMPLE *33.583*

291

291 Gold Mourning Ring, 1779

D. 13/16 in.

MARKS: *b* after age and before seam.

A plain band on which three engraved curves and two punches for eyes make a winged death's-head.

Engraved inside *Mrs. T. Gordon. ob. 21 April 1779 AE 48.*

HISTORY: Descended in the family of the donor's husband.

GIFT OF MRS. GORDON DEXTER *38.771*

DANIEL PARKER
1726–1785

Son of Isaac and Grace (Hall) Parker of Charlestown, Massachusetts, Daniel Parker was born November 20, 1726. He married on October 8, 1751 Margaret, daughter of Elias and Mary (Sunderland) Jarvis. Three children are recorded to them: Daniel in 1757, Mary in 1759, and Elias in 1760. In 1759 he was robbed of "Three large Silver Spoons stamp'd D.Parker, 12 Tea Spoons, most of them stamp'd D.P., 3 pair Silver Tea Tongs, not stamp'd, one large Gold Locket . . . 14 pair large open-work'd Silver Shoe Buckles with Steel Chapes. . . ." In 1761 he was again robbed, but the culprits were found. He also then advertised importations of jewelry and gold-smiths' tools from "his Shop near the Golden Ball." Between 1763 and 1767 he mentions only his Union Street address and his tools included "Forging & raising anvils for tankards, canns & creampots," and "Death head & heart in hand ring swages." In 1771 a child of his had fallen "thru the scuttle at Christ's Church" and in 1772 he was mentioned as a merchant. Although he is said to have gone to Salem in 1775, H. W. Belknap in his *Artists and Craftsmen of Essex County* does not mention him.

Parker's initial and surname mark is found with a rather high pellet *(a)* and drawn with a colon, both in rectangles. One initials mark, in a rectangle, has a colon *(b)*; another, on a cann in the First Church in Billerica, has a pellet and is in a shaped punch.

a   b

292

292 Creampot, c. 1750

H. 3⅞ in.; Wt. 4 oz., 1 dwt.

MARK: *b* on bottom.

Bulbous body, narrow neck, slightly notched rim, and applied rather long lip. Three shell feet on curved legs, a lady's mask with flower headdress as body joinings. Double scroll handle affixed over rim, slight grip, forked scroll and pointed tip. Center point on bottom.

Engraved IHS on bottom.

HISTORY: John Hathorne, m. Susanna Towzel, October 16, 1746; either their son John or their daughter Susanna Ingersoll; descended in the family to the Misses Bailey, from whose heirs the piece was bought.

REFERENCE: *Comstock 1958*, opp. p. 65, pl. 48b.

EXHIBITIONS: *MFA 1911*, no. 818; *ESU 1960*, no. 61.

THE H. E. BOLLES FUND *54.658*

293 Cann, c. 1760

H. of body 5¹¹⁄₁₆ in.; D. of base 3¹⁵⁄₁₆ in.; D. of lip 3¹¹⁄₁₆ in.; Wt. 16 oz., 2½ dwt.

MARK: *a*, broken punch, tangent to and below center point on bottom.

Bulbous body, everted lip with incised line; on cast splayed foot, the surface molded (and edge applied?). Edge damaged at front. Double scroll cast handle with scroll tips, lower forked, vent hole in molded extension (resoldered?) for upper joining, cylinder forms lower joining on elliptical disc.

293

Engraved FCA on handle below grip; *1770* added below mark.

HISTORY: Foster Cruff (Cruft), m. Ann Breck September 22, 1757; descended in the family to the donors.

GIFT OF THE ESTATES OF THE MISSES EUNICE MCLELLAN AND
FRANCES CORDIS CRUFT 42.385

294

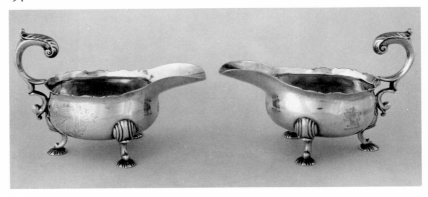

294 Pair of Sauceboats, 1760–1770

42.240: H. 5⅛ in. (inc. handle); L. 8 in. (inc. handle); Wt. 13 oz., 17½ dwt.;
42.241: H. 5¼ in. (inc. handle); L. 7¾ in. (inc. handle); Wt. 13 oz., 15 dwt.

MARK: *a,* very poor stamp, across center point on each.

Elliptical with long and apparently drawn lip, everted rim with cyma curves. The three legs have vertically molded bosses on body, short scroll, and circular pad feet with rayed lines in clusters; rare if not unique, one is under the handle instead of at the front. Cast handle, its open C scroll with acanthus grip affixed over rim, forks to small reverse C joined to body just above leg and terminates in forked scroll with vent hole beneath.

Engraved at right of handle in shell, scroll, and floral cartouche are the Hall arms; on other side a lion rampant on a torse (perhaps the Dudley coat, and added; both families had lion crests); under lip is script monogram *BHH* in decorated letters.

HISTORY: Benjamin and Hepzibah (Jones) Hall, m. 1752; their son Benjamin, m. Lucy Tufts, granddaughter of William Dudley; descended in the family to Vernon L. Hall, 1911.

NOTES: The inventory of Benjamin Hall of Medford, probated in 1817, gave no weights or values but included "2 sauceboats".

REFERENCES: *Avery 1930,* p. 81; pl. XIV opp. p. 86; *Hipkiss 1943,* pp. 62–63, illus.; *Wenham 1949,* p. 82; *Buhler 1957,* fig. 8.

EXHIBITIONS: *MFA 1911,* no. 813 (one; as with Hall arms and Dudley crest).

PHILIP LEFFINGWELL SPALDING COLLECTION. GIVEN IN HIS MEMORY BY KATHERINE AMES SPALDING AND PHILIP SPALDING, OAKES AMES SPALDING, HOBART AMES SPALDING 42.240-241

295

295 Teaspoon, c. 1750

Attributed to SAMUEL HALEY

L. 4⁷⁄₁₆ in.

MARK: *SH* or *HS* with pellet between in rectangle on back of stem.
Very short ridge on upturned tip, rounded drop and shell on back of bowl. Engraved on curve of tip *LF.*

HISTORY: Louis Foye (born c. 1730); for subsequent history see Cat. no. 45.

NOTES: The mark has been read as Samuel Hough's, but he was too early for this style. Samuel Haley, a goldsmith mentioned in the estate of Jonathan Reed in 1748, is surely a candidate for consideration, but his work is unknown. George Francis Dow, in *Arts and Crafts in New England* (Topsfield; 1929), records the death of "Mr. Healey, goldsmith" in 1773, and Hollis French gives in his list of goldsmiths Samuel Healy with this death date, but no mark. Probably all are one and the same.

GIFT OF MISS HARRIET A. HILL *15.914*

BARNABAS WEBB
c. 1729–1795

The first child of Benjamin Webb (Harvard 1715), who was minister of the First Parish in Eastham, Massachusetts, and Mehetabel, daughter of Thomas and Mary Williams, Barnabas Webb married Mary Homes. It is probable that he learned his craft from her father, William (q.v.), whose firstborn she was. Their intentions were published May 10, 1759, three years after he had advertised a ring which he had found in Cambridge, calling himself "Goldsmith, near the Market." In 1761 he "informes his Customers, that since he was burnt out near the Market he has opened a Shop in Back-Street, opposite Mr. Brown's Meeting-House, formerly occupied by Mr. Edward Whittemore."

He advertised in 1765 having "stopped" a spoon on the suspicion that it had been stolen; in the first Boston Directory in 1789 Barnabas Webb, retailer, was on Ann Street. Presumably he went shortly thereafter to Maine, where his tools and stamps were sold circa 1965.

Two initials marks are given for Webb; that of his initials, a pellet between, in a rectangle *(a)* is on Cat. no. 296.

a

296 Sugar Scissors, c. 1760

L. 4⅝ in.; Wt. 1 oz., 7½ dwt.

MARKS: *a* in each tip, but poorly punched in one.

Circular finger holes with short scrolls, broken scroll to circular pivot hinge, reversed scrolls to shaped shanks with shell (?) tips (neatly hollowed inside, but one is very pitted).

Engraved ᴛᴅʜ on pivot.

HISTORY: Said by the donor to have been owned by the Donnell family of Portland, Maine.

GIFT OF J. VAUGHAN DENNETT *38.981*

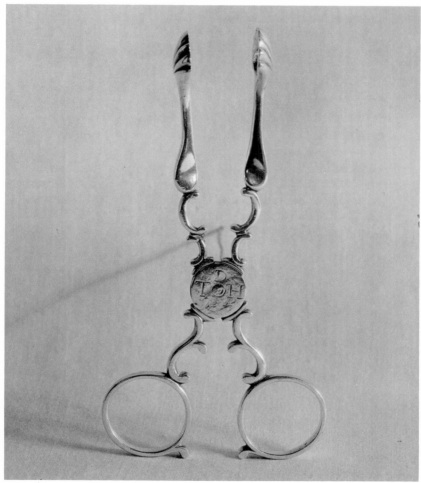

296

BENJAMIN BURT
1729–1805

The birth of Benjamin Burt was recorded in the family Bible as follows: "Benjamin Burt a Twin Borne y^e 29 Decem^r 1729" following "Sarah and Willm Burt, twins . . . 1726." With their brother Samuel (q.v.) the two boys at least started their training under their father, John Burt. William died in 1752, his important published piece being the Cunningham flagon for the Old South Church, Boston. Benjamin married Joan, daughter of John Hooton, oarmaker, in October 1754. In 1759 he was commissioned to make two flagons for the First Congregational Church in Marblehead matching those his brother Samuel had made in 1748/9. He served in town offices and was bondsman for his sister Sarah's husband, Francis Shaw, becoming Collector of Taxes. Esther Forbes (*Forbes 1942*) recounts Hannah Crocker's childhood impressions of him, "A respectable goldsmith and a very large man. . . . He weighed three hundred and eighty pounds . . . a very pleasant man". The directories list him on Fish Street; in 1800 he was selected to lead the goldsmiths in the memorial procession for George Washington. He died in 1805 mentioning his deceased sister Sarah's children and left "all my Goldsmiths working tools now in my shop" to Samuel Waters and one hundred dollars to "my trusty friend Joseph Foster, Goldsmith," who was named sole executor. Ebenezer Moulton was one of the appraisers of his estate, which included a share in the Charles River Bridge.

His full name mark in capitals in a cartouche is in two lines *(a)*; his initial and surname in capitals, a pellet between, is in a rectangle *(b)*, without a pellet in one with a shaped end *(c)*, and in a rectangle with a device between the initials *(d)*.

 *a*    *b*

 *c*    *d*

297

297 Punch Ladle, c. 1750

L. 15¾ in. (does not include ring); Wt. 7 oz., 14 dwt.

MARK: *a* on back of short stem.

Hollow cast handle, upper section angled at sides, has paired lines at broadest part and tapers to angled collet-under-ball finial with loop for wire ring. Molding at top of long tapering shank and paired moldings above a short stem rectangular in section, chamfered on upper edges, with rounded drop and shell of thirteen lobes on back of deep almost elliptical bowl. Edge of bowl cracked, minor dents, vent hole below collet.

Engraved DMA / *Wei 7:18.0* below shell.

HISTORY: Captain Daniel and Ann (Fudge) Malcom; William Mackay, executor of their estate; his daughter Elizabeth, m. Tristram Barnard 1779; their niece Frances, m. Thomas Carter Smith; their daughter Frances (b. 1832), m. Thomas David Townsend; their son William Smith Townsend, father of the donors.

NOTES: There is no published Boston marriage record for Daniel and Ann Malcom, but their daughters were Sarah Fudge (b. September 28, 1751) and Susan (b. September 6, 1753). Daniel in 1755 and James Fudge in 1759 are also recorded to them. Daniel Malcom's inventory (1769) included "1 punch ladle" and "a Silver Pipe." The only other ladle by Burt of this type known to the author was, in 1966, on loan to the Cleveland Museum of Art.

REFERENCE: *Bigelow 1917*, pp. 276-279, fig. 179.

EXHIBITIONS: *MFA 1911*, no. 101, pl. 5; *MFA 1956*, no. 8, mark in error.

GIFT OF THE MISSES ROSE AND ELIZABETH TOWNSEND 56.675

298 Caster, c. 1750

H. 5⁵⁄₁₆ in.; D. of base 1¾ in.; Wt. 3 oz., 14 dwt.

MARK: *d* on side.

Vase form, hemispherical body on cast splayed molded foot; seamed curve with applied molding at rim and joining. Center point on bottom. Cover has alternating panels of diaper engraving centering simple holes, and scrolls outlined in engraving; applied molding forms bezel; disc set on curve of top for bell-form finial with high base.

Engraved RDM on side.

HISTORY: Richard Derby (1712-1783), m. Mary Hodges, February 3, 1734; their son, Elias Hasket Derby (1739-1799), m. Elizabeth Crowninshield; their daughter Anstiss, m. Benjamin Pickman (1763-1843), 1789; their daughter Anstiss Derby (1793-1856), m. John Whittingham Rogers (1787-1872), 1815; their daughter Martha Pickman Rogers (1827-1905), m. John Amory Codman (1824-1886); their daughter Martha Catherine Codman, m. Maxim Karolik.

298

REFERENCES: *Hipkiss 1941*, pp. 216-217, illus., no. 146.
M. AND M. KAROLIK COLLECTION *39.194*

299 Cann, 1750–1770

H. of body 5¼ in.; D. of base 3⅜ in.; D. of lip 3⅛ in.; Wt. 10 oz., 15 dwt.

MARKS: *d,* worn, at left of handle; *a* at center point on bottom.

Bulbous body, applied molded rim with paired incised lines below, broad belly, molded cast splayed foot. Double scroll cast handle, turned extension for upper joining, scroll tips flattened at sides, lower joining crudely repaired (soldering lines very evident between two halves); slight grip. Crude soldering of foot. Battered and poorly repaired.

Engraved ILE on bottom; scratched weight *10 - 17;* added to body at front, elaborate script monograms *HEW / to / IW* (or: *TW*).

HISTORY: Unknown.

BEQUEST OF CHARLES HITCHCOCK TYLER *32.374*

299

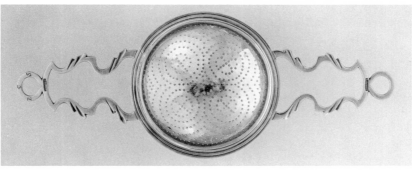

300

300 Strainer, 1750–1760

L. 11⅜ in.; D. 4½ in.; Wt. 4 oz., 1 dwt.

MARKS: *d* on each strap.

Shallow circular bowl with everted molded rim, pierced in four groups of circles enclosing crosses within circle with angles pierced. Flat notched or modeled and shaped strap handles ending in loop; their blunt tips are affixed under rim.

Engraved ᴇᶜs on one loop.

HISTORY: Unknown.

GIFT OF THE ESTATE OF MRS. FRANCIS B. CROWNINSHIELD *59.693*

301

301 Sauceboat, c. 1760

H. 4¾ in. (inc. handle); L. 7¹³⁄₁₆ in. (inc. handle); Wt. 11 oz., ½ dwt.

MARK: *a* on bottom.

This sauceboat is the mate to Cat. no. 302. Elliptical with center point on curved bottom, bulbous sides incurved below everted shaped rim, long broad drawn lip. Three short legs, rectangular in section, joined with scrolled and molded boss, on hollow shell feet. Double scroll cast handle, upper C curve with acanthus grip and scroll tip affixed over rim; short curve to reverse C affixed at widest part of body; forked tip; both scrolls flattened at sides.

Engraved RDM on lower curve of body between legs on pourer's side; added under initials *1734* and near mark: *E.D. / 1881* by the same hand. Under edge of foot on right side *oz* over *11-3*.

HISTORY: Richard Derby, m. Mary Hodges February 3, 1734; descended in the family (see Cat. no. 298) from John Whittingham Rogers (1787-1872) to a "Mr. Rogers" of Canaan, Connecticut, from whom it was bought.

REFERENCE: *Hipkiss 1941*, pp. 216-217, illus., no. 147.

M. AND M. KAROLIK COLLECTION *39.145*

302 Sauceboat, c. 1760

H. 4⅝ in. (inc. handle); L. 7⅞ in. (inc. handle); Wt. 10 oz., 11½ dwt.

MARK: Same as Cat. no. 301 but not tangent to center point.

This sauceboat is the mate to Cat. no. 301, which see for its description.

Engraved RDM over *1735;* added between legs on right side *M.C.D. / -TO- / J.G.P. / 1881,* not in the same hand as on Cat. no. 301; on front foot edge all that shows of the weight is *8.*

HISTORY: Richard Derby, m. Mary Hodges, 1734; their son Elias Hasket Derby (1739-1799), m. Elizabeth Crowninshield; their daughter Elizabeth,

m. Nathaniel West and was divorced, resuming her maiden name; descended in the family to Mrs. William P. Derby, from whom it was bought.

REFERENCE: *Hipkiss 1941*, pp. 216-217, no. 147.

M. AND M. KAROLIK COLLECTION 39.229

303 Salt, c. 1760

H. 1½ in.; D. of lip 2⁹⁄₁₆ in. (uneven); Wt. 2 oz., 8½ dwt.

MARK: *a* on bottom above center point.

Circular with incised lines below everted rim, almost flat bottom. Three cabriole legs with molded joinings and pad feet.

Engraved sHA on curve of base, the S perhaps over another, illegible, initial.

HISTORY: Samuel Hastings (1750-1834), m. Anna or Nancy Lush August 2, 1778; descended in the family to the donor.

GIFT OF MRS. JAMES H. SLADE 53.136

303

304

304

304 Cann, c. 1760

H. 5⅛ in.; D. of base 3⅜ in.; D. of lip 3⅛ in.; Wt. 10 oz., 18 dwt.

MARKS: *d* at left of handle; *a* at center of base.

Bulbous body, double incised lines below molded rim, on cast splayed molded foot. Modeled extension for upper joining of double scroll handle, vent hole under flattened scroll at tip, slight grip, disc at lower joining, bulb tip with applied curl beneath.

Engraved coat of arms and crest of a beaver with a fish in its mouth, in shell-and-foliate cartouche with drapery below on front; in semiscript on bottom: *Ex Dono T:F* between very faint guidelines, presumably for Thomas Fayerweather.

HISTORY: See *Notes*.

NOTES: The mate to this cann, which has identical arms, was exhibited *(R.I. 1965)* as bearing "Payne [?]" [*sic*] arms. The Paine-Hubbard coat of arms with crest of a beaver in carved and painted wood framed in a lozenge was illustrated in the catalogue of an exhibition at Harvard (*Harvard 1936,* no. 470). Here the Paine coat of arms is as shown in Guillim's *Display of Heraldry* (p. 89), described as granted to Robert Paine of Widlowe in Hunting-donshire. In the same position on the facing page of Guillim is the Everard coat of arms, which more nearly matches the design on the canns, although its fess is not engrailed. The heraldry is a puzzle which we cannot solve; the painted wood carving belonged to Thomas Hubbard (Harvard 1721), yet neither his parents nor his wife Mary Jackson explains the impaled Paine coat. Their daughter married Thomas Fayerweather (1723-1805), and the Paine arms with beaver crest has been published by Charles Knowles Bolton as for the Fayerweather family.

EXHIBITION: *MFA 1906,* no. 32, pls. IX, XVI (initials in error).

GIFT OF MRS. ARTHUR W. WELLINGTON IN MEMORY OF HER HUSBAND 44.81

305 Cann, 1760–1770

H. 5¼ in. (inc. finial); D. of base 3½ in.; Wt. 13 oz., 10 dwt.

MARK: *a* near center point on bottom.
Bulbous body, molded rim, on cast and lathe-turned splayed molded foot.
Double scroll handle, extensions for both joinings, disc at lower joining; vent
hole below tip of acanthus grip.
HISTORY: Early history unknown; owned by Adeline M. Soule in 1924.
REFERENCE: *Hipkiss 1941*, no. 148.
M. AND M. KAROLIK COLLECTION 39.237

305

306

306 Pair of Porringers, 1750–1800

39.236: H. 1⅞ in.; D. of lip 5½ in.; L. of handle, 2¹¹⁄₁₆ in.; Wt. 7 oz., 10 dwt.
39.238: H. 2 in.; D. of lip 5⁷⁄₁₆ in.; L. of handle 2¹¹⁄₁₆ in.; Wt. 7 oz., 18 dwt.

MARKS: *a* in bowl; *d* above initials on handle on each.

Rather narrow everted rims, curved sides, stepped and wide domed bottoms.
Center points in and on bottoms. Keyhole handles, soldered on top.

Engraved TWE with device below W on handle toward bowl. On 39.238,
added in script on battered front of bowl, *MHCH to MFS.*

HISTORY: Early history unknown; owned by Adeline M. Soule in 1924.

REFERENCES: *Hipkiss 1941,* pp. 218-219, illus., no. 149.

M. AND M. KAROLIK COLLECTION *39.236 and 39.238*

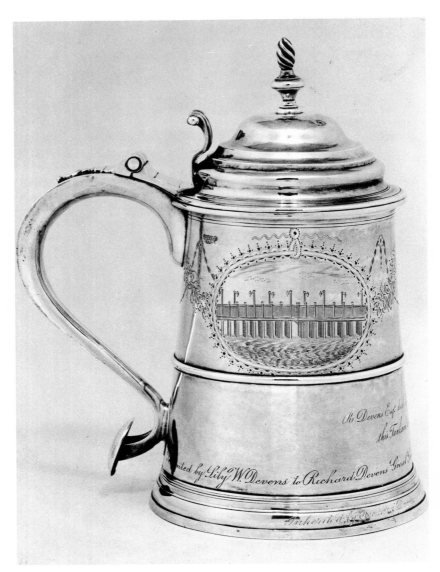

307

307 Tankard, 1786

H. 9⅛ in. (inc. finial); D. of base 5¼ in.; D. of lip 4³⁄₁₆ in.; Wt. 30 oz., 14 dwt.

MARKS: *a* on body at each side of handle.

Raised straight sides tapering to molded rim, incised lines below; applied half-round midband; molded baseband seamed near front. Center point on bottom. Shaped and molded plate on handle for five-part hinge, slightly angled hinge plate to scroll thumbpiece on domed and molded cover with turned-over flange cut at back, bezel soldered within. Turned and flame finial soldered to dome. Hollow scroll handle with rounded body drop and disc at lower joining has curved disc tip and small vent hole almost at body disc.

Engraved RDE on handle; on bottom *OZ* over *31* =. Bright-cut ribbon-hung horizontal ellipses at sides joined by floral garlands and incised short lines, tiny wreath (?) centered at front. View of Charles River Bridge (perhaps the builder's drawing) in one ellipse; in the other, script: *Presented to / Richard*

Devens, Esqr. / by the Proprietors of / CHARLES RIVER BRIDGE, / in
Testimony of their entire Approbation / of his faithful Services, / as a special
Director of that Work. / begun A.D. 1785, / and perfected / A.D. 1786.
Added at front in script: R. Devens Esqr. died Sepr 20. 1807. Aged 86 &
bequeathed / this Tankard to his grandson, John Harris. Added in another
script cutting beginning at right of handle near baseband: Presented by
Lily W. Devens to Richard Devens Great-Great Grandson of Richard Devens
Esq. April twenty second 1908. A modern cutting on curve of baseband:
Inherited by Richard Devens' Great Great Great Grandson November 3d
1922. On the bottom and in lettering differing from the others, curved at the
back: Presented by Charlotte Harris / = TO = / Richard Devens, great-
grandson of Richard Devens, Esq. / 1868.

HISTORY: See inscriptions.

NOTES: The same medallion design and inscription is to be found on a teapot
by Zachariah Brigden (Cat. no. 331). See Cat. no. 331 also for a contemporary
description of the completion of the Charles River Bridge.

REFERENCES: Hipkiss 1941, pp. 220-223, illus., no. 150; Hipkiss, MFA
Bulletin, no. 235 (1941), illus. p. 86; Buhler, Antiques, no. 6 (1945), pp.
351-352, fig. 12; Phillips 1949, pp. 111-112, illus. pl. 26, p. 100.

EXHIBITIONS: Harvard 1939; N.Y. 1947; R.I. 1965, no. 31.

M. AND M. KAROLIK COLLECTION 36.459

307

308

308 Sauceboat, c. 1790

H. 5¼ in. (inc. handle); L. 8 in.; Wt. 13 oz., 17½ dwt.

MARKS: *b* on bottom near center point.

Elliptical with high broad drawn lip, molding applied to rim. Double scroll open handle, acanthus grip, affixed at molding and to disc below. Three scroll legs with stylized shell joinings and feet.

Engraved with bright-cut medallion with garland at side enclosing script C.

HISTORY: Descended in the Curtis family.

NOTES: One of a pair, the mate still owned by the family. *Bigelow, 1917,* p. 417, illustrates a similar sauceboat with punched beads instead of the molded rim, and initials of Nathaniel and Rebecca Pierce, who were married in 1770 (Yale University Art Gallery, Garvan Collection).

GIFT OF MRS. RICHARD CARY CURTIS 59.32

309 Teapot, 1790–1800

H. 6⅜ in. (inc. finial); L. 11½ in. (overall); Wt. 21 oz., 17 dwt.

MARKS: *c* on bottom.

Set with Cat. nos. 310, 311, and 312. Elliptical, with eight flat flutes to a side, seamed at right of back flute, very neatly soldered almost flat base. Top perimeter flat for elliptical low domed lid with narrow flange; finial of wooden oval has silver rayed tip on long screw with separate whorl of leaves at base and small nut beneath; vent near screw hole. Five-part hinge applied with plate triangular in section underneath, flat bezel inside to ends of hinge. Tapering straight spout applied almost at bottom over small strainer holes. Slanting circular handle sockets, molded above pins for wooden scroll handle with scroll grip.

Engraved with bright-cut border above tasseled garlands around base and top, including sockets and spout; border around lid; rayed and dotted design on cover, designs on sides of spout.

HISTORY: Joanna Sigourney, m. first Newman Doane, July 5, 1777, second Nathan Bond, June 11, 1783; her daughter Eliza (1795-1876), m. Isaac Green Pearson; their daughter Elizabeth Parsons Pearson, m. Peter Kemble Paulding; their daughter Alice, m. William Henry Haldane, from whom the set was bought.

REFERENCES: *Hipkiss 1941*, pp. 224-225, no. 151, illus. (ownership as Parsons, Pearson, Haldane families); *Buhler 1950*, p. 59, fig. 44; *McLanathan 1956*, illus. p. 64, fig. 24.

EXHIBITIONS: *MFA 1956*, no. 9 (as a set); *Richmond 1960*, no. 6 (as a set); *R.I. 1965*, no. 35, fig. 68 (as a set).

M. AND M. KAROLIK COLLECTION 39.231

310 Stand for Teapot, 1790–1800

H. 1⅛ in.; W. 4⅞ in.; L. 7¾ in.; Wt. 6 oz., 12 dwt.

MARKS: None.

This stand is for teapot Cat. no. 309. It conforms to that piece, with applied raised rim forming longer flutes at end; added brightcut border. Four supports are curved brackets the width of a flute, incurved sharply to claw-and-ball feet. Bright cutting, matching that of the set, the tasseled garlands an ellipse within a dotted border.

HISTORY: See Cat. no. 309.

M. AND M. KAROLIK COLLECTION 39.232

311 Creampot, 1790–1800

H. 8¹¹⁄₁₆ in. (inc. handle); W. of base 2¹⁄₁₆ in.; Wt. 9 oz., 11 dwt.

MARKS: None.

Set with Cat. nos. 309, 310, 312. Urn form, raised and fluted to concave neck high at front and back, applied molding under edge. Lip slightly grooved

309, 310

for pouring. Pointed body fits into high splayed foot with turned-over edge set in square plinth with applied vertical rim. High curved molded strap handle, affixed to interrupt molding at back, has a hinge pegged through for strap on slanting flange of domed cover with reverse groove over pouring spout. Tiny turned and pointed finial pegged through dome. Lower tapering end of handle affixed within garland below dotted border, its rounded tip curving free. Border on neck and foot, corners decorated. No visible center point.

HISTORY: See Cat. no. 309.

NOTES: A "cream jug" in this rare covered form, but not fluted, was thus charged by Paul Revere in 1784 to Colonel James Swan (The Paul Revere Insurance Company, Worcester, Massachusetts).

M. AND M. KAROLIK COLLECTION 39.233

312 Sugar Urn, 1790–1800

H. 9½ in. (inc. finial); W. of base 3⅛ in.; Wt. 14 oz., 3½ dwt.

MARKS: None.

Set with Cat. nos. 309, 310, 311. Body matches creampot (Cat. no. 311) in form but is quite different in decoration, with less planishing underneath, and simpler corner designs. A dotted ellipse on the body matches that on the lid —at no other point do the flutes fit. Convex lid with domed cover, molding at joining, crudely soldered inside. Turned and pine-cone finial soldered through the dome, rayed lines at base. No visible center point.

HISTORY: See Cat. no. 309.

M. AND M. KAROLIK COLLECTION 39.234

311

312

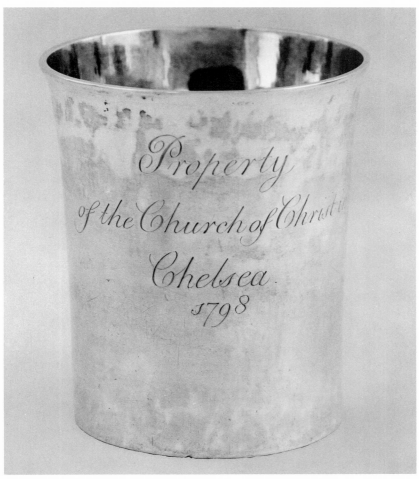

313

313 Set of Six Beakers, 1798

H. 3⅞ in.; D. of base 2¹¹⁄₁₆ in.; D. of lip 3³⁄₁₆ in.; Wt. of *51.1517:* 4 oz., 14 dwt.; of *51.1518:* 4 oz., 12 dwt.; of *51.1519:* 4 oz., 13 dwt.; of *51.1520:* 4 oz., 13 dwt.; of *51.1521:* 4 oz., 9½ dwt.; of *51.1522:* 4 oz., 15 dwt.

MARKS: *c* on bottom of each.

Raised straight sides flaring at lip, center point on very slightly domed bottom.

Engraved in script on front of each: *Property / of the Church of Christ in / Chelsea. / 1798.* (See *Notes,* Cat. no. 119 for names of this congregation.)

NOTES: Domestic beakers in the same form were made by Benjamin Burt for John Bray (Harrington Collection, Dartmouth College) and by Paul Revere II for Ozias Goodwin (Cat. no. 418).

REFERENCES: *Jones 1913,* pp. 402-403, pl. CXXII; *McLanathan 1956,* p. 50, fig. 2; *Comstock 1958,* p. 84, fig. 11.

EXHIBITIONS: *51.1517-1518: Cranbrook 1952,* no. 24; *51.1521-1522: Towle 1954.*

GIFT OF THE FIRST UNITARIAN SOCIETY OF REVERE *51.1517-1522*

NATHANIEL HURD
1729/30–1777

Born February 13, 1729/30, Nathaniel was the third son of Jacob Hurd but the first to follow his father's craft. He became particularly proficient as an engraver and styled himself "Goldsmith & Engraver" in his will. His portrait by John Singleton Copley shows him with Guillim's *Display of Heraldry* in its 1724 edition, and probably Symp-son's "New Book of Cyphers . . ." of 1726, both of which might well have belonged to his father. Revere's account book (Massachusetts Historical Society) in 1762 debited Hurd for "2 small scolop^d Salvers," a chafing dish, a pair of canns, a silver frame for a picture, and, uniquely, a "Silver Indian Pipe." The following year, "mending a Picture frame" and making a snuff box complete the transactions, for which payment was prompt. Hurd cut a variety of plates for Harvard College, and a table of coins (*R.I. 1965*, fig. 45) which must have been helpful to his contemporaries. He cut for James Breck, who dedicated the view to the Hon. Thomas Hubbard, a "South Prospect of the Court House, Boston" published for the first time in *R.I. 1965* (no. 115, fig. 44). He died unmarried in 1777 leaving among other bequests to "Brother Benjn Hurd £30 in tools, cloathes & some money"; to his brother-in-law "Jno Furnass . . . my Volume of the Universal Dictionary of Arts & Sciences," and to his nephew "Jno Mason Furnass . . . my large printing press & some tools in considera-tion for the love I bear to him & the genius he discovers for the same business which I have followed & to which I intended to have brought him up to." The residue of his estate was divided between Benjamin Hurd and his sisters, Elizabeth, wife of Daniel Henchman, and Ann, wife of John Furnass.

He used his initial and surname, with pellet between, in a cartouche *(a)* and a similar mark in a plain rectangle; he also used his initials divided by a pellet in a rectangle.

a

314

314

314 Teapot, 1755–1760

H. 6¼ in. (inc. finial); D. of base 3⅜ in.; Wt. 19 oz., 7½ dwt.

MARKS: *a* above and below center point, both in same direction, on bottom.

Transitional form, between globular and pear-shaped, fashioned in reverse; rounded shoulder flat on top, sides taper to inset base with seemingly unnecessary center point and rather conspicuous hammer marks on bottom. Cast and lathe-turned splayed molded foot with strengthening edge. Flat rim on slightly domed cover, no bezel but band inside body; tiny vent hole near turned and spiral finial pegged through top. Three-part hinge with heavy plaque under shaped cutting. Curved spout rather high on body molded at joining with turned body drop and molded lip; three vertical lines of six, seven, and six small holes for strainer. Straight handle sockets with shell engraving surrounding the upper one, wherein left pin is missing from the wooden handle, which is repaired at the base with a band of silver and a screw into lower socket.

Engraved with Stoddard arms and crest in a scroll, shell, and foliate cartouche on pourer's side, foliate scroll-and-shell border on rim, narrow leaf-band on lid, ray-and-dot design around base of finial. *1731* added on base.

HISTORY: Prudence Chester (1699-1780), m. Colonel John Stoddard of Northampton; their daughter Prudence (1734-1822), m. Sheriff Ezekiel Williams of Wethersfield; their daughter Prudence (1767-1853), m. Rev. Bezaleel Howard of Springfield; their son Hon. Charles Howard (1794-1875), m. Elizabeth "Betsy" Dwight of Springfield; their daughter Elizabeth (1828-1907), m. William Shaw Tiffany of Baltimore; their son Charles Howard Tiffany, from whom the donor bought the teapot.

NOTES: Although the final on this piece is more characteristic of a tankard than of a teapot, Nathaniel Hurd used the same type of finial on a coffee pot engraved with impaled arms of Chauncy and Stoddard (illus. *MFA 1956,* no. 101).

REFERENCES: *French 1938,* p. 52, no. 319; *Buhler 1963,* pp. 52-55, figs. 1, 2.

GIFT OF MISS MARGARET HALL 63.1044

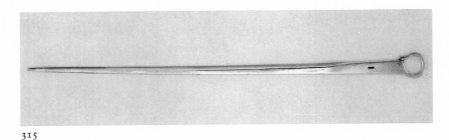

315

315 Skewer, 1755–1775

L. 13¼ in.; Wt. 1 oz., 18 dwt.

MARK: *a* near loop.

Tapering blade, rectangular in section; slight double chamfer on one edge starting two inches below circular loop with scroll tip.

HISTORY: Unknown.

NOTES: Skewers are surprisingly rare in American silver. See Cat. no. 407.

REFERENCE: *French 1938,* p. 52, no. 311.

EXHIBITION: *MFA 1956,* no. 102.

GIFT OF MRS. HENRY R. CHAPIN AND EDWARD H. R. REVERE 56.584

DANIEL HENCHMAN
1730–1775

The second son of Rev. Nathaniel Henchman and his first wife, Deborah (Wagner) of Lynn, Massachusetts, Daniel Henchman was born November 23, 1730 (see teapot and sugar bowl by Jacob Hurd, Cat. nos. 180-181, made for Nathaniel Henchman). He was apprenticed to Jacob Hurd, whose daughter Elizabeth he married in 1753. His best-known, most ambitious piece is the monteith made to be presented to the president of Dartmouth College and his successors in that office. It was engraved by his brother-in-law Nathaniel Hurd with an inscription dated 1771 and signed with his initials and a calligraphic bird. Henchman's plaintive advertisement in the *Boston Evening Post* of January 4, 1773 (*MFA 1956*, fig. 3) doubtless reflected the feelings of many craftsmen "bred to the Business" against "those Strangers among us who import and sell English Plate." He died in 1775; there is no will in Suffolk Probate Court, where his inventory was filed February 10, 1775, appraised by Daniel Boyer, Zachariah Brigden, and Joseph Russell. He left tools but no silver in a very small estate.

Henchman used a mark of his initials, separated by a pellet, in a rectangle *(a)* as well as that of his surname in capital and lowercase letters in a rectangle.

a

316

316 Caster, c. 1755

H. 5⁷⁄₁₆ in.; D. of base 1¾ in.; Wt. 3 oz. 7 dwt.

MARKS: *a* on bottom (very clear quatrefoil marks of *IE* and *IA* inside seamed section).

Hemispherical body on cast molded and splayed foot with strengthening edge; seamed section curves at joining with applied molding wider than that at rim. Domed cover with rayed design below turned bell-form finial and bright-cutting over edge above six panels of diaper design with three vertical rows of small holes in each.

Engraved *S • R* in small letters on body near applied molding.

HISTORY: Unknown.

NOTES: The marks of John Edwards and John Allen in their partnership era (c. 1700) appear clearly on the inside of the seamed section and lead one to wonder how Henchman acquired silver with such unworn and earlier marks. Since we know that Henchman was Hurd's apprentice, this piece of silver may be further substantiation of the theory that Hurd was associated with the Edwards family (see biography of Jacob Hurd).

GIFT OF THOMAS L. SPRAGUE *13.324*

317 Gold Mourning Ring, 1767

D. ¹³⁄₁₆ in.

MARK: *a* inside at end of inscription.

Gold band, outer surface slightly curved; very worn death's head with long wings.

Engraved in semiscript inside: *N Henchman Esqʳ ob • 30 May 1767 AE:39*

HISTORY: Nathaniel first son of Rev. Nathaniel Henchman, born 1728, Harvard College class of 1747. A practicing physician and Justice of the Peace. Married Margaret Mansfield 1750/1. *Boston News-Letter,* June 4, 1767: "A Gentleman, whose superior Abilities, render'd him not only very useful to Mankind, but greatly endear'd him to all his Friends in Life, and universally lamented in Death."

BEQUEST OF MAXIM KAROLIK *64.858*

317

THOMAS GRANT
1731–1804

H. W. Belknap in *Artists and Craftsmen of Essex County, Massachusetts* (Salem, 1927) records that Thomas Grant was baptized on October 3, 1731 in Marblehead, and probably married Hannah Corral on July 1, 1751. He died before August 7, 1804.

His similar marks, of his initial and surname in capital letters in a rectangle, are given with *(a)* and without a pellet.

 a

318

318 Creampot, c. 1760

H. 3¹¹⁄₁₆ in. (inc. handle); Wt. 2 oz., 15½ dwt.

MARK: *a* on bottom.

Bulbous body with rounded bottom, repaired at center point; slightly everted scalloped rim cut straight across front, the long lip added. Triangular body joinings for three cabriole legs with trifid feet, one under handle, as was usual on creampots. Double scroll handle affixed over rim, slight grip, scroll and rounded tip.

Engraved JCM, the *M* partially covered by a small patch.

HISTORY: Unknown.

EXHIBITIONS: *MFA 1911*, no. 528.

GIFT OF MR. AND MRS. WILLIAM BELTRAN DE LAS CASAS 30.733

JOHN HANCOCK
1732–1784

Born in Charlestown, Massachusetts, on October 10, 1732, John Hancock was the son of John and Susanna (Chickering) Hancock. He married Martha Sparhawk in 1760. Pleasants and Sill in *Maryland Silversmiths* (Baltimore, 1930) record him in Providence, Rhode Island, in 1767 and in June 1774 as "of Talbot County, silversmith" probably in Oxford, Maryland. There he died in 1784, but he is not known to have left any southern made silver. His children, John Jr. of Malden, Massachusetts and Nathan Sparhawk Hancock and Martha, wife of Phineas Brentnal, of Barre, Massachusetts, were living in 1788. His relationship to the more famous John Hancock has not been traced.

Hancock's other mark, initial and surname in capitals in a rectangle, bears little resemblance to the script initials in a shaped punch *(a)*.

a

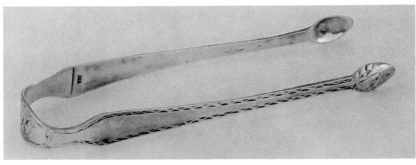

319

319 Sugar Tongs, c. 1780

L. 5¹¹⁄₁₆ in.; Wt. 1 oz., 2½ dwt.

MARKS: *a* inside top of each arm.
Bow form, shaped bow thicker than tapering arms with bright-cut edges, acorn shaped and incised hollow tips.
Engraved with script monogram *NRG* on bow.
HISTORY: Nathaniel (1738-1796) and Rebecca Gorham; descended in the family to the donor.
NOTES: In a similar pair of tongs by Hancock (privately owned), the bright-cutting forms a heart at the shaping of the bow.
EXHIBITION: *MFA 1911*, no. 685.
BEQUEST OF HENRY W. CUNNINGHAM 31.421

SAMUEL MINOTT
1732–1803

SAMUEL MINOTT is said to have bought tools from Edward Winslow's estate, which would have been just as he was completing his apprenticeship to an unknown master. He began his career as a fashioner of tutorial plate at least as early as 1758. In August 1762 he was debited by Paul Revere for silver, and in October of that year he was married in the Church in Brattle Square to Elizabeth Davis. According to the church records, their children, Elizabeth in 1763, two Samuels, Mary, and an unnamed child followed at two-year intervals; elsewhere he is said to have had six daughters and one surviving son. His mark is found with Josiah Austin's and with William Simpkins', suggesting successive partnerships; a strainer in a private collection has his mark over Joseph Coolidge's. In 1772 he advertised "at his Shop opposite William's Court, Cornhill" assorted groceries and pottery and was pursuing "the Goldsmiths Business in all its Branches as usual at his other Shop Northward of the Draw Bridge". He was a loyalist; he appears in the first Boston Directory in 1789 as "Minot Samuel, goldsmith, and importer of plated and jewellery-ware, Ann-street". He was still there in 1796, but had added his house address on Court Street. His estate was inventoried October 17, 1803; there was 84 oz. of plate and the appraisers were Samuel Belknap, Stephen Howe, and Azor G. Archibald.

Minott's surname, in semiscript in a rectangle *(a)*, often appears with the smaller semiscript *M* in a square *(b)*; his initials mark, in a rectangle and separated by an elongated pellet *(c)*, appears with that of his surname on a tankard in the Rhode Island School of Design. Church pieces owned in greater Boston marked *SM* also have the elongated pellet of *c*.

b

a

c

320

320 Gold Mourning Ring, 1754

D. 13⁄16 in.

MARK: *c* at end of engraving, quite worn.
Plain band.
Engraved inside in semiscript *F. Brattle ob • 10 . July . 1754 . 11 years.*
HISTORY: Unknown; F. Brattle has not been identified.
ANONYMOUS GIFT *55.108*

321

321 Communion Dish, 1764

H. 1⅜ in.; D. 13¼ in.; Wt. 24 oz., 7 dwt.

MARK: *a* on bottom below center point.

Large plain dish with shallow depression, slightly domed in center; flat rim with slight molding on underside. Center points on bottom and in dish.

Engraved with the Hancock arms and crest in scroll-and-foliate cartouche opposite a winged cherub's head in widespread wings with curling fronds below. On rim *The Gift of the Hon;ᵇˡᵉ THOMAS HANCOCK ESQ;R* (arms) *to the CHURCH in Brattle Street Boston 1764.*

HISTORY: Made for the Brattle Street Church, Boston, 1764.

NOTES: Six dishes, three by John Coburn (one of which is owned by the MFA, Cat. no. 272) and three by Minott, were presumably purchased with Thomas Hancock's bequest of £100 to the church. Minott's other two plates are in the Clearwater Collection, Metropolitan Museum of Art, New York, and in the Worcester Art Museum, Worcester, Massachusetts.

REFERENCES: *Jones 1913,* p. 69; *Paull 1913,* pp. 23-24, illus.; *Bigelow 1917,* pp. 243-244, fig. 148; *Avery 1920,* p. 93; *Eberlein and McClure 1927,* p. 163, illus. opp. p. 124; *McLanathan 1956,* illus. p. 56, fig. 9.

EXHIBITIONS: *MFA 1906,* no. 187; *Jamestown 1907,* no. 472; *MFA 1911,* no. 724, pl. 25; *Cranbrook 1952; Towle 1954; Minneapolis 1956,* no. 255, fig. 48; *Richmond 1960,* no. 94; *ESU 1960,* no. 66; *Buffalo 1965,* no. 99.

GIFT OF THE BENEVOLENT FRATERNITY OF CHURCHES *13.393*

322 Tankard, c. 1770

H. 8⅞ in. (inc. finial); D. of base 5⅜ in.; D. of lip 4 in.; Wt. 26 oz., 16½ dwt.

MARKS: *b* above and *a* below and touching center point.

Raised tapering sides, molded rim, applied bead on body and molded base-band seamed at right of handle, solder smoothed and rounded. Stepped and domed molded cover, the flange turned over, bezel soldered from outside. Turned and flame finial pegged through flattened top. Hollow scroll handle with rounded body drop and disc at lower joining, curved disc tip over vent slit, molded hinge plate and turned drop on shoulder, five-part hinge, tapering curved support for scroll thumbpiece soldered to step of cover.

Engraved on front in rectangular frame of scrollwork, in block and script: *HARVARDINATIBUS / Anno Domini MDCCLXX initiatis / Tertium sub ejus tutela annum agentibus, / Hoc poculum acceptum / Refert JOSEPHUS WILLARD.* On bottom within guidelines: *Josephus Willard / Coll: Harv: tutor / Cal: Septembris electus fuit / Anno MDCCLXVI.* Faintly scratched on bottom. £20-10.

HISTORY: Joseph Willard (1738-1804), tutor in Harvard College, President (1781-1804); descended in the family by 1907 to Susanna Willard, who sold it to the donor.

NOTES: Other tutorial silver of this era is a tankard given to Timothy Hilliard, made by Benjamin Burt in 1769 (Henry Ford Museum and Greenfield Village, Dearborn, Michigan) and its accompanying cann (private collection). Also privately owned are a tutorial cann and pair of salts by Minott made in 1758 for William Kneeland. A pair of canns by Paul Revere was given to tutor Stephen Scales in 1768 (The R. W. Norton Art Gallery, Shreveport, Louisiana). See Cat. no. 323.

322

REFERENCES: *Hipkiss 1943*, pp. 67-69, illus.; Buhler, *Antiques*, no. 6 (1945), pp. 349-350, fig. 7; H. Maxson Holloway, "American Presentation Silver," *The New-York Historical Society Quarterly*, XXX, no. 4, pp. 215-233; *McLanathan 1956*, p. 53; *Buhler 1957*, p. 50.

EXHIBITIONS: *Park Square 1925*, no. 294, illus.; *Harvard 1936*, no. 153; *Harvard 1939*; *Minneapolis 1956*, no. 256.

THE PHILIP LEFFINGWELL SPALDING COLLECTION. GIVEN IN HIS MEMORY BY KATHERINE AMES SPALDING AND PHILIP SPALDING, OAKES AMES SPALDING, HOBART AMES SPALDING 42.246

322

323

323 Cann, 1770

H. of body 5⅜ in.; D. of base 3⁷⁄₁₆ in.; D. of lip 3⅛ in.; Wt. 12 oz., 4 dwt.

MARKS: *a* above and *b* below center point.

Bulbous body, with scribed lines on flaring rim, on cast, molded, and splayed baseband. Acanthus grip on cast double scroll handle, extensions for joining below rim and disc on curve; the vent hole is in the upper part of the lower curve, which ends in a forked scroll.

Engraved as on Cat. no. 322.

HISTORY: See Cat. no. 322.

NOTES: The mate to this cann was lent by R. T. Haines Halsey to the MFA in 1906 and to the Hudson-Fulton Exhibition, Metropolitan Museum of Art, New York, in 1909; it is now in the Yale University Art Gallery, Garvan Collection.

REFERENCES: *Hipkiss 1943,* p. 70; *Buhler 1957,* p. 50.

EXHIBITIONS: *Park Square 1925,* no. 1052; *Harvard 1936,* no. 154 (with mate); *Harvard 1939;* N.Y. 1946.

THE PHILIP LEFFINGWELL SPALDING COLLECTION. GIVEN IN HIS MEMORY BY KATHERINE AMES SPALDING AND PHILIP SPALDING, OAKES AMES SPALDING, HOBART AMES SPALDING 42.247

324 Gold Mourning Ring, 1770

D. 1¾₆ in.

Mark: *c* at end of inscription.
Very carefully modeled winged death's-head (dots in upper part of wings) in slightly curved surface, flat inside for inscription.
Engraved in script *W Fisher Obᵗ 19 Septʳ 1770: AE 43.*
History: Unknown.
Bequest of Maxim Karolik 64.859

324

EBENEZER AUSTIN
1733–1818

NATHANIEL AUSTIN
1734 or 1739–1818

Born in Charlestown, Massachusetts, Ebenezer Austin was the son of Ebenezer and Mary (Smith) Austin. The latter's sister Sarah married the goldsmith Samuel Edwards. Ebenezer's younger brother Nathaniel, a pewterer, was long confused with their cousin of the same name. Ebenezer is said to have moved to Hartford, Connecticut in 1764. In the 1780s he is said to have moved to New York, where in 1818 he was listed among the pensioners of the Revolution.

Recorded variously as 1734 or 1739-1818, Nathaniel Austin is also listed as the son both of Josiah Austin and of Thomas and Ruth (Frothingham) Austin. In 1759 he married his cousin Anna, daughter of Ebenezer and Ann (Smith) Kent, the latter a sister of Mary and Sarah. Nathaniel appears in the Boston Directories from 1789 through 1816.

This mark (a), the surname *Austin* in script in a rectangle, appears with the initials *EA*, separated by a pellet in a rectangle, on a piece owned by the Yale University Art Gallery (Garvan Collection). However, since the style of this spoon (Cat. no. 325) is of the period after Ebenezer had moved to New York and since the Gorhams for whom it was made were a New England couple, it is likely that Nathaniel also used the mark.

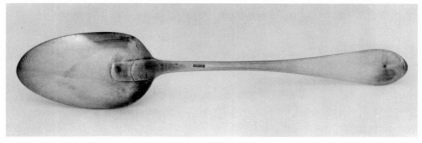

325

325 Tablespoon, c. 1790

Ebenezer Austin or Nathaniel Austin

L. 8⁷⁄₁₆ in.; Wt. 1 oz., 13½ dwt.

MARK: *a* on back of handle.
Almost pointed handle bent backward; slight ridge; double drop on oval bowl.
Engraved script monograms *NRG / MBV* on handle.
HISTORY: Nathaniel (1738-1796) and Rebecca Gorham; their great-granddaughter, Mary Bartlett Vose; descended in the family to the donor.
NOTES: Rebecca Gorham in 1797 left "138 1/2 oz of plate at 6/ 8" according to the Middlesex County Probate Court.
BEQUEST OF HENRY W. CUNNINGHAM 31.424

ZACHARIAH BRIGDEN
1734–1787

Born in 1734, Zachariah Brigden was the ninth child of Michael
Brigden (1698-1767), blacksmith, and his wife Winifred Sprague.
Thomas B. Wyman in *Charlestown Genealogies and Estates,* 1879,
lists him as fifth generation from the immigrant Thomas Brigden who
arrived with his wife and two children in the *Hercules* to become an
inhabitant in 1634. Zachariah is believed to have been apprenticed to
Thomas Edwards with whose daughter Sarah his marriage intentions
were recorded December 9, 1756. She died aged forty-four in 1768,
and in 1774 he married Elizabeth Gillam. He advertised as a goldsmith in 1764 "at his shop opposite the West Door of the Town
House" imported materials for goldsmiths' use and jewelry. He died
intestate in 1787; Moses Gill and Benjamin Burt were bound with his
widow in the settlement of his estate. His "pew in Revd Doctor
Howard's Meeting House" was in the West Church, his "mansion
house and land" was in Cornhill, and he owned a share in the Charles
River Bridge which was sold for £150, ten pounds more than its
appraisal. His silver is owned by eight churches ranging geographically from East Hartford, Connecticut to Springfield, Hadley, Salem,
and Duxbury, Massachusetts, and Kittery, Maine. His chocolate pots
and teapots (including a privately owned pear-shaped one dated 1760;
see *MFA 1956,* no. 4) are his most ambitious pieces known today,
wrought with a skill worthy of the family with whom he almost
surely trained.

Brigden's two marks consisted of his initial and surname in capital
and lowercase letters separated by a pellet and contained in a cartouche *(a),* and his initials with a device between, in a rectangle *(b).*

a   b

326

326 Chocolate Pot, c. 1755

H. 9⅞ in. (inc. finial); D. of base 4¹¹⁄₁₆ in.; Wt. 27 oz., 7 dwt.

MARKS: *a* on bottom and left of handle; *b* on edge of cover.

Tapering cylindrical body, center point on bottom, incised lines at very slightly flaring rim, molded baseband applied and seamed at right of handle. High domed cover, incised lines on step and flange, has narrow bezel from rim and deep bezel at top for stirring rod; removable turned finial on molded disc has bezel of same depth. Open-link chain attached to finial holds pin with turned tips for five-part hinge at right angles; the upper plate curls at cover into vestigial thumbpiece; the lower is arched to fit over cylindrical handle socket, incised lines at edge, and turned body drop. Lower socket is affixed at top of oval disc on body. Wooden scroll handle with grip has additional brass pin in center of upper socket and angles above lower socket. Cast hexagonal spout, over relatively small hole, with modeled animal's head tip, molding below paneling at smooth ellipse on body, turned drop below.

Engraved with coat of arms used by Ebenezer Storer in scroll-and-wheat cartouche with drapery below. Added to bottom *Storer / 1720*, and in script *EHS / 1863*.

HISTORY: Ebenezer and Mary Storer, m. 1723; their daughter Elizabeth, m. Isaac Smith; their son William, m. Hannah Carter; their son Thomas Carter, m. Frances Barnard; his sister Elizabeth Hall Smith (d. unmarried); her sister Frances, m. Thomas Davis Townsend; their son, William Smith Townsend, was the father of the donors.

NOTES: A similar chocolate pot found in 1965 in England is larger but has the same paneled spout; there is slight variation in its molding. The drapery of its cartouche is held at the left by a bird's head, and the arms are quartered. It is now in the Heritage Foundation, Deerfield, Massachusetts.

REFERENCES: *Bigelow 1917*, pp. 372-373, fig. 266; *Jones 1928*, pp. 35-36; *Phillips 1949*, p. 76; *Wenham 1949*, pp. 214-215, fig. 83; *Buhler 1950*, pp. 40, 48, illus. back cover.

EXHIBITIONS: *MFA 1911*, no. 78; *MFA 1956*, no. 5, fig. 60; *Richmond 1960*, no. 2.

GIFT OF THE MISSES ROSE AND ELIZABETH TOWNSEND 56.676

327

327 Pair of Sauceboats, c. 1760

H. 4½ in. (inc. handles); L. 6¼ in.; Wt. of *62.190:* 10 oz., 15 dwt.; of *62.191:* 10 oz., 12 dwt.

MARKS: *a* on bottom of each.

Almost circular bodies with everted scalloped rims and wide, drawn lips. Center points on bottoms. Each has triangular body joining for three short paneled scrolled legs and shaped pad feet. Slight cracks in rim of each sauceboat. Double scroll open handle affixed with slight fork over rim, and short scroll with forked tip to body.

Engraved with crest of running hare on pourer's side.

HISTORY: Unknown.

EXHIBITION: *R.I. 1965*, no. 24.

GIFT OF DR. J. H. MEANS 62.190-191

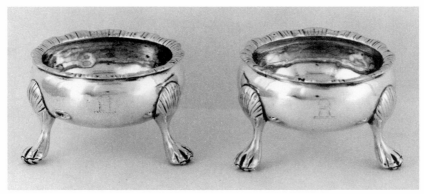

328

328 Pair of Salts, c. 1770

H. 1⅝ in.; D. of lip 2½ in.; Wt. 2 oz., 9½ dwt. each.

MARKS: *b* at center point on bottom of each.

Each circular with applied everted scalloped and gadrooned rim, three radially grooved pad joinings for short legs and paw feet.

Engraved with Bliss crest, a garb, on the side.

HISTORY: Jonathan Bliss (Harvard 1763); his son William Blowers Bliss, m. Elizabeth, granddaughter of goldsmith John Blowers and daughter of Sampson Salter Blowers; their daughter Elizabeth, m. William Hunter Odell; their daughter (d. 1937), gave this piece to the persons from whom it was bought.

NOTES: Jonathan Bliss, a loyalist, went to New Brunswick about 1784 and became Chief Justice of the Province. Another salt by Brigden has a scalloped edge on almost straight sides and pad feet (Cleveland Musum of Art, Hollis French Collection).

EXHIBITION: *ESU 1960,* no. 68.

DECORATIVE ARTS SPECIAL FUND *55.210-211*

329 Porringer, 1755–1785

H. 2⅛ in.; D. of lip, 5⅜ in.; L. of handle 2¾ in.; Wt. 8 oz., 18 dwt.

MARK: *a* at center point inside.

Everted rim, curved sides, stepped and domed bottom, center point inside and on base. Keyhole handle, pitted solder beneath and trace of solder on top.

Engraved ITR toward bowl.

HISTORY: Unknown.

NOTES: See Cat. no. 451 for a piece with the same initials. Doubtless they are both from the donor's family.

CHARLES T. AND SUSAN P. BAKER BY BEQUEST OF THE LATTER *21.1260*

329

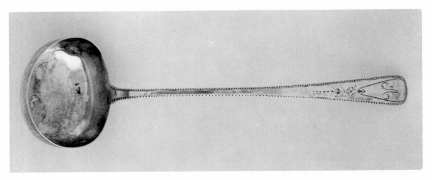

330

330 Ladle, c. 1785

L. 13¼ in.; Wt. 5 oz., 13 dwt.

MARK: *a* on back of stem.

Rectangular stem broadening to backward bent rounded tip with short ridge on back, and to double drop applied on back of deep elliptical bowl, bent, with center point on bottom. Edges of handle lined and punched to simulate gadrooning.

Engraved on tip script *A* in pointed ellipse, which has a flower at its base and a pendent design.

HISTORY: John Amory, Jr. (1759-1832), m. Catharine Willard (1761-1831); their daughter Catharine Willard Amory, m. Henry Codman; their daughter Martha Codman m. Maxim Karolik.

REFERENCE: *Hipkiss 1941*, pp. 214, 216, no. 145.

M. AND M. KAROLIK COLLECTION 39.196

331

331

331 Teapot, 1786

H. 4¾ in. (inc. finial and ball feet); L. 10¼ in. (overall); L. of base 5 in.;
Wt. 16 oz., 10½ dwt.

MARK: *a* on bottom.

Elliptical body seamed under handle; concave shoulder seamed at right of
handle; slightly domed base not quite flush with sides, flat lid, five-part hinge
affixed at back, very narrow bezel around sides and front. Fixed concave-
sided elliptical applique under turned wooden finial with pointed cap on
screw through lid; small nut; vent hole in surrounding rayed decoration;
upper handle socket has U applique for joining (perhaps a repair) but corresponding disc at lower joining for wooden handle. Four ball feet, probably
added early in the nineteenth century, serve as insulation.
Engraved with bright-cut and dotted borders on lid and neck, wider ones on

body; engraved floral garlands on body suspend horizontal ellipses at sides; flower designs on sides of spout. On pourer's side, in script and capitals in an ellipse: *Presented to / Capt. David Wood, / by the Proprietors of / CHARLES RIVER BRIDGE, / in Testimony of their entire Approbation / of his faithful Services, / as a special Director of that Work, / begun A.D. 1785, / and perfected / A.D. 1786.* On the opposite side is a view of the Charles River Bridge (see tankard by Benjamin Burt, Cat. no. 307, which shows one more lamp post).

HISTORY: David Wood (1742-1808), son of David, a baker, and Ruth (Hopkins) Wood, m. 1765 Margaret Sprague (d. 1807); from recent owner-ships it appears to have descended through his sister Mary, m. Thomas Edes (see Cat. nos. 241, 242).

NOTES: Deacon John Tudor (c. 1709-1795) wrote in his diary about the completion of the bridge:

> 1786 June 17 This day Charles River Bridge was finish'd, when a vast concourse of people passed over: There was two Tables of 320 feet sett up on Bunker's hill, the place where the Battle was foug't with the Brittons this Day 11 Years, on the Day Charleston was burnt. This Day of festivity & joy was Kept so as to Entertain 800 Gentlemen; the Governor's &c &c was present. 13 Tosts &c was drank &c &c. Sutch a Concourse of people, Carriages &c I never Saw at one Time before: Said Bridge is 1503 feet long encluding the abutments and is the greatest peice of Work ever don in Emerica. For the first pier of the Bridge was drove on the 14th June 1785 & the Bridge completed on the 17th June 1786 12 mo & 3 Days. The greatest depth of the river from the upper floring 46 feet 9 Inches. Small part 14 feet at high Water: The breadth of the Bridge 42 feet & Orna-mented with 40 Lamps, which make a Sparkling Show in the Night. The town & Contrey soon found the Advantage of this Bridge.

A teapot by Brigden in this form (privately owned) was exhibited in London (*ESU 1960*, no. 67, illustrated *Antiques*, LXXVIII, no. 3 [1960], p. 231).

REFERENCES: *Bigelow 1917*, pp. 347-348; fig. 248; *Phillips 1949*, p. 112; *Buhler 1963*, pp. 55-57, figs. 3, 4.

EXHIBITIONS: *MFA 1906*, no. 12, pls. XVIII, XXVII; *Harvard 1936*, no. 155, pl. 25; *R.I. 1965*, no. 25, fig. 66.

GIFT OF MISS PENELOPE BARKER NOYES IN MEMORY OF HER FATHER, JAMES ATKINS NOYES 63.634

ALEXANDER CROUCKSHANKS
working 1768

A goldsmith who arrived in Boston on August 29, 1768 from Glasgow on the *Snow Catherine,* Alexander Crouckshanks had left for an unknown destination before the first Boston directory was published. This mark, of initials in a rectangle *(a),* is on a piece with Boston provenance and of the proper period, and it seems a logical attribution.

a

332

332 Punch Strainer, c. 1770

H. 1⅛ in.; L. 11⁹⁄₁₆ in.; D. of bowl 4⅛ in.; Wt. 4 oz., 9 dwt.

MARKS: *a* on back of each handle curve at junction of pointed loop.

Shallow bowl, sides incurved under horizontal flange, upper side molded (bent above area of initials). Two flat strap handles, rounded ends affixed under flange, in parallel reverse curves, slightly modeled, with curve below pointed loop and circular tip. One strap is broken. Bowl pierced with six interlocking circles of plain holes, design of plain holes in each, and small inside circle, all within row of plain dots.

Engraved THPE under flange at side.

HISTORY: Thomas Handasyd and Elizabeth Peck (d. 1777); their grandson Thomas Handasyd Perkins (b. 1764); descended in the family to the donor.

NOTES: Similar strainers are known by Daniel Parker (*MFA 1911,* no. 816); by Paul Revere for John Templeman in 1792 (Minneapolis Institute of Arts); by Benjamin Burt (Cat. no. 300); and by Joseph Loring (Cat. no. 434).

REFERENCE: John D. Kernan, Jr., "The Mystery of AC Silver," *Antiques,* June 1957, p. 554 (when it was considered as by a New York maker).

EXHIBITION: *MFA 1911,* no. 816.

GIFT OF MISS CAROLINE E. CABOT 64.1992

HOUGHTON PERKINS
1735/6–1778

HOUGHTON PERKINS was the son of Isaac Perkins (d. 1737) goldsmith of Charlestown, Massachusetts, and his wife Sarah Hurd, whom he married in 1732. Perkins was apprenticed to Jacob Hurd. Although he is supposed to have moved to Taunton, Annie Thwing (The Thwing Catalogue, Massachusetts Historical Society) records that in 1770 he bought the house and land of John Hurd in Boston, and in 1772 he and his wife Elizabeth deeded land. In that year Joseph Eyres (Ayres) mortgaged a house and land on Essex Street to Houghton Perkins, goldsmith, which was canceled in 1783.

Perkins used two marks: his initials, with pellet between, in a rectangle *(a)*; and his initial and surname, a device between, in semiscript *(b)*.

a   *b*

333

333 Teaspoon, 1750–1760

L. 4⁷⁄₁₆ in.

MARK: *a* on back of stem.

Stem, semicircular in section, flattens and broadens to forward-bent tip with short ridge on front; long molded drop on back of elliptical bowl.

Engraved *AH* on back of handle.

HISTORY: Ann Hurd, daughter of Jacob Hurd, m. John Furnass, 1762; descended in the family to the donor.

NOTES: A spoon by Samuel Casey (Cat. no. 491) is also engraved for Ann Hurd.

EXHIBITION: *MFA 1956*, no. 113.

GIFT OF MISS LAURA FURNESS 43.1349

DANIEL ROGERS
1735–1816

The son of Richard and Mary (Crompton) Rogers, Daniel Rogers was born August 29, 1735. His first wife was Elizabeth Simpkins, probably daughter of William Simpkins, goldsmith, who was probably Rogers' silversmithing master. They had three daughters, the last born in 1765 when her mother died. His second wife was Elizabeth Rogers, daughter of the Rev. Nathaniel and Mary (Leverett) Rogers; of their seven children only two survived infancy. His third wife was the widow Mary Appleton Leatherland (1745-1832), who bore him five children. A daybook which he kept (now in the Essex Institute) shows among other activities that he made quantities of gold beads for fellow goldsmiths. His will left "To my Sons Daniel and Richard Rogers all my Shop Tools, except such of them as are calculated for Plate work, which I order to be Sold." His wife and six daughters are mentioned in the will. This silversmith and the facts concerning his life and work were first published by Martha Gandy Fales (Essex Institute Historical Collection, CI, No. 1, 1965). Previously the silver now attributable to this Daniel Rogers, of Ipswich origin, had been given to a silversmith of the same name in Newport, Rhode Island.

For his many marks, see Mrs. Fales' article mentioned above showing variants of those of his initials in a rectangle *(a)*, and of his initial and surname, in capital letters, separated by a pellet and enclosed in a rectangle *(b)*.

a   b

334

334 Gold Locket, c. 1760

L. $^{15}/_{16}$ in.; Wt. 3 oz.

MARK: *a* on back.

An elliptical plaque engraved with line at edge surrounding a small flower of curled scrolls, its vertical edge fastened to conforming back with extension at one side for three holes (for stitching) to match those of wedge fastener, which slips into the hollow box.

Engraved *RC* below mark on back.

HISTORY: Unknown; the donor by 1933.

REFERENCE: *Hipkiss 1943*, pp. 73-74, illus.

THE PHILIP LEFFINGWELL SPALDING COLLECTION. GIVEN IN HIS MEMORY BY KATHERINE AMES SPALDING AND PHILIP SPALDING, OAKES AMES SPALDING, HOBART AMES SPALDING *42.248*

335

335 Cann, 1775–1800

H. of body 6 in.; D. of base 3⁷⁄₁₆ in.; D. of lip 3⅝ in.; Wt. 17 oz., 16½ dwt.

MARK: *b* at left of handle.

Bulbous body, three incised lines below slightly everted lip, on molded splayed foot with very thick solder. Double scroll cast handle, scroll tips flattened at sides, extension for upper joining, disc at lower joining; slight grip; forked tip. Center point on bottom.

Engraved JÇE below grip on handle; added *J•D* above center point on bottom.

HISTORY: Unknown, but probably Crowninshield-Derby families.

REFERENCE: *Hipkiss 1941*, pp. 236-237, no. 164 (as Newport goldsmith).

EXHIBITION: *R.I. 1936*, no. 170.

M. AND M. KAROLIK COLLECTION *39.122*